REFORMATORY SCHOOLS

PATTERSON SMITH REPRINT SERIES IN
CRIMINOLOGY, LAW ENFORCEMENT, AND SOCIAL PROBLEMS

A listing of publications in the SERIES *will be found at rear of volume*

PUBLICATION NO. 106: PATTERSON SMITH REPRINT SERIES IN
CRIMINOLOGY, LAW ENFORCEMENT, AND SOCIAL PROBLEMS

REFORMATORY SCHOOLS

FOR THE CHILDREN OF THE
PERISHING AND DANGEROUS CLASSES
AND FOR JUVENILE OFFENDERS

BY

MARY CARPENTER

Reprinted with Index Added

MONTCLAIR, N. J.

PATTERSON SMITH

1970

Originally published 1851

Reprinted 1970 by
Patterson Smith Publishing Corporation
Montclair, New Jersey 07042

New material copyright © 1970 by
Patterson Smith Publishing Corporation

SBN 87585–106–1

Library of Congress Catalog Card Number: 72–108223

This book is printed on three-hundred-year acid-free paper.

PREFACE.

THE enormity and amount of juvenile depravity is
a subject which now most painfully engages the
public mind. The mature and headstrong character
which it exhibits has been unveiled and presented
to the public eye in colours, fearful because true, by
various recent publications, which must make every
Christian heart shudder and tremble. Statistic
tables prove to us its appalling progress, in a ratio
far exceeding that of the population generally ;—but
even these, clear as they may appear to be, and
forcible in their appeals, are less powerful to convince of the dreadful truth, and to demonstrate its
results, than the daily experience of our great cities,
as it can be attested by our magistrates,—our governors and chaplains of gaols,—our police,—or even
the common readers of our newspapers.

These things have long been known to the few ;—
now they are made evident to the many ; and it is
equally clear that if the evil is not checked it must

increase.   Now we see : — therefore our sin re-
maineth if we strive not to remove the evil.

But what can be done ?   Is there any remedy ?
If so, how can it be applied ?

None, probably, will hesitate to acknowledge that
education, — the early nurture, and the sound,
religious, moral, and industrial training of the child,
is the only curative that can strike at the root of the
evil, by infusing a fresh and healthy principle,
instead of that which is now so rotten in our state.
But can it be given, so as to influence these degraded
children; and if it can, ought it to be bestowed
gratuitously upon them ?   Have we not already done
enough in this country for the prevention of crime,
by providing Schools, Penitentiaries, and Gaols ?.

These are important questions, which it will be
attempted in this work fully and satisfactorily to
answer; while it will be proved that Reformatory
Schools, adapted to the various conditions of the
" perishing and dangerous classes " of children, both
can, and under Providence, will produce the desired
effect of *checking the progress of crime in those who
have not yet subjected themselves to the grasp of the
law, and of reforming those who are already convicted
criminals.*   Such Schools occupy a middle ground
between educational and penal establishments, and
are liable to misunderstanding from a double source;
such misunderstanding it will be the aim of the

following inquiries to remove, placing them in their true position with respect to society.

It is earnestly entreated that all who have within them any desire to promote the welfare of their fellow beings, or any sense of the high responsibility which every Christian lies under, to do something to prepare the way for the coming of his Lord's kingdom on the earth, — will seriously and candidly peruse this volume, and, excusing its many defects, will allow due weight to the truths it contains,— truths which all may test for themselves.

Then let every one go forth to do what he can in this great cause ;—all may find a way ;— and what they do, let them " do quickly ;"— the hour is fully come ; the harvest truly is ripe;—may the Lord send many labourers to gather it in faithfully.

CONTENTS

INTRODUCTORY CHAPTER.

CHAPTER I.

FIRST PRINCIPLES.

98876

CHAPTER II.

EVENING RAGGED SCHOOLS.

CHAPTER III.

FREE DAY SCHOOLS.

CHAPTER IV.

INDUSTRIAL FEEDING SCHOOLS.

CHAPTER V.

THE GAOL.

CHAPTER VI.

PENAL REFORMATORY SCHOOLS.

REFORMATORY SCHOOLS.

INTRODUCTORY CHAPTER.

It is not needed, at the present day, to demonstrate the immense importance of the juvenile portion of the community to the future, and even to the present welfare of the state,—or to show the need of education to prepare the young to be good citizens and useful members of the community. The days are past when it was requisite to prove that the labouring classes can work better in light than in darkness, and that even if they cannot, the more favoured few have no right to withhold from the many God's best gifts. These questions we shall suppose to be settled. Nor shall we, in any way, touch on the topic at present so interesting to the public mind,—National Education, or refer to the systems pursued in the various public schools already existing for the labouring portion of the population, any further than to consider how far they can or cannot be applicable to the classes which form the subject of our enquiry. In like manner, if houses of correction and common prisons are alluded to, it will not be to offer any opinion on the plan and principles adopted in them, except as they bear on juvenile offenders.

The subject of the present work is solely,—The children of the "perishing and dangerous classes,"—and the means to be adopted to raise them from that condition. Many remedies, more or less effectual, have been applied to mitigate or remove the evils, so multiplied and varied in form, amid which the infant population is springing up, rank and noxious as in a hot-bed of vice;—philanthropists of varied powers and in different walks of life, have laboured, and are labouring devotedly, for the removal of the causes of crime, however and wherever it manifests itself. We wish them all God speed, and sympathise warmly in their efforts. Yet none can prove effectual without setting right the main-spring of life, which can be done only by education.

That part of the community which we are to consider, consists of those who have not yet fallen into actual crime, but who are almost certain from their ignorance, destitution, and the circumstances in which they are growing up, to do so, if a helping hand be not extended to raise them;—these form the *perishing classes:* —and of those who have already received the prison brand, or, if the mark has not been yet visibly set upon them, are notoriously living by plunder,—who unblushingly acknowledge that they can gain more for the support of themselves and their parents by stealing than by working,—whose hand is against every man, for they know not that any man is their brother;—these form the *dangerous classes*. Look at them in the streets, where, to the eye of the worldly man, they all appear the scum of the populace, fit only to be swept as vermin from the face of the earth ;—see them in their homes, if such they have, squalid, filthy, vicious, or pining and wretched with none to help, destined only, it would seem, to be carried off by some beneficent pestilence ;—and you have no hesitation in acknowledging that these are indeed dangerous and perishing classes. Behold them when the hand of wisdom and of love has shown them a better way, and purified and softened their outward demeanour and their inner spirit, in Schools well adapted to themselves, and you hardly believe them to be separated by any distinct boundary from the children who frequent the National and British Schools. Yet there is, and will long be, a very strongly defined line of separation between them, which must and ought to separate them, and which requires perfectly distinct machinery and modes of operation in dealing with them.

In the present chapter an idea will first be given of the amount of crime among the juvenile portion of the population in our large cities; and it will be shown that this is co-existent in a great degree with absolute ignorance of the lowest kind, but still more with a striking deficiency in the nature of the education they have received. It will thus be proved that the present educational establishments for the labouring classes neither can nor will affect these perishing and dangerous ones, and that if we would effectually influence them, gratuitous ones of a different character must be provided for them. The objections made by political economists to such Schools will afterwards be considered and answered.

In order to become somewhat acquainted with the extent and heinous nature of the juvenile depravity existing in our very midst, we shall not have recourse to general statistical tables of crime, and for the following, among other reasons :—

The returns are generally of the number of committals, not of the number of individuals committed. Instances are known of one person having been committed 100 times, and among juveniles, re-commitments of 6, 8, or 10 times, are not unfrequent : hence the number of committals may show the frequency of crime, but not the number of criminals. But it will be only an approximation even to this. A clever young thief will go on for years committing daily depredations before his case is recorded in the annals of crime.

Even if we have the numbers before us of the juveniles committed during a series of years, we shall still be in danger of forming very erroneous opinions of the actual amount of crime, from ignorance of circumstances which have led to some particular course of conduct in the acting magistrates. For instance :—when we find that the number of boys from 7 to 14, committed to the Houses of Correction at Westminster and Cold Bath Prisons, and tried by jury in 1837, was only 67, and that in 1846-47, it was 277, we are appalled at the fearful increase ; and not less so when we find that in this last year the summary convictions were 621, making a total of 898, while in the next, 1847-48, when Ragged Schools were in operation, the summary convictions rose to 1,129, the trials by jury being 131, making the fearful amount of 1,260. Might not the inferences be plausibly drawn from such facts, that in the ten years from 1837 to 1847, juvenile crime in its more serious aspect had quadrupled, and that in the very next year, when Ragged Schools were in active operation, it had increased by nearly 200, thus showing the ill effects of that movement.   Sergeant Adams, in his excellent " Charge to the Grand Jury, of the Quarter Sessions of the County of Middlesex," 1849, satisfactorily explains this.   In the year 1837, he tells us, " the rage for summary conviction was at its height, during the year of the parliamentary inquiry ; and several police magistrates gave evidence in its favour, and the returns show the consequent rapid increase of committals, although the trials by jury remain stationary." (The summary convictions in 1837 were 1,031, making a total increase of 200 juvenile offenders over the preceding year.)   " By degrees, summary convictions decreased, and the old constitutional tribunal was resorted to ; and the consequence was that in the last year before the Larceny Act was passed, 1846-47, the number of committals *had decreased* 200 *on the committals of* 1837, *though the trials by jury quad-*

rupled the number of trials in that year. The Larceny Act has brought summary conviction again
into action in another form; and the consequence
has been that the committals of the first year of its
operation (1847-48,) exceed the committals of 1837
by 162." The effects of the Larceny Act will be
again referred to; but we make this extract here, to
afford a clue to the detection of the fallacies which
may be and have been founded on apparent facts.
Another illustration may be given :—The numbers
of juvenile offenders in Bristol during the last three
years, have been 202, 164, 315 ; these figures would
indicate a great increase of crime since the Ragged
Schools have been in operation. But this increase
is fully accounted for by the fact, that during the
last two years a change has been made from 14
to 16, as the age under which young persons are to
be regarded as children, thus including in the last
returns a period peculiarly prone to crime; these
figures cannot, therefore, give us any certain result
as to the increase of juvenile crime, or as to the
effect of Ragged Schools in checking it. On the
other hand, the last report of the Bristol Ragged
School Society, states, "In the Schools in Temple
parish, 9 boys were committed in 1848, only 4
were committed in the last year. Of boys attending
the St. Philip's Evening School, 12 were committed
from April 19, 1847, when the School was opened,
till the close of the year; 11 in 1848; and only 4 in
the last year. The diminution may in part be attri-

buted to the influence of the institution, and of the wholesome discipline of the Industrial School." Those, however, who are fully conversant with the actual working and progress of such Schools, with the individual characters of the boys frequenting them, and at the same time with the existence, at least undiminished, of a very great amount of juvenile crime in that city, will probably attribute the diminution of the number of committals from the Schools to the fact, that though boys of vicious character will frequent such Schools at their first opening, and while they continue in a somewhat disorderly state, yet that they will seldom persevere in attendance, or endure the discipline of a well-conducted School, and hence cease to go to it.

Again: statistical returns may give a very erroneous idea of the amount of the criminal population in any district; this is shown in the following extract from the evidence of F. Hill, Esq., Inspector of Prisons, before the Committee of the Lords in 1847.*

"With reference to the numbers of habitual offenders, in saying that it is smaller than is generally supposed, I do not mean to say that compared with the number of occasional offenders it is smaller, but that the criminal population is much smaller than is generally imagined, in consequence

---

* " First and Second Reports from the Select Committee of the House of Lords, appointed to inquire into the execution of the Criminal Law, especially respecting Juvenile Offenders and Transportation; together with the Minutes of Evidence taken before the said Committee, and Appendix and Index, 1847."

of the very large number of distinct offences which any one habitual offender commits where crime is his trade. I may mention in illustration of this, a case that came to my knowledge some time ago, of three families, consisting of 15 members. They were the families of three brothers, and it was ascertained that of those 15 members, 14 had been in the constant habit of making and uttering false coin. I made an estimate of the number of distinct offences which this body of criminals had committed; and it appeared highly probable, considering the issue of every separate coin as a distinct offence, that not fewer than 20,000 separate offences had been committed by those three families, considering every separate issue of a false coin a distinct offence. So large a number being issued by those families, and the families moving about, and appearing first here and then there, it would probably create in the minds of the public who could not put these facts together, a supposition that there was a much greater number of persons employed than was really the case. In many instances I have ascertained by inquiries of the police, the precise number of habitual offenders in a given town—for in small towns the criminals are frequently well known—and I have generally found the prisoners to be very small. By a reference to my second report, which contains much information on this subject, it will be seen, for example, that the town of Kinghorn, in Fife, containing a population of about 1,500, there were at the time of my inquiry just 9 thieves. Even in places of much larger size, the number of offenders appears to be often very small."

While, then, we shall not enter on a minute statistical examination of the amount of juvenile crime, referring all who wish to do so to 'the published tables, and to such valuable works as Mr. Fletcher's "Moral Statistics of England and Wales" (which, however, is not published), it will be important carefully to consider a few tables and statements on the subject, which, having been made by individuals who have had peculiar opportunities of accurately investigating the subject, and delivered in to parliamentary committees, may be regarded as having great weight, as well as calculated to give a more distinct impression than mere general statements.

From a paper delivered in by Mr. Pearson, as part of his evidence before the Select Committee of the House of Lords, the following most important facts are selected :—

" It appears from parliamentary returns and other authentic documents, that during the present century the number of commitments and convictions for crime has increased in this country greatly beyond the increase of population. In a period of 40 years, the population, 10 years old and upwards, has increased 65 per cent., while the proportionate commitments for crime have been augmented 494 per cent., and the convictions 625 per cent. Until the last 10 years, the returns do not specify the ages of the prisoners ; but, as appears by these later documents, the number of juvenile criminals has increased in a greater degree than even the mass of criminals at large. Thus the number of criminals under 20 years of age, committed to prison in the year 1835, was 6803, or 1 in 449 of the population, between 10 and 20 years of age ; while in 1844 they amounted to 11,348, or 1 in 304 upon the population of the same age. This increase of crime cannot be attributed to an increased degree of poverty and ignorance, for it has gone on in an inverse ratio to the accumulation of national wealth, and to increased means of education afforded to the masses. It is likewise worthy of remark, that although the last 3 years show a decrease in the number of commitments and convictions in respect of the whole population of England and Wales, (which the Premier and Secretary of State have, in Parliament, truly ascribed to the increased prosperity and industrial occupation of the masses of the people,) yet the stated decrease during those years is in respect of the adult population only ; as upon comparison of the two periods, the number of commitments and convictions of juvenile offenders has increased in the 3 latter years upwards of 7 per cent."

Mr. Pearson remarks, however, that though crimes have increased in number, they have been less aggravated in character, and that various changes which have taken place between the two periods of comparison may have had effect on the numbers of convictions, and prevent our considering the amount of actual crime, as truly indicated by them. Yet, on the other hand, he adds, " It is believed that the number of summary convictions for petty offences, in England and Wales, which do not find a place in the returns of commitments and convictions from which the foregoing calculations have been made, amount to more than three times the number of convictions at the assizes and sessions which form the basis of such evidence."

" I am very desirous," says Sergeant Adams, " of having this return in my evidence before the committee of the Lords. The number of summary convictions under the Metropolitan Police Act, of children under the

age of 16, in 1834, was	1557	}1820
The number of convictions of those tried by juries	263	
Summarily convicted in 1835 . . .	1624	}1806
Tried by juries	182	
Summarily convicted in 1836 . . .	1662	}1825
Tried by juries	163	
Summarily convicted in 1837 . . .	1819	}1958
Tried by juries	139	

" Among those summarily convicted as ' reputed thieves,' there are no less than 32 children of the age of 7 years ; and it is singular, that though these children have been convicted as reputed thieves, there is not one case tried by a jury under the age of 8 years.   Of the age of 8, there are no less than 90 who are summarily convicted as reputed thieves, and there are in the same period but 3 tried by juries ; so that there are 32 children of 7, and 87 of 8 years, who have acquired the reputation of reputed thieves, making altogether 119, during a period in which 3 only are tried for theft."

What are these poor children to become, who have acquired a reputation for thieving at so early an age, —who have been inured to the police-court and the prison, while others, the children of the same Heavenly Father, are tenderly watched over in the nursery ?

It is stated in Mr. Neison's " Statistics of Crime," that in the whole of England and Wales the number of persons under 15 years of age who are tried and convicted, only form about one-seventeenth part of the total numbers of all ages.   But this gives a very inadequate idea of the proportion of juvenile to adult offenders in our large cities.   Sergeant Adams states, that in the Midland Circuit, which he attended, he found few juvenile offenders, and he believes that the large towns are where they are to be chiefly found, few being met with elsewhere.   In saying this, we are not of course to understand that ignorance and sin do not exist in as great, perhaps in a greater degree, in the rural districts,—this would be the subject of a very different inquiry ; but that large towns are more favourable to that precocious development of crime which brings the young offender under magis-

terial correction.   The metropolis exhibits this early
training to vice in an overwhelming extent; next to
it are some of our large seaport towns.   Mr. Rushton,
in his evidence before the Lords, gives the following
extract from the report of Captain Williams, Inspector of Prisons, for 1840, respecting the state of
juvenile delinquency in Liverpool:—

"During one year, the number of male juvenile prisoners
committed to the Liverpool Borough Prison, was, in proportion to the whole number of male prisoners, much greater
than in any of the gaols selected for comparison, and the proportions of juvenile re-committals was, in Liverpool, nearly
double that of the average proportion of the metropolitan
prisons, and more than double the average of the five remaining English prisons ; whilst of the worst class of re-committals,
(those who had been in gaol four times or oftener,) the proportion in Liverpool was upwards of seven times the average
proportion in the metropolitan gaols, and nine times more
than in the five provincial gaols.   The proportion of male
juveniles to the whole number of male prisoners committed
to the Liverpool Borough Gaol, was 4 per cent. more than the
average proportions in the six metropolitan prisons ; $8\frac{1}{2}$ per
cent. more than the proportion in Salford New Bailey Prison;
$10\frac{1}{2}$ more than Bristol ; 10 more than Warwick ; $12\frac{1}{3}$ more
than Wakefield ; $7\frac{1}{2}$ more than Hull ; and 4 per cent. more
than Glasgow ; or about 9 per cent. more than the average of
6 of the largest provincial prisons attached to the most
populous manufacturing and commercial towns and cities in
the kingdom.   The character of the offences for which they
were committed will be evident from the fact, that of 709
juvenile prisoners committed during the year to the Liverpool
Borough Prison, 316 were committed as known or reputed
thieves, and 256 as vagrants.   The proportion of male juvenile
re-committals to the whole number of male juveniles during
the year, was, in Liverpool, 66 per cent.   Of these, $28\frac{1}{2}$ per

cent. had been in prison four times or oftener ; so that 66 out of every 100 boys committed to this gaol had been previously imprisoned ; and more than 28 of each 66, who had been previously committed, had been in gaol four times or oftener. In the Metropolitan districts the proportion of re-committals to the number of juvenile prisoners, averaged 35½ per cent., and in the other five gaols in England 32¾. The number of re-committals to the Glasgow Bridewell does not appear in the returns. *Compared with the proportion of re-committals in the adult class of male prisoners, the proportion in the male juveniles was much greater generally,* the average number per cent. having been in the Metropolitan gaols 35½, whilst of adults it was 23 ₁₀th, and in the other five gaols the average re-commitments of juveniles was 32½, and of adults 18½ per cent. In Liverpool the proportions were, of adults, 36 ; of juveniles, 66 per cent. The returns of the preceding year exhibit nearly similar results. Of the 2740 juvenile re-committals to 203 prisons in England and Wales, 299, or about 1-9th of the whole, occurred in Liverpool ; and of the 506 juveniles who had been in gaol four times or oftener, the number in Liverpool was 138, or upwards of 1-4th of the whole number of this class in 203 prisons from which the returns were made. It is a cause of satisfaction to learn from the last report of the Chaplain of the Liverpool Borough Gaol, that there is some improvement since that time, but the per centage still remains very high. ' It is pleasing to notice,' he says, ' that whilst the instances of relapse of juveniles into crime, in the years ending 30th Sept., 1843, 1844, and 1845, have been 52, 50½, and 49 per cent. respectively, those of the year to which this report refers (1847) have been little more than 41 per cent.' This improvement is ascribed by Mr. Rushton, ' in great measure to the care and vigilance of the Chaplain, and also to the great care on the part of the Governor of the Borough Gaol, who has taken much pains, and has in a very beneficial manner bestirred himself about this matter, in taking care of the lads who are there, and delivering them up to their parents, and so forth."

Here is a specimen of a prison return, which must make the blood thrill:—

Paper delivered by Captain Groves to the Select Committee of the Lords. Return of two boys sent to Milbank Prison, under sentence of seven years' transportation.

Name and Age.	Crime.	When and where tried.	Remarks by judge.	Whether before convicted.	Time supposed to have lived on crime.	Character of Parents.	Remarks by Chaplain.	Remarks.
John Nicholls aged 7.	Stealing monies.	June 12, 1846, at Warwick.	None (!)	Not known.	Not known.	Bad: Connections bad.	None.	Sent to House of Correction, under the provisions of a conditional pardon.
Dominick Rafferty, aged 8.	Stealing 9d in copper.	Oct. 21, 1846, at Preston.	"Must be separated from his family and connections."	Not known.	Lived by crime, from the time he was capable of committing it.	Thieves and vagabonds; father tramps about the country; an elder brother transported; another 12 years old who has been eight times in prison.	"The habits and society in which this poor child has lived, render it almost impossible to develop, in his short stay here, any good tendency in his feelings or disposition.	Rejected by order of the Secretary of State, as unfit to be received.

These two children were believed, from their appearance, to be little more than six years old.

The subsequent history of poor little Dominick, the "prison nursling" of the excellent Chaplain of Preston Gaol, to which he was returned, will be given hereafter. No wonder is it that sheriffs and judges feel perplexed how to deal with such cases!

" The most puzzling part of our duties," says R. Wigham, Esq., Sheriff of Perthshire, in his evidence before the

Lords, " is, how to deal with juvenile offenders ; there is nothing which is so difficult of solution." He tells us that there is a boy at present in prison, who says he will not go out at the expiration of his twelve months. He is ten years of age, and had been before imprisoned in Edinburgh. This poor child is an orphan, having no one to look after him. He was quite ignorant when he came in, and has not learnt much during the six or eight months that he has already been in prison ; though a clever boy, he is one of the worst behaved in the gaol. The fare of the prison is porridge and milk, good wheaten bread, broth and meat on alternate days. Having been " in a state of destitution," and leading a miserable life in the street, what wonder will it be if the miserable little outcast, when again turned out on the world, should by crime again seek admittance to what is his only comfortable home."

Now let us hear a few facts respecting the ages of these juvenile offenders :—

" Sergeant Adams states before the Select Committee of the Lords, that of the 100 prisoners whom he has to try every fortnight, from 16 to 40 are boys ; some even of the age of 7 ; a few of 8, and a great number of 9 and upwards ; of these children the offences are, for the most part, of a pilfering description, to which the young children are tempted by older persons. 'A large proportion of these poor children,' says Mr. A., 'are wholly and entirely without friends and relations of any kind ; others have profligate parents who neglect them ; another class have stepfathers and step-mothers, who abuse and ill-treat them ; some have parents who encourage them ; and almost all are quite uninstructed in religious, moral, and social duties. I should say the evil is far more deeply-seated than in the natural disposition of the children themselves. I do not think they are naturally worse than other children ; but that these offences spring from the want of proper moral and religious education, and in the want of proper friends to attend to them.'"

The Right Hon. J. Shaw holds sessions, he states, at Dublin twelve times a year, trying on an average about 2,000 prisoners, of whom from 300 to 350 are boys under 15; there are some girls, but not many.

"I generally give them," he says, "for the first offence, three months; for the second offence, six months; and if it is a young boy I do not generally transport him, but give him perhaps twelve months imprisonment for the third offence; sometimes, not often, I pass sentence of transportation upon a boy under 15 years of age, if he is a very hardened offender, and has been convicted frequently before. About a third of those tried before me have been convicted of former offences. I have sentenced many boys between 10 and 12; but I do not recollect any younger. The greater part are destitute and abandoned children, or the offspring of profligate parents, but many may be the children of small tradesmen; I have sometimes dismissed children on the promise of the parents to look after them."

The maturity in crime, exhibited by these poor children is appalling.

"There is an extraordinary precocity as regards crime," says the Rev. Whitworth Russell, Inspector of Prisons, in his evidence before the Lords, "observable in children whose moral training has been neglected. I have recently conversed with one of 7 years of age. I conversed this morning with one under sentence of transportation who is only 9 years of age, and that child is a girl. I have written to the Secretary of State this morning, to authorize me to send back the child from the Transport Depôt, as being utterly unfit, under any circumstances, for transportation. There is an older sister convicted with her, a child of fourteen years of age, and a sister-in-law. I have had no time to investigate the particulars of the case, except that it was a case of housebreaking:—the only fact I ascertained was, that they said "all our misfortunes have arisen from the loss of our mother, and our having a bad stepmother." Though such juvenile delinquents are mostly found in towns, I have found the same premature advancement in criminal habits in rural districts. One of the most artful offenders I ever saw was a girl, who came from one of the rural districts of Buckinghamshire, where the child, though not more than 10 or 11 years of age, had secreted a small light ladder, with which she used to go to cottages when they were left by families to work, get in at the upper window, which was often left open to ventilate the house whilst the lower part was locked, steal different things out of the house, and carry them away to her parents, profligate people who had urged her to pursue this guilty course."

Cases of this kind might easily be multiplied as those can testify but too well who have familiarized themselves by actual contact with the juvenile part of the criminal population. We will take only one other example, given by Alexander Nichol Caird, in his "Cry of the Children." (1849.)

"A creature," he says, "*six or seven years old, was recentl brought up for housebreaking.* Its age manifestly put punish ment out of the question, and the only practical resource left to the administrators of the law, under the guidance of the highest authorities, was a solemn reprimand from the judge,— a measure whose propriety no one will dispute. Behold, then, the majesty of offended justice adequately personified on the bench, and surrounded by all the circumstantials which are calculated to affect the imagination,—the grave deportment of a public prosecutor, armed with authority to denounce or to spare, and then most fitly exercising his office of forbearance,— the anxious countenances of the bar, stirred by unwonted feelings,—the attendant lictors ready to execute the behest of the law, the crowded spectators eager to catch a glimpse of the prisoner:—and thus,—"*parturiunt montes*," turn to the great depredator who has put all in motion, elevated on a table to bring him into view, answering to his name with infantine pipe, on being prompted,—and studying with intense satisfaction the dress in which he has been equipped for the occasion. With this hopeful subject the judge had to deal ; and after feeling his way with all the tact and patience for which he is distinguished, and anxious to test the little culprit's ideas of a court of judicature, he put the question, " Do you know that I am a judge ?"   The shrill, simple, Scottish answer, " What's that ?" electrified the court, upset its gravity, and showed all too clearly the hopelessness of dealing effectually with such a creature in the imposing forms of law.   But it was not all a mockery : for thus was tried and found wanting the society of which that child was an outcast, and there was written in the record of a higher tribunal, " Inasmuch as ye did it not to one, the least of these my brethren, ye did not to me !"

Without at present considering how far society can and ought to remedy the fearful ignorance existing among these outcast children, let us endeavour to gain some idea of its extent and nature. It may at first surprise us to hear a gentleman of great experience, and possessing ample opportunity of gaining information on the subject, express some doubt of the amount of ignorance existing in our criminal population.

"When engaged in my office of Under-Sheriff," says Mr. Pearson, in his evidence before the Lords, " I paid great attention to the subject of juvenile delinquency ; the enormous increase of crime generally, and of juvenile crime in particular, arrested my attention.   Mr. Cotton, the late Ordinary of Newgate, had a register of many hundreds of the juvenile prisoners that had passed through Newgate.   During the time I filled the office several hundreds passed under my observation ; I spent much time with them in conversing with them, separately and together ; and the conviction produced on my mind was in entire accordance with the experience of Mr. Cotton, that the juvenile delinquents, as a class, were not destitute of education, but that, on the contrary, a very large portion of them had received a considerable degree of instruction."

Now, though many circumstances may make Newgate no fair criterion for the educational condition of the prisoners through the whole of the kingdom, yet, if we form our judgment only from the "reading and writing" tests, we may come to the same conclusion from the examination of gaol returns, and doubt whether ignorance has so much to do with crime as is generally supposed. But of the danger of trusting to such records, which, however carefully made, cannot give an idea of the real condition of the subjects of them, Mr. Pearson gives the following caution:

" The returns received from the prisons as to the state of the acquirements and education of prisoners, are to a surprising extent in contradiction to what I believe to be the actual facts of the case. The amount of instruction a child has received when brought into gaol, is by no means to be estimated by the answers he gives, and the answers the chaplains return. The juvenile classes of thieves are the most subtle, crafty, acute, mendacious body you can possibly imagine. They are perfectly aware that they are now objects of great compassion; that ignorance is supposed to be the cause of their position. For the purpose of the prison returns the question to them is, ' Can you read ? ' ' No.'—Can you write ? ' ' No.' Prisoners recommend themselves to the compassion of the officers of the prison, who place them under the chaplain, and the schoolmaster of the prison. In the course of a month or two they acquire a degree of intelligence, and a capacity for reading and writing, which would seem to show that the prison school far surpasses any other seminary for education that the mind can conceive of, such is the rapidity of their progress. But let them get into the world again, and be brought again to prison, the same questions are put to them, —' Can you read ?' ' No.' ' Can you write ?' ' No.'—I have been from my earliest infancy a devoted advocate for education ; but I am satisfied that the cause of juvenile crime is not the absence of education ; and that any education of the children of the labouring classes that is not accompanied with industrial training, and their actual employment in manual and useful labour, will entirely fail in checking the growth of crime."

Instead, then, of referring to the ordinary educa-tional statistics, let us avail ourselves of the carefully analysed records of chaplains of gaols, from which we shall also be able to gather not only the degree, but the nature of the education the prisoners have received.

Though it may be impossible from mere statistic tables to form a true estimate of the real relation between ignorance and crime in this country,—so variable are the criterions on which such tables are founded, so easily may the most accurate be led into error by the misstatement, intentional or otherwise, of the prisoners,—yet the testimony of such a man as Mr. Clay, who for more than a quarter of a century has been anxiously and watchfully fulfilling the painful yet most important duties of Chaplain at the Preston House of Correction, must be entitled to great weight. The wise and careful manner in which, by judicious questions and skilful experiments, he has ascertained the nature of the instruction which his prison inmates had received, will show that the mere statement of the numbers who can read or write well, indifferently or not at all, will give a very inadequate idea of the degree of real education they have received.   In his evidence before the Committee of the Lords, in 1847, he states that the cases of extreme ignorance among the juvenile and adult prisoners, amount to 43 or 45 per cent.

" I call it," he says, " extre meignorance, when a man, or woman, or child, cannot repeat a word of prayer—when they cannot do it intelligibly.   They attempt sometimes to repeat the Lord's Prayer, but they make gibberish of it.   I call it extreme ignorance when they cannot name the reigning Sovereign, or the months of the year.   I have found a great number that did not know the months of the year ; and when I have put the question to them in the plainest way I can ' Do you know who is reigning over us ? ' the answer has been ' No.'—' Do not you know the name of the Queen ? ' " Prince Albert, is it not ?"   I have conversed with 1,301 men and boys, and 287 women and girls, out of about 3,000, in this state of ignorance.   I have found 1,290 men and boys, and 293 women and girls so incapable of receiving moral or religious instruction, that to speak to them of virtue, vice, iniquity, or holiness, was to speak to them in an unknown tongue.   They have a vague impression of the immortality of the soul, and that when they leave this world for another they will be rewarded or punished, but they know little or nothing of the conditions of the reward or punishment.   As respects mere ignorance, I cannot say that I have known many instances of persons who did not believe in the existence of a God at all, and that is the ground of our hope, but they have no sense of a God constantly present and superintending them."

" In the month of February last," says Mr. Clay, in his report for 1848, " I requested the schoolmaster to procure specimens of writing and spelling from all the male prisoners

(185) then incarcerated, who professed the ability to give
such specimens. A copy of the Lord's Prayer was the exercise required. Sixty different attempts were made by as
many different men, to comply with my wishes, and the result
may be thus classified.

Class No. 1.—1, accurate in every particular.
    „   2.—2, deficient as to capitals and punctuation.
    „   3.—2, only 1 error in spelling.
    „   4.—5, 2 errors in spelling.
    „   5.—7, 3 or 4 errors in spelling.
    „   6.—6, from 5 to 8
    „   7.—15, exhibiting great ignorance.
    „   8.—22, scarcely intelligible.

"The only accurate specimen was written by a young man
of 17, who had been well instructed in a school of superior
character." After speaking of the other classes, he gives the
following specimens of the 7th : "Hour father witch hart in
haven, &c.," "Our father wicth chart, &c." "Our father
which heart, &c." "Oure father Wich art, &c." 12 of the
specimens of the 8th class were utterly unintelligible. " I
copy," he says, " some of the others, were it only to exhibit the
real amount of knowledge in persons who might be hastily set
down by some inquiries "as able to read and write" and therefore fit to be included among the " educated." " Hour father
with har in heven, thy Cingdom come," and (written in a fair
hand ; writer aged 39). " Ower father who art in heven all
wead be thy neama, thy will dun on erth," &c. (writer aged
17.) Eighteen prisoners of the 7th and 8th classes had been
convicted of felony, and were noted in our calenders as able to
read and write " imperfectly." The description cannot be
said to be wrong, when all the degrees of instruction possessed
by prisoners are comprised under four heads, viz.: " n,"
" neither read nor write ;"—" imp," able to read and write
imperfectly ;"—" well," able to read and write well ;"—" sup,"
" superior education ;" but certainly no sufficient idea of the
actual want of knowledge is conveyed by the " imp," of our
calendars, when it is made to comprise such instances as I
have presented. It would seem indeed that some of the im-

perfect reading and writing, when tested, only serves to demonstrate an amount of ignorance greater than could be supposed possible, even in persons who are marked in the calendar as capable of neither one nor the other."

The following tables are from the same report :—

Religious Knowledge of Prisoners :—

	Sessions. Per cent.	Summary. Per cent.
Ignorant of the Saviour's name, and unable to repeat the Lord's Prayer . . .	37·5	37·0
Knowing the Saviour's name, and able to repeat the Lord's Prayer, more or less imperfectly	51·7	59·0
Acquainted with the elementary truths of religion	10·0	7·6
Possessing that general knowledge level to the capacities of the uneducated . .	·6	·1
Familiar with the Scriptures and well instructed	·0	·0

Ignorance in prisoners on the most ordinary subjects, as compared to their direct or indirect acquaintance with demoralizing literature :—

Unable to name the months	61·8	60·5
Ignorant of the name of the reigning sovereign	59·1	59·1
Ignorant of the words, "virtue," "vice," &c.	61·5	58·4
Unable to count a hundred	6·8	12·8
Having read, or heard read, books about Dick Turpin, and Jack Sheppard . . .	52·6	44·0

Whole number of prisoners—Sessions, M., 265 ; F., 73.
Summary, M., 859 ; F., 186.

Can there be a stronger proof than is presented by these tables, of the utter deficiency of any moral and religious training, or even of any ordinary culture of mind in these 1383 persons, who came under the penalty of the law at Preston; yet nearly half of them, however deficient in other knowledge, had found the means of access to such books as would stimulate their worst passions and encourage them in crime. It will also be noticed, that while the continual proportions of the Sessions cases, and the Summary convictions, are nearly equal in all other particulars, a much larger proportion of the former, which may be considered the most heinous, have become acquainted with these demoralizing productions.

Let us now take the evidence of another Chaplain, in whose district society may be expected to wear a very different aspect from that of the manufacturing population of North Lancashire.

The following is an analysis of tables presented to the committee of the Lords by the Rev. John Field, of Reading Gaol.

"In 1846, of 631 prisoners, 3 only had received a superior education; 11 could read and write well; 192 could read and write imperfectly; 189 could read but not write; 236 could not read; 204 were ignorant of the Saviour's name, and could not repeat the Lord's Prayer, of these last 65 could read; 2 only of the whole number were familiar with Scriptures, and had been well instructed in religious truths: 398 were imperfectly acquainted with the simple truths of religion; 27 had learnt the creed, commandments, and catechism, remembering the most important parts.

" The offences committed by these culprits,,' he says, most truly, " have been the natural and almost necessary consequences of neglect. A greater number had received some measure of instruction, yet so wretchedly defective had been the character of their education, that for restraining vice, or directing in the practice of duty, it had been altogether inadequate. Children—or still childish men—have learnt to read or write, but they have not learnt to think about, or to understand, any thing which they have been taught. Words are to such men sounds; they are not signs. The ear has heard them, and the tongue has learnt to give utterance to them, but the mind has received no ideas or impressions from them. Hence these criminals have no realizing sense of any important truths, which it is supposed they have been taught, and consequently, though acquainted with terms, they remain ignorant of motives. Conscience, indeed, once whispered approval, or condemned, but its voice has been stifled—it has ceased to warn. Thus, men who might be, and if properly educated would have been, rational, really live without intelligence."

Similar to this testimony is that of the Rev. W. C. Osborne, Chaplain of the Bath Gaol. The following table is selected from the Educational Statistics for the year ending Sept. 30, 1849, in the *Fifteenth Report of the Inspectors of Prisons of Great Britain*, and is very valuable, as founded on constant, careful observation. It will be observed, that while six-sevenths could repeat the Lord's Prayer, nearly one-half knew nothing of the gospel history, and three-fourths could not repeat the Ten Commandments; while nearly one-half had been at a Sunday School above a year, three-sevenths could not write their name, and only 21 had received a good national education:—

In the gaol Sept. 30, 1848, 83; admitted during the year, 625; total, 708.
608 could repeat the Lord's Prayer, . . 100 could not.
173 could repeat the Ten Commandments, 535 could not.

374 knew something of the gospel history, 334 knew nothing.

344 had been at a Sunday school for 12
      months and upwards . . . . } 303 not at all.
 61 for less periods . . . . }

515 could spell easy words . . . . . 193 could not.

296 could read the Bible . . . . . . 412 could not.

400 could write their name . . . . . 308 could not.

194 could write a letter . . . . . . 514 could not.

 39 could write well . . . . 669 could not.

 30 were acquainted with the first four }
      rules of arithmetic . . . . . } 678 were not.

 21 had received a good national education 687 had not.

"During the last year, 1850," Mr. Osborne states
in a recent lecture, " of the prisoners brought under
my own care, 222 had never attended a Day School,
—303 had never attended a Sunday School at all.
With regard to the most commonplace elementary
knowledge, such as the name of our Queen, the day
of the month, the name of the county and kingdom,
as to how many months, weeks, and days there are
in a year, I found that 473 could give no satisfactory
answers. And so it was with regard to religious
knowledge of the simplest character. As to the
questions, 'Who made you, and all the world?'
'What book teaches us to know God?' and 'Who
is Jesus Christ?' there were upwards of 100 entirely
ignorant."

It is evident, from a careful examination of these
statements, that a depth of ignorance almost incredible to those who on the one hand have thought
but little respecting the condition of the lower classes
of the community, or on the other have taken a per-

sonal interest in it, is consistent with crime, and doubtless in great measure the cause of it ; but that at the same time the mere circumstance of having attended a Sunday or some other School for twelve-months or more, produces very little effect in opening the faculties to the true reception of knowledge, or even communicating the most simple elements of it. We shall, however, discover another truth not less important from what follows ; namely, that the mere mechanical power of reading and writing, unaccompanied by sound moral, industrial, and religious training, really prepares the ill-disposed for greater audacity in crime,

" The number of prisoners," says Mr. Smith, the Governor of Edinburgh Gaol, in his evidence before the Lords, " during the year ending the 30th of September, 1846, who could neither read nor write, was 317 out of 4,513 ; 292 could read well; 85 could read and write well, and 3 had received a superior education. There is a remarkable fact elicited by the table from which this statement is derived, viz., *that the number of re-commitments of those who can read well*, is much greater than the number of those who cannot read at all."

Parkhurst Prison, in the Isle of Wight, was built for the reception of juvenile offenders sentenced to transportation, with a view of reforming them previous to sending them to people a new country. "Three qualifications are now necessary to qualify a juvenile for admission into that reformatory," says Sergeant Adams in his charge, 1849 ; "he must be fourteen years of age, four feet six inches high, and of a character so depraved that he would be sentenced by the Court to transportation if Parkhurst Prison did not exist." But for some years before these regulations were fixed, so great was the difficulty of judges respecting these poor children, that they frequently condemned them to transportation with a view of placing them under the discipline of Parkhurst. It will then be important to ascertain the educational condition of these boys, who are selected on account of their very depravity.

" Captain Hall, Governor of Parkhurst Prison, states before the Committee of the Lords, 'that the great majority of the boys sent there are uneducated ; the proportion who could read and write with tolerable readiness would be but small, and the proportion of those who have any real understanding of what they read is very small indeed. Yet it is a remarkable fact, that of between 1100 and 1200 boys that have been received into Parkhurst from 1838 to 1847, there have been only 36 who have never been to school at all. But though the very large majority, 96 or 97 per cent., have been at school they have learned little or nothing ; they were truants : there are here truants from schools in all parts of the country. Many have been at the National Schools ; many have been at private, or Lancasterian Schools !"

Mr. England, the Chaplain of Parkhurst, has ascertained the following important particulars, not only in reference to the actual amount of education in the children coming under his care, but the length of time that they had been at School. It is extracted from the Parkhurst Report for 1839 :—

Digest of acquirement.	Knowledge of Scripture.	Table showing the period during which the prisoners attended Day-schools previous to conviction.
Read tolerably 20	Considerable 7	
" indifferently ...38	Some 16	
" scarcely at all...14	A little...............20	
" not at all.........30	Scarcely any or none 59	Under 1 year ... 22
Write tolerably 11	*Knowledge of the meaning of words in use.*	From 1 to 3 years 44
" indifferently 27	Some 15	From 3 to 5 years 21
" scarcely at all...12	A little...............74	From 5 to 8 years 5
" not at all.........52	Very little 13	From 8 to 12 yrs. 2
Cipher tolerably ...11	Scarcely any or none 60	Never at school ...8
Add and subtract ...12	*Information from general reading.*	——
Scarcely at all.........79	Some 16	102
Repetition of Church Catechism.	A little............... 9	
Well... 24	None 55	Longer than 1 yr. 69
Tolerably 26	Forgotten 22	Of these schools 35 were connected with
Imperfectly 33	——	the Church of England;
A small portion......29	102	25, private schools; 27,
All can repeat the Lord's Prayer.		Scotch and other free schools.

Those who are aware of the very irregular habits of children such as these, will feel that this time-table can by no means give a true idea of the period during which a boy was actually at School; but, even making this allowance, it is painfully evident that such instruction must have been very inefficient. While 69 have been longer than a year at School, and 28 from three to five years, only 20 can read tolerably; of these, only 16 have "some" general information from reading, and knowledge of the meaning of words in common use: the rest of the 102 have little or none;—and only 11 can write and cipher tolerably. The religious instruction also must strike every one as injudiciously given, and quite inadequate to influence the life; 24 can repeat the Church Catechism well, and all have more or less a knowledge of it; while only 7 have any good knowledge of Scripture, and 69 have scarcely any or none.

Even more striking results are derivable from more recent observations in the Report of Parkhurst Prison for 1844. It is a table showing the number of convicts who had been in the establishment, and the period and description of School at which they had received instruction.

Period.	National.	Lancasterian.	Infant only.	Factory.	Regimental.	Workhouse.	Private.	Sunday only.	Total.
Under 1 year	42	43	4	—	—	5	39	27	160
1 and under 3 years.	116	95	17	6	2	6	86	30	358
3 „ 5	120	56	2	3	3	12	46	4	246
5 „ 8	71	27	—	2	—	4	40	1	145
8 „ 12	11	1	—	—	—	—	6	—	18
Never at school.	—	—	—	—	—	—	—	—	30
Total.	360	222	23	11	5	27	217	62	957

Numbers attending day-schools longer than one year...... 732
Average period of schooling received by these 732.... 3 years 10 months.

On comparing together these various tables, the conclusions must necessarily follow that the mere " reading and writing" test will not indicate the real amount of ignorance in the criminal population of our gaols; that professed attendance at Day and Sunday Schools, is still less a safe criterion; and that the absolute ignorance of even the most simple truths of religion and the Gospel history, as well as the undeveloped state of their faculties respecting the subjects of their reading, or the most common elements of knowledge, affords the strongest proof, were others wanting, of the utter deficiency of this class in sound education. The elaborate and closely-reasoned essay of Mr. Fletcher, on the " Moral Statistics of England and Wales," gives results quite in correspondence with the foregoing.

" These numbers," he says, " afford but feeble testimony in favour of much of the instruction which is now being given." And from a number of carefully drawn tables he arrives at the following important result :—" The proportion of the wholly uneducated in gaol, is *less* than the proportion of the population at large, equally in the most purely agricultural districts of the south and east, and in the most purely mining and manufacturing districts of the north and west, which are respectively the most positively ignorant and criminal ; while in the most instructed counties, whether of the north or the south, and whether metropolitan, agricultural, mining, or manufacturing, the converse is seen. The only explanation of this fact which suggests itself to my mind, is, *that there is no less difference in the quality than in the amount of instruction given* in the most and least instructed portions of the kingdom respectively ; *and that it is only a degree of careful uptraining of the young, far higher than that which can be tested by the lowest attainments in reading and writing, that is alone blessed to the good end of righteous living in a Christian hope.*"—" The conclusion," he says, " is therefore irresistible, that *education* is not only essential to the security of modern society, but that such education should be solid, useful, and above all Christian, in supersedence of much that is given by the weakest of the Day Schools, and attempted by the most secular of the Sunday Schools."

But we are not now to consider the subject of education generally, but only that lowest and most neglected portion of society from which the wholly uninstructed criminals are derived; and that other portion, which, having received some degree of instruction, when it has once fallen into the criminal class and received its brand, sinks lower and lower still, to swell the tide of vice that overwhelms us. We would inquire whether the existing Schools are not open to them as to all, and whether the extension of these by a more general system of education will not meet the existing want. That it will not is incontestably proved by the fact, that in New England, where the experiment of a national education has been tried with the best success, and under the most favourable circumstances, it has failed to reach this class.

Here is a revelation from Massachusetts, dated, "Boston, April 27, 1849":—

"During the past year, more than one thousand children, between six and sixteen years of age, were registered by the Day Police as truants and vagrants. In February and March, no less than eight fires were found to have been set by minors in different parts of the city, some of which destroyed much property. Many lads have lately been arrested for drunkenness, some under seven years of age.

"Both the City Police and the Ministers at large, and others who have much knowledge of the condition of our community, are convinced that there is need of a mission to the destitute and morally-exposed children of this city, that they may be rescued from evil, and surrounded by good influences."

This emanates from a minister of the gospel; in New York, in the next year, the "Chief of Police" is moved to make a yet stronger appeal to the Mayor of the City. After giving the total number of arrests for the year (14,274), he goes on to call the attention of the Mayor to a deplorable and growing evil existing in that community, of vagrant, idle, and vicious children of both sexes, who infest the public thoroughfares, hotels, docks, &c. From reports made to him, he estimates the number of these children at three thousand, of whom two-thirds are between the ages of eight and twelve years. After enumerating the different classes of juvenile criminals, he thus concludes :—

" In presenting these disagreeable facts for the consideration of your honour, I trust that I may be pardoned for the suggestion in conclusion, that, in my opinion, some method by which these children could be compelled to attend our schools regularly, or be apprenticed to some suitable occupation, would tend, in time, more to improve the morals of the community, prevent crime, and relieve the city from the onerous burden of expenses for the Almshouse and Penitentiary, than any other conservative or philanthropic movement with which I am at present acquainted."

The existence, then, of a number of Free Schools is not alone a preventive of juvenile vagrancy, still less will any number of National or British Schools, where the weekly payment, however small, would be an insuperable obstacle to those who required every farthing to supply their physical wants, or would be unwilling to spend it for what they did not value. But would any good Day Schools receive these children ; to the poor and inefficient ones we should not

care to send them? We know that the masters or
superintending committees of such would generally
exclude, as undesirable associates for those under
their care, the outcast or vicious children, young in
years, old in all the arts of crime; and rightly so,
for the strength and independence of character so
early developed in these would have a most powerful
and evil influence over the spirits of the young, who
are not yet hardened by vice or strengthened by
principle. Nor would these ill-clad children feel at
ease in the company of the clean and neat ones;
there is a very strong feeling of aristocracy pervading
even the lowest classes, manifested, though it may be,
in ways which to the more favoured ones may appear
absurd; perhaps, indeed, it exists even more strongly
in those who have nothing to be proud of *but themselves*. They *will not* come to be looked down on by
those whom they feel superior to themselves in external advantages only. The experiment was tried
by Sheriff Watson at Aberdeen. He details his experience in a speech at the third Annual Meeting of
the Glasgow Industrial and Ragged Schools :—

" About ten years ago, his (Sheriff Watson's) attention was
particularly called to the case of the destitute outcast children
found in great numbers wandering about the streets and
throughout the county of Aberdeen. It was then constantly
said that education was the great means by which the children might be reclaimed and made better. He accordingly
resolved to test the power of education, and endeavoured, if
possible, to have every child in that town sent to school. It
was not difficult there to organize a society for any scheme
that might be proposed. It was, therefore, determined that

an association should be formed for the purpose of enabling every child of poverty, every child of destitution, to go to school. The houses of the destitute were visited, and wherever it was found that the child could not obtain education on account of poverty, a ticket was given to admit such child for a certain period to any school, without exception ; and if it remained there during the period specified, the ticket was renewed. Of course, all the children being sent to school, education, had it stood the test, must have put an end to juvenile vagrancy and delinquency ; but it did not do so. He was met by two objections, different in their nature, but very serious in their aspect. The first objection was, that they were filling the schools frequented by the higher class of scholars—children of respectable parents—with the children of those who were known to the police to be 'habit and repute thieves,' and compelling the children of honest parents to associate with those who were taken from the streets, and accustomed to the habits of vagrant delinquency. But another objection presented itself still more serious. In visiting the abodes of the destitute, they found the wretched inmates, as in all large towns, in a condition in which they could not avail themselves of the means of attending school ; so that placing a ticket in their hand was, as one of the visitors had observed, very much like offering the child a stone instead of bread."

There is another reason even stronger than these, which renders the existing School establishments absolutely unavailable for this class of children. Were we to undertake to clothe them, and to keep them clothed, (a still more difficult · undertaking,) during their attendance at School,—did we use such precautionary measures while there, and on their way to and from School, as effectually to prevent their contaminating the other children,—a thing almost impossible,—*they would not attend*. The whole system of our good British Schools is utterly unfitted for them, and would not be endured by them. Their habits of independent and wild freedom, accustomed as they are "every one to do what is right in his own eyes," without any regard to others, would render the discipline there enforced utterly abhorrent to their natures; while a different system, such as will be hereafter described, may render them as docile, and as susceptible of instruction, as any other children. Again;—the attendance of such children at School must necessarily be irregular. The parents are seldom engaged in any fixed, regular occupation, and though a large proportion of them may offer no objection professedly to their children attending Schools, they care in reality so little about it, that they will not take the slightest trouble to facilitate it, and will constantly keep them away for their own convenience. While at a good Infant School, and a British School, in one of the worst localities of a large city, the bulk of the children are sent clean, neat, and with tolerable regularity, even by parents in the lowest depths of poverty,—inquiry being anxiously made by them if anything seems amiss,—in a Ragged School, distant but a few minutes' walk, the master asserts that there is scarcely a parent who takes any trouble to send the child to School, numbers proving utterly careless of the most earnest entreaties to keep their children from the contamination of the streets ; and that the regularity of attendance at the School, which is now considerable, is almost entirely owing to the interest in it excited in the children themselves.

It is evident, then, that not only for the well-being of our existing British, National, and other Schools, for the labouring classes of the community, but to effect our object at all of providing instruction for these children, Schools specially adapted to them must be provided for them. But there is a large portion of these children who will not be induced voluntarily by any means to attend School, and it is peculiarly from these that the criminal class directly emanates, if they do not already, at the tender age of seven or eight, glory in being distinguished members of it, having served out their apprenticeship for transportation by numerous convictions, as we have already seen. Surely these call more loudly for a restraining, as well as a helping hand;—they have already shown us that if we withhold it they will exact from us a heavy penalty. For these the large towns of England as yet afford no refuge from that school of vice in which they are such proficients; though individual effort has in some places attempted to provide a remedy, which has been inefficient from want of power and means. In some of the large towns of Scotland, the experiment has been tried under more favourable circumstances, and its success removes from us all excuse for not making similar efforts.

After thus stating the principles which should regulate all Schools for the children of the perishing and dangerous classes of the community,—we shall consider :

First.   The necessity of establishing good *free Day Schools*, for such children as cannot attend other Schools, from the poverty of their parents, or from their own want of character or necessary clothing. Under this head Ragged Schools will be noticed, as the only attempt which has hitherto been made to supply this need; their inefficiency, as generally carried on, to prove an effectual check to ignorance and vice in the lowest population, will be shown, and the principles investigated on which they are conducted.

Secondly.   The establishment of *Industrial Schools*, with food given, for those children, who, through extreme poverty or vice, subject themselves to the interference of the police, for their vagrant and pilfering habits ; the attendance at these should be *compulsory* on all who will not attend the Free School.   These, as they are to deliver the public from a serious nuisance, *should be supported by a municipal or parochial rate.*

But these Schools provide only for those children who have not yet come within the iron grasp of the law.   When, by crime, they are constituted " children of the state," the gaol is the only nursery, the only School provided for them by their stern step-mother.   Strong are often the misgivings of those who, in the discharge of their duty, are *compelled* to commit these young creatures to an imprisonment and a discipline, which, however admirably calculated for the reformation of adults, they feel, *they know,* by long years' experience, is quite inefficacious to check juvenile crime; and if so is worse than useless. But it is the law,—the law which has forgotten the distinction once acknowledged between infants and adults, and which now treats both alike, giving only the added power to the magistrate, in the case of the child, to inflict the degradation and suffering of corporal chastisement, as well as incarceration. We shall then—

Thirdly, consider the prison system in reference to juvenile offenders, and prove its uselessness, as well as costliness, from the testimonies of persons eminently qualified to form a correct judgment on the subject. Having shown the inefficiency and the injurious tendency of the prison system for juvenile offenders, various *Reformatory Schools* will be carefully examined, both as to their principles and their details; and their applicability as substitutes for prisons, under suitable restrictions, will be shown.

But before proceeding to these inquiries, we are met by objections strongly felt by a large class of persons, and those whose co-operation would be most important in carrying out the plans here proposed,—persons of really benevolent mind, but who have seen so much mischief arise from injudicious giving of alms, and from apparently excellent charitable institutions, that they look with a suspicious eye on any new effort which may disturb, as they imagine, the ordinary course of nature, or interfere with those maxims of political economy which they hold sacred. The objections of such persons deserve our serious consideration, and we shall now attempt to answer them, while we entirely disregard the cavils of those who have no faith in human nature, no practical belief in Christianity, no real knowledge of the subject on which they treat, and who only desire an excuse for doing nothing to help their fellow-beings.

The first objection is mainly this; and it applies particularly to the proposed Free Schools. " Unless the training and proper education of the poorer class at large were undertaken as a state duty, and similar Schools, with at least equal advantages, esta-tablished and maintained at the general cost for them, you are acting unjustly to the self-denying and industrious poor, who are struggling to educate their children by their own efforts : if you freely give to the profligate and careless what they are obliged to toil for, you are conferring a bonus on vice."

How little a sound political economy has to do with such objections, may appear from the following answer given to them by the ablest economist of the present day :—

" It may, indeed, be objected, that the education of children is one of those expenses which parents, even of the labouring classes, ought to defray ; that it is desirable that they should feel it incumbent on them to provide by their own means for the fulfilment of their duties, and that by giving education at the cost of others, just as much as by giving subsistence, the standard of necessary wages is proportionally lowered, and the springs of exertion and self-restraint in so much relaxed. To this argument there could be no reply, if the question were that of substituting a public provision, for *what individuals would otherwise do for themselves*. If all parents in the labouring class recognized and practised the duty of giving instruction to their children at their own expense, no one would seek to undermine so virtuous a habit by volunteering a needless assistance. It is because parents do not practise this duty, and do not include education among those necessary expenses which their wages must provide for, that the general rate of wages is not high enough to bear those expenses, and that they must be borne from some other source. And this is *not one of the cases in which the tender of help perpetuates the state of things which renders help necessary*. Instruction, when it is really such, does not enervate, but strengthens as well as enlarges the active faculties : in whatever manner acquired, its effect on the mind is favourable to the spirit of independence ; and when, unless had gratuitously, it would not be had at all, help in this form has the opposite tendency to that which in so many other cases makes it objectionable : it is HELP TOWARDS DOING WITHOUT HELP."—*Principles of Political Economy, by John Stuart Mill.*

With respect to the discouraging effect which these Schools are alleged to have on the industrious labouring classes, we believe it is not the fact. They have been receiving a benefit which they can fully appreciate, in the enlightened exertions which are being made to enable their children to receive, for a very small weekly stipend, advantages of education which four times the sum would not have procured for them in their younger days ; and thousands of them have come forward to give their unpurchased services to these untaught children. And will not they derive a certain benefit from this to themselves and their children, independently from that which must arise from every act of self-sacrifice? Do not many of them live in near proximity to these outcasts, and are they not liable to be themselves exposed to continual annoyance and injury from them, and to have their children infected by the corrupting influence of bad example? In justice, then, to the industrious labouring classes, such Schools *ought to exist;* and on them, and on their children, directly and indirectly, they are conferring a boon.

But a more serious objection presents itself in the minds of many to the Industrial Feeding Schools, and to the Penal Reformatory Schools. " We cannot, without danger, interfere with the universal laws of Providence, which entail on parents the care of providing for the physical wants of their offspring. By such institutions you are relieving parents from the only check on their vicious indulgences. The profligate and idle will be led into parental neglect by the hope that others will supply their deficiencies, or will even incite their children to crime to relieve themselves from the burden of them. You are increasing the spirit of dependence which has been already engendered by charitable institutions, and offering a bonus to vice." This objection is valid, and the danger a real one; but both may be removed.

With respect to those parents who are absolutely unable to provide for their children, no greater encouragement to dependence is presented to them, than is already given by parochial relief. If, as is already done in some parishes of Glasgow, [Vide *Report of Industrial Schools*, 1849,] the same allowance were made to an Industrial School, as is now given to the parents or guardians, dependence and neglect would be checked, instead of increased, by such Schools. " It is undeniable," the report states, " that a large portion of the funds formerly granted for the maintenance and education of the children, was misapplied through the vices of their parents or guardians. Instances have not unfrequently occurred, in which boys and girls have been apprehended by the police for begging in the streets, whose parents, while thus encouraging their children in habits of idleness and dishonesty, have been in the regular receipt of an allowance for their maintenance and education." A similar instance has recently come under the notice of the master of a Ragged School :—A widow was receiving parish pay for each of her three little boys, whom she left entirely to their own guidance, to pilfer or indulge in lawless habits. The master used every persuasion to them to attend School, but unavailingly ; their rags and occasional starvation were more than counterbalanced to them by the charms of liberty ; two got into Bridewell, but it was no effective warning. The elder soon was again in prison, now for more than four months, *during the whole of which time the mother continued receiving the allowance,* without any remonstrance for thus rearing up her children to vice.

Was not this an encouragement to parental neglect, which would have been removed by Industrial
Schools, to which the young vagrants should have
been taken by the policeman, and to which her
allowance for them should have been paid?

There are again parents who can support their
children, and who might, by a system of Industrial
and Penal Reformatory Schools, be relieved of the
responsibility which nature has laid upon them. The
objection would be just, if they were allowed thus to
escape from their duties. But, if a man is compelled
to support his family if able, and punished if by his
own neglect he throws the burden on the parish,
why should not equally stringent regulations enforce
the charge of maintenance on those who not only
throw the charge of their children's bodily wants,
but of their moral training (the most expensive
item), on the state? Such a provision ought to form
an important feature in any government regulation
for such Schools; it was contemplated so long ago as
1846, by a committee appointed at the sessions of the
justices of the peace for the county of Middlesex,
to report to the court their suggestions for checking
the growth of juvenile crime, and promoting the
reformation of juvenile offenders. Petitions founded
on the report of the committee, were presented to
both Houses of Parliament. It was desired that
various clauses of a proposed Act should provide that
" an Asylum should be established by legislative en-
actment, for affording religious and moral training to

such children of the destitute and dangerous class as may be brought before the local magistracy, and proved, on oath, to be in the class specified, and des-- titute of proper guidance ;—that this Asylum should be under the control of the visiting justices, subject to the approval of the Secretary of State for the Home Department, and to government inspection ;— and that the cost of erecting and maintaining the establishment be defrayed out of a county rate, *the parents of the child being compelled to pay for his maintenance, as directed by the Poor Law Act.*" In a printed proposal for an Act recently prepared in Scotland, it is especially provided that "it shall be competent for the treasurer, or other officers of such institution, to prosecute the parents of such young persons for the cost of their support therein, and to recover the same from the means and effects of such parents; and in respect to the alimentary nature of the claim, with power to imprison on the decree ; and such debt shall be preferable to all and every other claim."—Similar suggestions were laid before the Committee of the Lords in 1847 :—

" If, on the one hand," says Mr. F. Hill, Inspector of Prisons, " by the general introduction of industrial occupations, edu- cation were made as cheap as I believe it may be rendered, and its advantages made apparent even to the most ignorant, and, on the other, a *parent were held responsible for his child's support in prison if the child should afterwards fall into crime*, as I have ventured to suggest in some of my reports, a very powerful motive would be given to every parent to attend to the proper education of his children, instead of allowing them to grow up, as is now too often the case, in idleness and ignorance, without the means of earning an honest livelihood, or the power of resisting temptation."

" It appears to me," says Mr. Sergeant Adams, in his evidence before the Committee of the House of Lords, " *that our* PRESENT *system is a premium upon persons in low life to make their children thieves.* We know that the provision for children presses very hard upon persons in low life. The moment a child is convicted of theft he ceases to be a burden to his parents. In like manner all expense is taken from the parish. It is all thrown, if you sentence him to imprisonment, upon the county at large; if you sentence him to transportation, upon the country at large. The effect of this system is, that you embark all the lower and more sordid feelings of the human mind against you, instead of for you." Mr. A. recommends that the parish should be made liable for the expenses attendant on the placing a young offender in a Penal Reformatory School, and that it should have the same power of enforcing payment from the parent, as in case of desertion. Matthew Davenport Hill, Esq., Recorder of Birmingham, also states :—

"This suggestion is by no means new to me. I have considered it much, and am strongly of opinion that it would be a wholesome provision." In reply to the question, " Do you think, from the experience you have in the particular district in which you have administered justice, that it would be applicable to a large proportion of the cases brought before you, and that in a large number of such cases the parents are in such circumstances, that practically such a power could be enforced?" he answers, " I think it could be enforced to some extent. If the parent could not afford to pay the whole, he might afford a part ; *at all events I would bring him before a magistrate and give him a feeling of responsibility, which at present he does not possess;* and after a sufficient amount of experience had been obtained by a provision of that kind, it would remain to be considered whether a very careless parent ought not to be regarded as an accessory before the fact, and if he should not have the means of maintaining his child be punished himself. I do not mean to say that it would be wise to attempt that *per saltum*, because there has not yet been a sufficient amount of experience upon the subject ; but I look forward to the possibility of its being found reasonable and practicable after a time."

If these moral objections are satisfactorily removed, we hope that no others would be allowed to weigh seriously against such Schools as are proposed, should they be proved to be an effectual remedy to the moral disease existing; yet as there is in the minds of many a certain "idolatry of figures," especially in reference to pecuniary outlay, we will now proceed to show that the expense to the county, to the government, and to the public at large is much greater on the present plan, than if reformatory measures were vigorously adopted.

"The first is an estimate of the expense to the county of 55 juvenile prisoners committed to prison for the first time at the New Bath Gaol, during the year ending 1st July, 1844, prepared by the Rev. W. Osborn.

The probable or approximate cost of these is as follows :—
For maintenance of these 55 at different times in the
    New Bath Gaol, during the six years ending July 1st,
    1849, amounting to 27½ years of punishment then   £
    inflicted, which, at £20 a-year   550

		£
For maintenance of ten of them, who have been transported from Bath, calculating that they will be a public burden for only half of their sentences, 50 years, at £25 a year		1,250
To 183 summary convictions by magistrates for warrants, summonses, &c., estimated at 5s. each ...		50
To 64 committals for trial, prosecutions, averaging £10 each		640
To maintenance of those 55 for six years, while out of gaol unemployed, living at unions, or by begging, supposing that they honestly maintained or supported themselves for half the time of the 252½ years while out of gaol (the 77½ years under punishment being deducted), which gives 126¼ years for this item, at £8 per annum		1,039
To property destroyed, robbed, or lost, over and above the amount for their support, supposing this item to be equal to the preceding		1,039
To rent for cells in gaols, at £6 per annum, for 77½ years		465
To maintenance of five of them known to have been transported from other places, calculating only half of the usual sentence of ten years		625
To maintenance of some of these known to have been in other gaols for offences committed and punished elsewhere, for nearly 5 years, at £20 a-year ...		100
To expense of prosecutions elsewhere ; five are known to have taken place, at £25 each		125
Rent of cells for these during 29½ years, at £6 per year		180
		£6,063

Mr. Sergeant Adams presented to the Select Committee of the Lords a " Summary of a Return showing the number and age of prisoners up to sixteen years inclusive, committed for trial at the Middlesex Sessions during the year 1846; the offence, sentence, value of property stolen, cost of prosecution, and cost of maintenance in prison after conviction." From

this the following important facts may be derived.
The ages are as follows :—

	OFFENCES.								PUNISHMENT.									
Age.	Sex.		Simple Larceny.		Stealing from the Person.		Other Offences		10 years Transportation.		7 years transportation.		From 6 to 9 months.		From 1 to 6 months		14 days and under.	
	M.	F.	M	F.	M.	F	M.	F.	M.	F.	M.	F	M.	F.	M.	F.	M	F.
8	2	1	2	—	—	1	—	—	—	—	1	—	1	1	—	—	—	—
9	10	1	8	1	1	—	1	—	—	—	—	—	3	—	5	—	—	—
10	16	0	16	—	—	—	—	—	—	—	—	—	4	—	6	—	4	—
11	31	1	29	—	1	1	1	—	—	—	—	—	15	—	8	1	2	—
12	50	2	44	2	5	—	1	—	—	—	1	—	17	1	23	—	4	—
13	60	7	49	4	10	2	1	1	1	—	—	—	24	3	25	2	3	—
14	90	9	76	9	14	—	2	—	—	—	6	—	28	4	38	3	1	—
15	61	11	46	11	12	1	2	—	2	—	3	—	23	5	28	4	—	2
16	151	27	107	16	41	6	3	3	9	1	9	3	60	6	39	10	1	3
Tot.	471	59	377	43	84	11	11	4	12	1	20	3	176	20	172	20	15	6
	530		420		95		15		13		23		196		192		21	

The value of the property stolen by these 530 juvenile
offenders, on the occasions for which they were committed,
was only £158 7s. 9d. ; the cost of their prosecution £445 17s.
3d. ; the cost of their maintenance in prison after conviction
£964 12s. 2d. ; hence the expense to the public, during one
year, of these 530 children was £1410 9s. 5d. ;—but to this we
must add, the expense of transportation of 36, which, reckoned
on the authority of Mr. M. D. Hill at not less than £82 each,
would amount to £3952 ; and besides, as 388 were sentenced
to imprisonment from 1 to 9 months, a large proportion of
their maintenance by the public cannot be included in this
estimate, as it would extend into the next year. Now, if this
sum were expended in the reformation of these young criminals, it might be deemed small ; but when we learn from the
statistics of Mr. Osborn, that only 5 of the 55 whom he noted
were in any degree reformed, and that the rest were a constant
expense to the country in repeated prosecutions ; when we
infer from the small amount of money stolen that a large proportion must be young beginners, who are likely, from the
testimony of a cloud of witnesses, to go forth from their imprisonment into the world hardened in crime, and taking their
place in the almost hopeless class of those who have ' lost
their character,' some, children of 9 or 10, many, young crea-

tures of 11 or 12, surely we should try to find some better way of ridding our large cities of this constantly increasing disease.

In 1846 a petition was presented to both Houses of Parliament by the Magistrates of Liverpool, which sets forth the expense of the present system in a yet stronger light.

" That at the Reformatory Institutions in Warwick, already much good has been effected. From the year 1833 to 1841, 77 boys between the ages of 14 and 16 years were admitted into the Warwick Asylum,—the cost of their clothing and maintenance was £1026.

" That, in order to enable your Honourable House to form a judgment of the cost of the present system, your Petitioners beg to record the actual cost attending fourteen cases of juvenile delinquents, who have from time to time been committed to the prison of this borough. The cases referred to were fairly selected, in the year 1842, from the mass of juvenile prisoners in the prison, by one of their body, who was at that time endeavouring to ascertain the charge incurred by the treatment of juvenile offenders in prison, in contrast with those in reformatory institutions.

" That the costs of prosecution, in the estimate, relating to these fourteen cases, are much less than the usual costs, because the Corporation of Liverpool are the public prosecutors, and all expenses are most economically conducted.

" That the costs of apprehension, maintenance, prosecution, and punishment of No. 1, was £129 5s. 6½d. ; of No. 2, £71 2s. 10½d. ; of No. 3, £74 1s. 10½d. ; of No. 4, £71 13s. 1d. ; of No. 5, £47 9s. 3d. ; of No. 6, £64 6s. 6½d. ; of No. 7, £99 2s. 5½d. ; of No. 8, £72 1s. 4½d. ; of No. 9, £52 9s. 7¼d. ; of No. 10, £64 18s. 9¼d. ; of No. 11, £28 10s. 4½d. ; of No. 12, £39 8s. 10½d. ; of No. 13, £26 10s. 10d. ; of No. 14, £47 7s. 7½d. : and thus the offenders cost the public £889 1s.

That for the more full development of the moral and financial results of the present system of punishing juvenile offenders, your Petitioners have traced, as far as it can be ascertained, the subsequent career of the above-mentioned fourteen prisoners.

" That at the time of the return, four of them, namely, numbers two, four, six, and ten, were under sentence of transportation; that number one died in prison; that number three, after being again once imprisoned, was transported; that number five, after two several additional periods of imprisonment, was also transported; that number seven, after six several additional periods of imprisonment, was also transported; that number eight, after six several periods of imprisonment, was also transported; that number nine, after one imprisonment, was also transported; that number eleven, after sixteen several additional periods of imprisonment, is again in custody for trial; and that number twelve has been imprisoned seven times since the return, but is now out of gaol a prostitute; that number thirteen has not been heard of in Liverpool since the date of the last return; and that number fourteen has been transported after an additional period of imprisonment.

" That it thus appears ten out of the fourteen children have been transported; that one is dead; that one is now in custody; that one is still among the criminal population, and of one only is there any hope of reformation, and of the last-mentioned nothing is known.

" That the costs of the various apprehensions, detentions, and imprisonments of these offenders, will have to be added to the costs already given, and, in addition, the cost of the final transportation of the ten prisoners must also be added.

" That none of these fourteen offenders could write, and only one of them could read, and that imperfectly.

" That an Asylum of the same character, though of but small extent, has for some time been established, with beneficial results, in the county of Warwick.

" That of these 77 boys, 41 have been reformed.

" That the cost, divided by the number of the reformed only gives about £25 as the cost of each reformation, whilst the costs of punishing offenders of the same class in the Borough of Liverpool, by the foregoing statement, cannot be much, if any, less than 100 guineas."

The following case of a single family will give
some idea of the expense which the public are now
supporting.

" Four Manchester pickpockets, O'Neil, aged 21, his wife,
aged 17, her brother, aged 18, and a companion, aged 18, were
convicted at Preston in April 1850, and sentenced to transportation ; and two of the gang were afterwards apprehended and
summarily convicted as rogues and vagabonds. A second brother of the girl was, at the same time, under sentence of imprisonment in Kirkdale ; and a third brother, aged 15, had just
been liberated from a seventh imprisonment in Manchester New
Bailey. The sentence of transportation, when it did come at
last, seemed, so to speak, to break them down ; a complete
change took place in them. They gave me their respective
histories independently, which, besides the intrinsic evidence
of their substantial truth, mutually corroborated each other ;
three of the parties made, independently of each other again,
estimates of the yearly plunder made by each individual of
the gang, and the following are the particulars. There is an
estimate made by Richard Clark ; an estimate made by his
sister, and an estimate made by her husband. The result is,
that during the 6 years for which Richard Clark had been
thieving ; the 9 years that O'Neil had been thieving ; the
$2\frac{1}{2}$ years that Ellen O'Neil had been thieving, always picking
pockets ; the $2\frac{3}{4}$ years that Edward Clarke had been thieving ;
the 5 years that John Clarke had been thieving ; the 5 years
that Thomas O'Gar had been thieving ; the 7 years that
John M'Giverin had been thieving ; the 20 years that Thos.
Kelly had been thieving, I make it out that they had robbed
the public to the amount of £16,640; from that may be de-
ducted £4,030 for the time they had passed in prison, leaving
a net sum of £12,600 ; but to that you have again to add
maintenance during their stay in prison, and the ultimate expense of transportation. In my own mind I am satisfied that
these eight thieves have mulcted the public to the amount
of £13,000."

Can we hesitate, then, to feel with Mr. Clay, who detailed the foregoing case in his evidence before the Committee of the House of Commons during the last year, and in whose last prison report even more startling particulars are given, that, "the most energetic measures are necessary generally, in order to obviate this tendency to crime at its very outset, and that something might be done by letting the responsibility rest painfully upon the parents : in the case of this family the whole is attributable to the ·father and mother."

Now it will be hereafter shown, that the expense of Penal Reformatory Schools, conducted on a good and economical plan, is much less than that of the system at present pursued, as well as being more effective; but as the Industrial Schools where food is given are now more immediately under considera-tion, we may quote the *Second Report of the Glasgow Industrial Schools* for 1849, as a proof of the very great saving to the public by such insti-tutions, especially if we take also into account the indirect but heavy expense of maintaining these children by thieving, if not in confinement. "It is well known that nearly the whole of the children admitted to these schools would, if left alone, become either paupers or thieves. The maintenance of these poor children, and the instructing them in religious and secular knowledge, does not exceed £4 each per annum; and when it is stated that the cost of maintaining paupers in the Town's Hos-

pital of Glasgow, was last year upwards of £13
per head, and that the average cost of prisoners in
all the prisons of Scotland is £16. 7s. 4d. per head
annually, it must be admitted that, apart altogether
from the good which has been effected in saving
many human beings from destruction and misery,
the money expended on these Schools has been a
measure of real public economy."

It is, indeed, to quote the same report, "a fixed
principle that, the more profligate the person, the
greater burden is he to the community;" and all
who have personally and philosophically examined
the subject, from the general philanthropist to the
chaplains and governors of gaols, bear the same
testimony, that to whatever extent other auxiliary
measures may be useful, from none but a good
industrial, moral, and religious training, can a real
and permanent effect be expected, in checking the
progress of crime. The same testimony was strongly
borne by the judges who sent in their opinions to
the Committee of the Lords in 1847. They all,
more or less strongly, express the same opinion as
Mr. Justice Cresswell:—

"*I am of opinion that good education, including infant training, as well as sound religious and moral instruction, will do
more to lessen the prevalence of crime than any mode of dealing
with convicts that can be devised.*"—"Our best hopes," says
Baron Alderson, "rest upon a good and religious course of
education for the people,—an education which shall mainly
be directed to teaching them their duties to God and man,
rather than merely giving them information. I do not under-

value the latter. I only think it of immeasurably less value than the former."—" My experience is," says Mr. Baron Rolfe, "from the marks affixed to the names of all the prisoners in the calendar indicating their amount of education, that at least a third can neither read nor write; at least a third more can read but cannot write, and very few indeed are able to read and write well. The inference is, I think, very reasonable, that education would have a very great influence. It may be that those who, included in the two first classes, have been committing crimes, have not done so from want of education; but I am persuaded a large portion of them have. *The union of a total want of education with criminal conduct is too general to be merely accidental;* and I must add that my experience does not lead me to believe that crime is generally the effect of distress or destitution. It much more frequently is the effect of recklessness, *arising from the degradation of ignorance,* and the total absence of self-respect."—" *I am confident that this education,*" says Lord Cockburn, "*must materially diminish crime.* It won't altogether prevent it—nothing ever will; *but it will lessen both its frequency and its enormity; and it immensely facilitates the reformatory process, when conviction makes its application necessary. It is our great hope.*"

Let us, then, with true and earnest spirit, full of Christian love, and with all the power which the highest wisdom can afford us, seek to carry to those that perish for lack of knowledge, healing and life-giving waters, without money and without price, even if they are so sunk in ignorance that they are not yet athirst for them. Yet let us, while striving thus to obey the precepts of the Christian's Lord, interpret them with that sound understanding which a careful study of the universal order of Providence, and the principles of good government will cultivate. Let us not withdraw from parents that responsibility which is the inalienable law of nature, and often the only curb which can in any way check them in a vicious career ; the parent should never be relieved from that responsibility,—that check,—that weight, —as long as he is in a position to bear it.   If his inability arises from his own fault, the state must punish him for that fault, which is producing such baneful effects, not only to his own children, who are to become members of it, and will be most diseased members if the remedy is not applied,—but to society in general.   If, however, his inability is no fault of his, but the effect of circumstances over which he has had no control,—the State,—the parent of all, —while endeavouring, if possible, to alter these circumstances, should give him a helping hand to enable his children to rise up to be, not a burden, but a support to the country ;—the Christian should fulfil the law of love, " Bear ye one another's burdens," " ye that are strong should bear with them that are weak."

These are no theoretic or visionary views, they are those on which men act in the ordinary affairs of life, on which the State already acts in parallel cases.   If a parent is afflicted with a dangerous and contagious disease, will not all having any interest, however remote, in the children, strive to remove them from him, however earnestly he may desire to have them near him?   Or if he is under the influence of mental derangement, especially if it be of such a kind as is likely to be injurious

to the children, will not friends interpose, and obtain
the sanction of the State to remove him from them,
to place him where he can no longer harm them,
and to subject the children to the guidance of
those who give evidence of being suitable protectors?
Yet we would leave children with a parent infected
with that disease which worketh death, and who
is madly striving to implant the seeds of it in
his offspring;—we would allow him to scatter the
plague-spot among them undisturbed, and make
them, too, centres of corruption, because, forsooth,
we would not abridge his liberty;—we would allow
him, unrestrained, when afflicted with the most
awful madness, that which must lead to the destruction of his soul, not only to be the scourge of
society generally, but to convert his young children
into firebrands, to kindle vice wherever they fall.
Can those be the principles of a true political economy which are in opposition to the plainest teachings of common sense, as well as to the most earnest
dictates of religion? It cannot be! If we impiously
exclaim, " Am I my brother's keeper?"—the Lord
will reply, in a voice we shall be compelled to hear,
" The voice of thy brother's blood crieth unto me
from the ground." A fearful retribution will come
upon us, which we shall find increasingly heavy to
bear, the longer we delay to fulfil towards these
" little ones" the commands of that Saviour, whose
words cannot pass away, though Heaven and earth
should be removed.

CHAPTER I.

HAVING now, it is hoped, shown the necessity of applying a system of sound moral and religious training to the children of the dangerous classes, we proceed to consider the principles on which Schools adapted to such a purpose should be established.

Let us, however, first endeavour to gain some insight into the real position and character of the children whom we desire to rescue from their moral degradation.

The external aspect of these poor children is calculated to excite compassion in any heart not rendered callous by absorption in the world's selfish interests ;—their tattered garments, their bare feet, their starved look, their mean and degraded aspect, on which the parent's vice has imprinted legible characters even in infancy,—must touch even those who regard them only as young beings, susceptible as our own children of privation and suffering. But let us look at them as the future actors in the world's theatre, destined to increase the vast amount of evil now existing if their course is not arrested,—and still more as the heirs of an immortality the condition of which is dependent on their life on earth,—and the painful external aspect loses its horrors in comparison with the infinitely greater dangers which attack the immortal spirits of these young creatures. Truly says Dickens,—

"There is not one of these—not one—but sows a harvest that mankind *must* reap. From every seed of evil in this bog a field of ruin is grown, that shall be gathered in, and garnered up, and sown again in many places in the world, until regions are overspread with wickedness enough to raise the waters of another deluge. Open and unpunished murder in a city's streets would be less guilty in its daily toleration, than one such spectacle as this. There is not a father, by whose side in his daily or his nightly walk these creatures pass ; there is not a mother among all the ranks of loving mothers in this land ; there is no one risen from the state of childhood, but shall be responsible in his or her degree for this enormity. There is not a country throughout the earth on which it would not bring a curse. There is no religion on earth that it would not deny. There is no people upon earth it would not put to shame."

Let us select a few out of the many pictures drawn by eye-witnesses, of the scenes that present themselves to those who attempt the work of juvenile reformation.

The following is from the diary of the master of a London Ragged School, and is extracted from the *Sunday School Teacher's Magazine,* April 1850.

"*October* 29,—On the way to the school this morning in company with ———, who has been appointed to act as my assistant, we were saluted by women and boys as we went along, in a most singular manner. I cannot say that the exclamations and gestures of these people were significant of displeasure, but rather the reverse ; however, their coarse and brutal manners had a most disheartening influence on me. I looked in vain for some manifestation of feeling that would enable me to 'thank God and take courage.' It was a dismal scene—no appearance of thrift or industry, nothing but squalid wretchedness and dirt and idleness ;—the lanes leading to the school were full of men, women, and children, shouting, gossiping, swearing and laughing in a most discordant and unnatural manner. The whole population seemed to be on the eve of a great outbreak of one kind or another ; ready for anything but work. These lanes are a moral hell. The place and the people beggars description. * * * No school can possibly be worse than this. It were an easy task to get attention from savages ; a white man's appearance would ensure him some sort of regard ; but here the very appearance of one's coat is to them the badge of class and respectability ;—for although they may not know the meaning of the word, they know very well, or at least feel, *that we are the representatives of beings with whom they have ever considered themselves at war. This is not theory, but fact."* Fearful scenes soon occurred. After separating two girls who had been fighting and yelling most furiously, and sending one home who was severely hurt, he continues, " I had not been quiet for ten minutes when a fearful outbreak took place. Seven women rushed into the school ; the stairs were full besides ; and outside at least fifty women had collected. These were the mothers and friends of the girls who had fought. Having abused me in no measured terms—and, if I mistake not, they collared me—they proceeded to fight. ——— remonstrated with one woman, and I with the others ; so we stopped their battle. Our boys cheered most tremendously. The women swore and shrieked. Those outside (several men among them) responded. Never surely was such a noise heard before. I did not believe that human beings resident in this most Christian metropolis could so behave."

Can we wonder if juvenile crime increases when the young are growing up under such influences ? Truly has it been said, "Train up a child in the way he should *not* go, and when he is old he will not depart from it."

But these had homes which they could claim ;—

many, perhaps the greater number, are early thrown on the world to fight the "battle of life" single-handed.   Here is a graphic description of such, who assembled at the opening of a Ragged School situated in Old Pye-street, Westminster; it is extracted from the *Ragged School Union Magazine*, January, 1849.

" One fine Sabbath afternoon, in the month of April, when the streets were unusually crowded, after having provided a large room, we went forth in the company of a poor tinker (the only person in the neighbourhood who would render us any assistance), to gather together these poor and outcast children of the streets.   After no small effort, forty were taken to the room, all of whom looked as wild as deer taken from the mountains, and penned up within the hurdles, when approached by man ; the matted hair, the mud-covered face, hands, and feet, the ragged and tattered clothes, that served as an apology to cover their nakedness, gave the group a very grotesque appearance, and would have been a fine subject for the painter's pencil. Little was done that afternoon besides taking their names, and even in this we had to encounter difficulties.   Beginning with the first bench, a boy was asked, ' What is your name ?'   He answered, ' They calls me Billy.'   ' Where do you live ?' ' I lives in that yer street down the way, at mother M——'s rag shop ; I have a tother brother, but I am older than he.' The next boy was ten years of age ; he said his name was Dick. ' Any other name besides Dick ?' ' No, they calls me Dick ; I sells matches in the streets, and live in that tother room next to Jimmy that sells oranges.'   Such is a specimen of the answers given to questions respecting names, age, and residence !"

No way strange is it that scenes like these should occur at the openings of Ragged Schools, when their life is such, as is derived from personal narratives, and facts elicited by careful examination, registered in the pages of the *Ragged School Maga-*

zine. The history of the " Arab of the City" contains
passages descriptive of a state of moral degradation
incredible to those who have moved only in the more
favoured classes of society; the reader who can
realize them as he peruses them, must shudder.
Here are a few specimens of the frequent position of
children of the class we are considering, and probably
not the most degraded, for they are from a number
selected for emigration :—

" W. L.—Slept at night under stairs, or behind doors on a
little straw with a sack to cover him. Only took off his clothes
to mend, or to go in the water to get clean. Father dead eight
years ; mother left him in a workhouse when two years old,
and does not know her ; saw her on Sunday morning going to
church, did not know her then ; was told it was his mother.
Runs messages for the stall-women in Westminster ; been in
this condition for at least three years.

" J. W.—No home ; sleeps at Mrs. B.'s lodging-house
when he has money ; pays threepence a night for his bed ;
when no money, sleeps in carts or on landings about four nights
a week. Father deserted mother fifteen years ; mother dead
two years. Occasionally employed as errand boy, or doing jobs.

" C. S.—Father dead four years ago ; was a drunkard ;
mother works at slop-work ; never went to any but the Ragged
School ; has two sisters and four brothers."

Where indeed could these seven poor children
gain any knowledge to help them through this world
to the next, but at such a school?

" D. F., aged about 14.—Mother dead several years ; father a
drunkard and deserted him about three years ago. Has since lived
as he best could ; sometimes going errands, sometimes begging
and thieving. Slept in lodging-houses when he had money,
but very often walked the streets at night, or lay under arches
or door-steps. Has only one brother, he lives by thieving.

Does not know where he is ; has no other friend that he knows ; never learnt to read ; was badly off ; picked a handkerchief out of a gentleman's pocket, and was caught by a policeman. (What follows is the remedy applied by society to cure this deserted boy of a sinful course to which circumstances seemed to impel him, with its results to the individual and to society.) Sent to Giltspur-street prison ; was fed on bread and water. Instructed every day by the chaplain and schoolmaster ; much impressed with what the chaplain said ; felt anxious to do better ; behaved well in prison. *Was 'well flogged' the morning he left ; back bruised, but not quite bleeding. Was then turned into the streets* ragged, barefooted, friendless, homeless, penniless. Walked about the streets till afternoon, when he received a penny from a gentleman to buy a loaf. Met next day with some expert thieves in the Minories; went along with them, and continues in a course of vagrancy and crime."—[*Ragged School Magazine*, vol. ii. p. 61.]

The following is a specimen of the ordinary Police Reports of a weekly paper in a large town.—[*Bristol Mercury*, Feb. 15, 1851.]

" J. S., a boy about thirteen years of age, was committed for a month, for stealing a piece of bacon from a shop. *The prisoner said that his father had been killed by a railway accident, and his mother had deserted him.* It being his first offence, the Magistrates remitted the whipping, which *generally* forms a portion of the punishment of juvenile offenders."

What *can* this poor child do when dismissed from the only home he now possesses—the prison, if no guiding hand is extended to him. Can it be matter of wonder if he avenges himself on that society which has thus cast him in tender years upon the world, homeless, friendless, and with a prison brand upon him? But retribution will assuredly come, sooner or later; for He, whose "words can never pass away," has said, " *Inasmuch as he did it not unto one of the*

least of these my brethren, ye did it not to me." But
again, and on the very same day,

" J. M., an intelligent little urchin, eight years of age, whose
head barely reached above the table, was charged with sleeping,
not on a ' bed of roses,' but on a bed of thorns which he had
selected for his couch, in a garden near. A policeman in passing by, hearing some one cough in the enclosure, at four o'clock
this morning, had detected the *youthful culprit*. In reply to
queries which were put to him, the prisoner said that his
father belonged to Sheffield, and had come down to this neighbourhood in the hope of finding work, but having had the misfortune to beg of a police-inspector in plain clothes, he was
taken up and lodged in Hanley gaol. Prisoner and his mother
went about selling needles ; she lodged in a court in Temple-
street, and was now suffering from a cold, and he not having
taken enough to pay for his lodging last night, was, it would
seem, afraid to go home, and preferred passing the night upon
the cold, cold ground. The magistrates determined on sending for his mother, and cautioning her as to how her son spent
his evenings out in future."

Without commenting on the unfeeling levity of
style of this paragraph, which is a painful indication of
the common mode of viewing such cases, we would ask
whether any thoughtful and Christian man can behold a young child, who in the more favoured classes
of society would be still in the nursery, first deprived
by the arm of the law of him who should have been
his support, next driven into the streets to find a
maintenance for himself and mother, and then compelled by fear to choose a night's lodging in the open
air of a winter's month, rather than incur the risk of
encountering his mother's anger. Is nothing but a
magisterial rebuke to be a remedy for this poor child's
position? But even this was not administered.

Bristol Mercury, March 1.—" J. M., was charged with sleeping in the open air ; the same boy who had been found the other day literally sleeping on a bed of thorns. The boy, *a good looking and intelligent child*, said, in reply to the bench, that when he went down to where his mother had lodged, he could not find her.

" *Q.* ' Do you mean to say that you have not seen your mother since ?'

" *Boy* (bursting into tears). ' No, sir, I have not.'

" *Q.* ' Where did you sleep the night before last ?'

" *Boy.* ' I slept out in the Park, sir.'

" The magistrates now said *it would not do for the boy to be about* exposed in that manner ; and they ordered an officer to take him up to St. Peter's Hospital."

How had the poor child passed his days since his last offence of sleeping on thorns ? If for those few weeks of neglect society is burdened with him for life as a rogue or a pauper, it is only a just reply to the question it had virtually asked respecting him, and thousands like him, "Am I my brother's keeper ?"

Now in all these cases it would really seem that a life of crime is inevitable ;—we know that a life of degradation must necessarily be the portion of beings sunk from childhood in such an abyss, if no hand is held out to rescue them ;—but a large portion of those who attain the higher ranks in crime, (for an aristocracy is observed even here,) are from among those who might, but for their vice, fill a respectable position in society, This is the testimony of one whose experience entitles his opinion to the highest respect.

" I speak not now," says Mr. Clay, " of the utterly destitute and unsheltered,—the friendless and the fatherless ; *it is very rarely that they appear in the felon's dock ;* but I speak of those young transgressors who have parents and homes ! Two brothers, the elder about thirteen, the younger nine, were committed, a few weeks ago, charged with obtaining money on false pretences. I ascertained that the father grossly neglected his children, leaving them for days together without food, and that they had committed their offence in order to procure it. Is this a case," he adds, " for the application of severity ?"

The narratives of prisoners contained in his Reports of Preston Gaol (Whittaker and Co., Ave Maria-lane, London), almost invariably give similar instances of gross parental neglect as the original cause of the commencement of a vicious course, and show that if society had interfered, as in justice to itself it should have done, many who are now transported at the country's expense might have been in a position to pay their own way to the colonies, had they been differently treated. We have here a picture of the home of one now a felon, drawn by himself :—

" Mr. Rev. John Clay,—I take the pleasure of writing these few lines, hoping to the Lord it will ease my mind a little. This I have had on my mind ever since I came here on the 7th of August last. My mother died of the cholera, and ·my father was drinking, and had been several days, and he came home on Saturday night, and begun to curse my mother as she lay ill in bed ! He cursed her as long as I could abide to hear him. I had a glass or two in me, so I got hold of him, and put him down stairs, and we started a-fighting, till the police came and my father went off. He came back again on Sunday morning, drunk, and started a-crying, ' whatever must he do if his wife died ?' He stopped at home all day, and on Monday, about two o'clock, he went off for another doctor, but he never returned of a week or more, when my mother was dead and buried."

Truly says the excellent Chaplain to whom this narrative was addressed—

" If a writer of fiction had described such a scene as this, who could tolerate the picture—could believe in the possibility of such wars, their savage brutality, and that it is generated in places sanctioned by law ? This over-true tale may be doubted, but it would not be doubted by any one who could have seen the pallid cheeks and the quivering lips of the strong, coarse-natured man of twenty-four, who has the memory of the terrible scene in which he himself was an actor, as the constant companion of his solitude."

The preceding sketches will fail to give any adequate idea of the reality to those who have not witnessed similar cases; but they contain important elements on which to base the principles which should guide Reformatory Schools, and they are types of various subdivisions of the classes for whom we destine them. These we shall briefly describe, as on the peculiar characteristics of each must depend the nature of the Schools appropriated to them.

In this review of the " perishing and dangerous classes" of children, we shall not here include those who have already subjected themselves to the grasp of the law, and who are inmates of our prisons ; these emanate from all the different grades that will be enumerated, and will be the subject of the latter part of this work on Penal Reformatory Schools ;— but we shall comprehend in it all those children who are *absolutely unable*, whether from poverty or vice, to receive instruction in the existing Schools, and who, without instruction gratuitously given, must

grow up utterly destitute of it, and will most probably become a burden to the State, either as paupers
or criminals.

First, then, are the children of those parents whom
extreme poverty prevents from sending their children
to School, but who yet desire education for them.
This poverty may be the result, to them unavoidable,
of external circumstances; it may be directly caused
by their own vicious habits; in either case it is
soul-crushing and degrading, and unless a hand is
stretched out to save the children, they will sink
into still lower depths of society. It is useless
for the charitable to defray the weekly payment of
such at the common Schools : their dress, and probably the habits they have already formed, will
expose them to the sneers of their school-fellows,
and they *will* not attend. Yet these very children
are raised and stimulated by the education given in
a good free School, so far superior to what they
were imbibing in the streets. The influence of such
an education has been often seen to be most valuable,
not only preparing the child to gain an honest livelihood, but indirectly stimulating the parents to exertions for their children which they before felt useless,
and inducing a self-respect which is the first step to
improvement. In such cases, education is felt by
the recipients of it to be a real boon, and there will
be that co-operation with the teacher on the part of
the parents which will make the good effects of it
most evident.

Next, are the offspring of parents low and ignorant, who are perfectly careless about the spiritual welfare of their children, and heed their physical condition no more than absolute necessity compels them to do. They have themselves felt no need of education; they are too debased even to understand what it means; they have, like the lower animals, been satisfied with obtaining, as honestly as they have been compelled to do by the laws of society, that food only which perisheth, and they leave their children to do the same. Were there not an indestructible germ of a divine nature in these unhappy little beings, their case would be indeed hopeless; *they* must be first lured to School, and patiently borne with for many a toilsome hour and long day, before the seed of life perceptibly springs up; but the happy influences of a School conducted in the spirit of " love, and of power, and of a sound mind," will be at length perceptible in them also. Many attempts may appear fruitless,—for "seventy times seven" may efforts have been made, and yet some cases of real and decided change of character and life will at last abundantly reward exertion, and the child who was learning to steal will gain his livelihood as a useful member of society. The children of this class cannot be expected to attend School regularly, but patient effort will work a change even in them; and the superior comfort, the more happy state of mind felt by these young creatures in a well-conducted School, obtains from them, even without any inducement but that of kind treatment, a degree of order and attention that would do credit to any School for the labouring classes.

Another and entirely separate class is formed by the Irish population, with whom our sea-port towns abound. They possess very distinctive peculiarities, both in habit and character; the worst parts of the national features are, of course, developed in them; indolent contentment with their condition, however low, excitability, unstableness of purpose, and a jealous yet blind attachment to the Catholic religion,— render it very difficult permanently to act on them; while their warmth of affection, grateful feeling, and quickness of apprehension, make them most interesting scholars when their faults are conquered. When Irish families become permanently settled in our cities, and can be induced to send their children to a School where no interference with their religion is attempted, and where the children of the two sister countries associate on an equal and friendly footing, the surest step is taken for correcting the national faults, and for softening the strong prejudice which now places a barrier between those inhabiting the same street, or even the same house.

For these three classes, good Free Day Schools will generally prove most valuable; and here, as elsewhere, the language of theory is not used, but of actual experience and observation. But it is utterly unavailable to those children of whom examples have been given, who are homeless, and friendless, who are barely maintaining themselves from day to day by hawking and jobbing. There are many among these of fine and noble spirits, early trained to independence and acuteness of intellect, whom the instruction given in the Evening Ragged School has led to a right direction of their energies, and to whom a degree of principle has been imparted, which might put to shame many of the higher classes of society; but for the greater part of them, nothing can be anticipated but that they must fall into the two last classes, the thieves and the beggars, and for these nothing can prove an effective preservation from vice but Feeding Industrial Schools, to which all shall be *compelled* to go, who from inability or from vicious inclination do not attend the Free Day School, and are addicted to vagrant habits.

We usually regard the juvenile thieves as a distinct class, and correctly so as respects those who have even in their youth formed a regular system for themselves, and are members of organized gangs; but there are a large number of boys in our large cities who merely fall into the practice from sheer idleness, or from that love of enterprize so natural to boys, and often lauded in the children of gentlemen;—a few, but comparatively few, are driven to the practice by sheer destitution. The thieves, as a class, would then be speedily diminished, and so marked as to impair their strength, if such a system were pursued as we are advocating;—and the determined culprits could then be submitted more readily to stringent reformatory discipline.

But the last class is even more difficult to deal with, because there is one stamp of degradation on them all, which must make them an hereditary burden to the country, if the young children are not early trained to a different course of life. This they will never adopt *voluntarily* ; their present mode of life is so lucrative and so pleasant, that they will not exchange it for another apparently presenting far greater advantages. Their filth and rags are no annoyances to them, for they are the implements of their trade ; the cold and hunger which they continually endure are most amply compensated by an occasional luxurious meal. The close and noisome dens in which they are stowed at night presents nothing revolting to their feelings, and they prefer them to a clean abode where they must resign their occupation and some portion of their liberty. The elasticity of spirit, the activity of youth, is changed for a degrading and dependent servility, which destroys all wish to rise. We have not known even a solitary instance in which a child who has been accustomed to beg has been induced to attend a Day School regularly, even though allured by promises of an improved condition ;—and if the children of beggars are induced to come they are soon withdrawn by the parents, except in very few cases.

This sketch is imperfect and faint. All who would more truly know these children must visit them in their homes, watch them unobserved in their daily goings, see them in groups planning evil, enter the

" gaffs," the sweetmeat shops, where they are early initiated into the mysteries of gambling,—the penny theatres, where, with all the accompaniments that excite the imagination and feelings, many have learnt their first lesson in crime,—the singing rooms, the nature of which, as given by Mr. Clay in his last Report, is too revolting to describe here,—and even the public-houses for children, for such there are, where the young rival the old in vice. Or they may read details of these things in the Reports of the Ragged School Union, and in the valuable Essays that have appeared on Juvenile Depravity. Enough has been said of their condition to prepare for a statement of general principles which must guide us in all Schools for their reformation, and which are essential to the success of our efforts.

First, and above all, there must be in the minds of those who plan, and of those who carry out the work, a strong faith in the immortality of the human soul, the universal and parental government of God, and the equal value in His sight of each one of these poor perishing young creatures with the most exalted of our race. We must feel even a reverence, blended with that intense pity which can never be separated from love, for these children, coheirs with ourselves of an eternal existence, and be able to discern under the most degraded exterior the impress of God's creative Spirit, one of those for whom Christ died. Such a statement as this at the outset may appear to many unnecessary, to still more absurd and wholly irrelevant. Few will venture to question its truth,—but still fewer uniformly act as though they believed it; seldom indeed are our institutions established with the direct and avowed object of preparing human beings for any other state of existence than what this world offers. But this must be the direct and avowed object of Reformatory Schools, or they will fail in their design, and will have but a short-lived existence. It is the Spirit only that quickeneth.

Secondly. Love must be the ruling sentiment of all who attempt to influence and guide these children. This love must indeed be wise as well as kind, but it must be so evidently the pervading feeling of the teacher to his charge, that no severity on his part shall alienate them from him. Truly has it been said, "There is one great instinct in every human breast, a weary longing for kindness from our fellowmen, and delight in finding it." But to children it is an absolute necessity of their nature, and when it is denied them, they become no longer children. None can tell but those who have witnessed it, the responsive love which is awakened in the heart of one of these forsaken ones by a kind look or word, or the purifying effect of the feeling, now by many experienced for the first time, that they are "loved for themselves." Love draws with human cords far stronger than chains of iron. While in the education of the young generally this element is a most essential ingredient, yet if wanting in the School, it may be supplied in the home;—but here?—if these poor children have a home, it is but too often one to crush rather than cherish any feeling of affection; and towards society in general, at any rate the more favoured portion of it, we have already seen that "their hand is against every man, and every man's hand against them." Law is to them only a natural enemy, whom it is most justifiable, and even honourable to elude. Would we teach them to respect the law of man, and reverence the law of God, it will not be by imposing on them a severe pressure, from which their elastic spirits will rise up more vigorous for evil whenever it is shaken off,—but by making them *feel* the brotherhood of man, and after teaching them to love man whom they have seen, they will learn easily to love God whom they have not seen, and to desire to obey His laws. It is love only which is the "fulfilling of the law." Love to the teacher will make what belongs to *him* sacred to the child who has hitherto thought all lawful booty; the same feeling is soon extended to the whole School property, which has been found secure when surrounded by young thieves: a desire to please the teacher will inspire a higher moral tone in his presence, and this, enlarged and strengthened by wise instruction, becomes a principle of action. Love to the teacher may be made the means also of awakening the spiritual affections towards the Heavenly Father. These have as yet been quite dormant. We have already seen that many are

barely acquainted with the existence of an ever present spirit, to them an "unknown God," one who
is not near to their hearts. But it is only from
the *known*, that we can form some comprehension of the unknown; only from the seen, that we can
pass on to the unseen. He *feels* the love of his
teacher who is making a constant sacrifice to benefit
him, and doing all for him that superior wisdom
directs,—he may now be led to understand that the
Heavenly Father is infinitely more loving, and more
wisely kind. Let the child once have a perception
of the "beauty of holiness," in the instructor, and of
the happiness of intercourse with such beings, and a
consciousness of a spiritual existence is excited in
him, which may be raised to a conception of God's
constant presence, and which may make him truly
desire the happiness of heaven.

These are the two fundamental principles which
must pervade all our Schools of Reformation; but
they must be guided by, thirdly, a careful study of
the laws of the nature, both spiritual and physical,
of the human being, especially as manifested in
childhood, and of the effect of different modes of
action on society. Space will not permit that such
inquiries should here be entered into; they have
engaged the attention of the wisest of our race,
whose works should be studied, and whose principles
should be tested by experience, by all who would
efficiently labour in this hitherto neglected field.

"To educate a man," says Dr. Channing, "is to

unfold his faculties, to give him the free and full use of his powers, and especially of his best powers. It is first to train the intellect, to give him a love of truth, and instruct him in the processes by which it may be acquired;—it is to give him a thirst for knowledge, which will keep his faculties in action through life." To all who engage in education it is most important thoroughly to study the nature of the mind, and the best means of so developing it as truly to educate it. But here we have an added task; we have to counteract evil strongly rooted, and to turn faculties and powers already perverted into a right direction. We have also to view the child, not only in his individual position, but in his relation to the class among which he is placed, and above which we desire to raise him. It must be, then, our steady and leading aim in these Schools, to train up children who will be fitted to gain an honest livelihood, being a benefit to society rather than its bane, and who will be prepared for an endless state of existence.

These principles appear to be hardly recognized, or, at any rate, seldom acted on in the ordinary Schools for the labouring classes, where, too frequently, the mere communication of a certain amount of know-ledge, with the power of reading and writing, appears to be the only object in view. Of how little value such is to the dangerous classes, and how little successful they have been in bestowing even these " beggarly elements," the foregoing tables, selected

from many others, will abundantly prove.—" Why,
they never taught me the meaning of the words,"
said a boy of sixteen to Mr. Clay, in a tone which
strongly expressed a sense of injustice done him,
when he proved quite ignorant of the sense of
passages in the New Testament which he could read
with fluency. But they must be constantly kept in
view in all Schools which are to be essentially reformatory, and we shall now attempt to develope them in
the general plans which should be adopted in all
Reformatory Schools, in the treatment of the
scholars, and in the mode of communicating instruction of all kinds, moral, religious, and intellectual.

The infusion of a moral tone into the School, one
of course based entirely on a sense of duty to God,
must, of course, be the first great object, to which all
others are subordinate. This will be the work of
time, and will not be effected by the enforcement of
slavish submission, of a compulsory obedience to the
arbitrary will of a master, but by a *well-arranged*
system, guided by undeviating order and regularity in
the whole School, to which it will be evident that the
master is bound as well as the scholars, and which
he will take opportunities of showing them are as
necessary for their comfort and well-being as for his.
When once this is fully established, it is no less
striking than encouraging to observe how soon the
most refractory and headstrong child will almost
insensibly yield, taking pleasure in what was before

most irksome. Mr. Clay gives a remarkable example of the power of this strict discipline, combined with a spirit of love, which of course must pervade all, in the case of a man who " had shown such a determined spirit of turbulence in the prison to which he had been removed after receiving his sentence of two years confinement, that he was removed by the Secretary of State's order to Preston Gaol, to undergo the latter half of his sentence. I chanced to be with the Governor when the man was brought into the gaol. The heavy irons with which he was loaded were instantly removed. It was explained to him, in a few clear words, that our discipline was more than a match for the most determined insubordination, that the past would not be remembered against him, and that he might derive benefit for the future by exercising the same self-control as the other prisoners. *During the entire year of his imprisonment his conduct was irreproachable."* Discipline, order, obedience, must, then, pervade the School, and must be maintained with firmness ; but the interests of the children must be engaged in maintaining them, and they will thus be prepared to submit to the laws of society, and to the still higher laws of God, to which they must constantly be referred.

Industrial training should form a part of all such Schools, whether the mere Day School, the professedly Industrial School, or the Penal Reformatory School. Not only is it valuable in aiding the development of various faculties, and preventing an undue exertion of the intellectual powers, unused to exercise of this kind, but it is calculated in many ways to have a direct moral influence. The idleness on the one hand, and love of action on the other, which have been among these children the causes of so much vice, may thus be corrected, and turned into a useful direction. The utility of such occupation has been widely felt in the Ragged Schools, and has been sufficiently proved. Industrial work, when carried out well, produces so valuable a moral effect, that it is usually easy to judge of the general progress of a boy or girl by observing the diligence and perseverance manifested in work. It may also be made conducive to what is a matter of no slight moment to the elevation of the child, improving its personal appearance by better clothing, and thus promoting its self-respect.

Personal cleanliness must form another great object in the general arrangements of such Schools; and not only for the obvious reasons of regard to appearance and the sanitary condition, but because it produces a direct moral influence.

"I have observed that even the act of washing," says a master, " seems to produce a subduing effect. . The other night Y. came into the School-room looking very wild, and with his hair standing on end ; I asked him if he would like to join my sister's class in the vestry, and if so, to go and wash and comb himself. The transformation was wonderful, and he behaved in a gentle and orderly manner—the feeling of self-respect, induced by his changed appearance, as well as the washing itself, so softened him."—" I now generally find my class of boys assemble, on Sunday evenings especially," says a teacher, " with clean hands and faces, and smooth hair ; indeed, it seems to be regarded by them as disgraceful to be dirty."

Nor should the cleanliness inculcated be a merely external one; it should be connected as much as possible in the child's mind with that feeling of purity which is essential to holiness, and he should be led to regard it not as a mere habit, but as a sacred duty.

Closely allied to this will be a careful observance of all matters connected with the *sanitary condition* of the scholars, remembering that the "meus sana" can seldom be found but "in corpore sano." This is peculiarly the case with children, and while they should be inured to hardships, and checked in habits of self-indulgence, which are peculiarly alluring to those who have no higher pleasures, the School regulations should be carefully framed, so as to promote the physical as well as moral health of the scholars. This, indeed, is needful in all Schools; it is quite essential in those intended for children who most commonly inherit the degraded physical, as well as mental condition, induced by the vices of the parents. "Many of the children of the criminal class," says the Chaplain of the Bath Gaol, who has had excellent opportunity of observation, " are labouring under bodily injuries ; most of them are old before they are young; they look haggard, pale, and emaciated. Many of them suffer from scrofula and cutaneous disorders, and indeed there are physically few who are capable of discharging any laborious occupation."—"About half a dozen boys," says Lord Ashley, as reported in the Times, "*who were selected* from one of the Ragged Schools to be examined by the surgeon of one of her Majesty's receiving ships at Portsmouth, were all rejected as being physically disqualified for a sailor's life."—"The children of convicts," says the Bishop of Tasmania, in his evidence before the Lords, 1847, "are not a fine race generally. I think that if you were to go to the Orphan Schools at New Town, you would agree with me, that a more painful sight is seldom witnessed than that of the ward or room appropriated to some of these children. There are many almost babies, others two or three years old, scorbutic and unhealthy in appearance." A similar testimony will be borne by most visitors to our large Union Schools, with but few exceptions.

Such, then, will be the general features of the system to be pursued in the arrangements of good Reformatory Schools of all kinds. Let us proceed to the treatment of the children.

We have seen them, in the former part of this chapter, low, degraded, miserable, perishing, or daring, vicious, dangerous; in either case lost, in their present condition, to moral sense; careless of the rights of society, because at enmity with it. Guided by our great principles of reverence for the germ of a Divine nature within them, and of a love awakened by their wretched state, we desire to save them, to raise them to their true position in society. Can we do this by any mere outward enforcements? still worse by that spirit of fear which is so opposed to the spirit of the Gospel? In order to prepare them for the due influence on the soul of that direct religious teaching of which we shall presently speak, the children should always be so treated as to excite and cherish in their minds true self-respect. By this feeling, we mean a sense of the high duty which each individual owes to himself as an immortal being, and to cultivate it in them is peculiarly important. These children have been hitherto so despised, that they hardly know whether there is within them anything to be respected. They therefore feel no respect to others. Yet let them be treated with respect, with true Christian politeness, and they will give a ready response. Nor let it be imagined an absurd thing to treat these poor little dirty children with respect. Their rags will disappear before those who look at them as young immortal beings; and so many good and beautiful traits of character in them will be revealed to those who treat them with Christian courtesy, that they will learn to respect them. This will, we believe, be the experience of all who treat these poor children with Christian courtesy; indeed the frank, easy, yet truly polite and respectful demeanour of children of the lowest grade who have been subjected to this wise treatment, has often been a matter of surprise when contrasted with the rough insolent conduct of children of the same class in the street, or the cringing civility too frequent in our Charity Schools. A true regard for the opinion of others will thus be generated, which is a motive to virtuous action not to be disregarded.

The principles already laid down will make it evident that love must be the ruling feature of the treatment of these children; this must not be a weak sentimental feeling, but a wise love which shall *evidently* have as its object the true welfare of the child. This should be made clear to him by a desire evinced to promote his innocent enjoyment, and a participation and sympathy in these will do much to draw out his affections; these once gained, a hold is secured on his future conduct. Let him once be made to *feel* that all the discipline to which he is subjected emanates from a spirit of love, and even the most severe will not alienate him from the teacher who enforces it, but rather bind him to him. "Few can conceive," says Mr. Clay, "the softening effect on a separated prisoner, when, in speaking the 'word in season,' an encouraging hand is laid on his shoulder." And could anything but love so touch the heart of a young criminal, as to draw from him at the prison grating, where only he was allowed to see his teacher once in his tedious confinement, "I have been doing wrong even here in prison, and have been punished, but I am resolved that I will not do wrong again all the six weeks that I shall still be here." The promise was kept; love had greater power over him than severity, and he was among the very few, who, after leaving prison, voluntarily withdrew from his bad associates, and placed himself again under the strict but loving influence of his School. " But," it will be said by many, "would you treat alike, with undiscriminating kindness, the bad and the good? would you confound all moral sentiment by receiving into your School a young culprit with a prison brand on him, in the same manner with which you regard the innocent?" Without here exposing the fallacy of supposing that *because* a child has been in prison he is more guilty than hundreds of others who constantly commit the same misdemeanours, and happen to escape—or the injustice of inflicting additional punishment in School, because the child has already suffered much in prison—we would earnestly insist on the principle that a penitent child who shows a desire to do right must always be treated with encouragement and love, and be no more reminded of his fault, than his own future conduct obliges us to do so. This, as we shall see in a future part of this work, has been the principle acted on with the greatest success in the best Reformatory Penal Schools; this is the course of conduct taught us by our Divine Redeemer in the reception given by the Father to the *returning* prodigal.

What rewards or punishments should then be employed in such Schools? As much as possible let them be of the same nature as those which the Heavenly Father has adopted in the treatment of

His children.   While with the ignorant, wilful and
rebellious Israelites He constantly presented temporal
and immediate rewards and punishments as the
consequences of obedience or disobedience, and
modified these with the altered conduct of the
people ;— but now, in these latter days, only more
distant though far higher motives are presented to
us, and the general order of His providence brings
most certain and inevitable consequences of our
actions, whether bad or good ;—so we must strive as
much as possible to make the natural consequences
of actions the reward or punishment of the child.
This will easily be arranged by a wise and experienced teacher.   Those who show themselves worthy
of confidence will naturally receive it, will enjoy
offices of trust, and what may be made the highest
reward, the feeling of the teacher's approbation ; and
those who are diligent will reap the fruits of it,
whether in higher intellectual enjoyment, or in improved personal advantages.   Such a system may be
made to offer a higher stimulus than any artificial
rewards.   If, on the other hand, a scholar is deceitful
or dishonest, he *cannot* be believed or trusted, till he
has afforded proof of true repentance ; if he is giving
a bad example to others by wilful infringement of
laws, and resistance of authority, he must be secluded
from his class, and *prevented* from diffusing a bad
influence ;—if he is quarrelsome in his plays, he
must not have the pleasure of society.   As much as
possible the act itself must be made to bring with it

its own necessary reward and punishment, and in all, a higher motive must, as much as circumstances allow, be made to blend with the immediate one.

In a School where such views are adopted, *no punishments of a degrading or revengeful nature will ever be employed.* The sense of shame, so keen in noble natures, is not extinct even in these, though often manifested in ways little understood by persons who think those only entitled to respect whose exterior commands it;—but the sentiment must be carefully guarded, and when excited should be cherished by screening it from observation, rather than hardened into indifference by public exposure. We have heard the master of a Union School congratulate himself on having discovered a punishment for refractory boys more terrible than flogging;—it consisted in forcing them to eat their food chopped in a trough, and with a spoon. The degradation was felt to be so painfully severe, that boys had run away sooner than endure it. Should such a means ever be used of crushing the spirits of children whom we would reform and elevate?

Nor less injurious is the practice of employing corporal punishment, which not only inflicts a disgrace most sensitively felt by all high-spirited children, but usually excites a vindictive spirit, which must utterly neutralize the influence of the master for good. What effect had the excellent instructions of the Chaplain on the poor boy, (p. 63.) when they were followed up by a whipping only so severe that his back did not bleed? We will not say that cases do not sometimes occur, in which the peculiar nature of the boy may render such a punishment more effective than any other; we have even heard of one who desired it at the hands of a master he loved, as the only means of subduing the faults he lamented. But we believe that in very few cases is it otherwise than most injurious, especially among children who are already but too well accustomed to harshness and severity, and that there are *very* few masters who could safely be trusted with such a power, or whose influence for good would not be seriously injured by it. So strongly is this felt in a large and excellent public School near London, that in the rare instances in which corporal punishment is inflicted, it is administered by the drill sergeant.

It is to be hoped that the time is gone by, when those who have an earnest desire for the reformation of juvenile offenders will agree with the opinion stated by Sir Peter Laurie, in his evidence before the Committee of the Commons (1850). " If there was a whipping-post at every police station in the metropolis, I am sure it would have a most beneficial effect. I am quite satisfied that nothing would deter juvenile offenders so much as corporal punishment."

Most of the judges examined by the Select Committee of the Lords, express an opinion favourable to corporal punishment, and speak of frequently awarding whipping. They have not of course had the opportunity of observing the effect of that punishment on juvenile offenders, possessed by Chaplains, and those who are more in contact with them. But the Lord Justice Clerk of Scotland states in his evidence :—

"Whipping is not now resorted to in Scotland. To whip and dismiss the boys *I believe would be utterly useless.* He would be immediately surrounded by his associates, consoled with drink, and only hardened and confirmed."

"Whipping, I have no doubt, would often be salutary," says Lord Cockburn, "but it is attended with two risks, which it is difficult to avoid ; one is the danger, especially in obscure places, of undetected cruelty ; the other, that where *the infliction fails to amend, it makes the culprit a greater blackguard than he was.*"

The Rev. J. Field of Reading Gaol, says :—

"I have never seen any reclaimed by corporal punishment ; I believe it has a hardening effect. Referring to the experience of the past we find that the most severe punishments have not operated to deter, as many have supposed." He gives the following illustration :—" W. W., aged 16, father and mother both absconded before he was a year old, leaving the prisoner to the care of an aged grandmother, by whom he was brought up under no control. *Was once publicly whipped, and has since appeared perfectly reckless.*"

Mr. Pearson, City Solicitor :—

"I think personal chastisement would not have the desired effect. We administered personal chastisement in Newgate. Boys convicted there were ordered perhaps to a week's imprisonment and to be flogged. We sometimes had those boys back again, after being flogged, in the next session. It occurred once at the Old Bailey, that in the very same session the same boy came back again, having committed another offence within a week of the time he had been flogged when he was discharged."

The following testimony, as being the statement of facts observed by Mr. Clay, (Report for 1849, p. 22,) will be more valuable than any mere theory as to the deterring effect of whipping, to say nothing of the reformatory one on juvenile offenders.

" For twenty years, boys convicted of a first crime were sentenced to be whipped ; the punishment being intended to deter them from repetitions of their offences, and the hundreds of other boys who heard the sentences passed, from venturing at all upon evil courses. *But the examples failed in both respects.* Whatever might be the fear of incurring such a punishment again, or at all, existing in the minds to the once sentenced or the never sentenced, it did not countervail the vicious confidence of escape and impunity which impelled one party to continue, and the other to embark in a career of crime. And even when this confidence was soon found to be illusory, and the sentence of transportation followed a second offence, *even this necessary severity failed to operate as a deterring example ;* and boys continued to crowd into prison, as if emulous (and I knew that very many of them, ' glorying in their shame,' were so,) of the base notoriety which a sentence of transportation conferred on them. In the two years ending with June, 1843—the last two years in which whipping was resorted to as the regular and best practice, and in which transportation was so much needed—71 boys were tried, and 29 were transported. In the two years ending last June, when no whipping took place, only 41 boys were tried, and only 4 sentences of transportation were passed on juveniles."

But not the least important testimony is that of Mr. M. D. Hill, before the Committee of the Lords, as his opinion is based, not only on his experience as Recorder of Birmingham, but on his long observation of the character of boys, and the effects of different treatment in the celebrated School at

Hazlewood, where he was associated with his venerable father, who fully shares his opinion.—" *The deterring effect of corporal punishment,*" he says, " *appears to me to be merely temporary, and it has a hardening effect; I certainly never have awarded it, and I do not think I ever shall.*"

Since, then, the experience and observation of those most qualified to form a correct judgment prove that not·only is corporal punishment unnecessary, but even injurious in the treatment of juvenile offenders, and the experience of years in a School of the lowest description of children shows that discipline may be obtained without it, even more effectively than with it—it is evident that it ought to form no part of the punishments inflicted in Schools, where not the spirit of fear, but of power and of love, and of a sound mind is to be the prevailing one.

With such general discipline and treatment as we have here described, our scholars will be prepared to receive that which is the great object of the education we are giving them—moral and religious instruction. This must be communicated in a manner perfectly different from the ordinary methods pursued. The religious teaching of the poor has hitherto proved so inefficacious, as to discourage the lukewarm, and furnish matter for sarcasm to the sceptical. The tables given in the Introductory Chapter shew us the large proportion of young criminals, as well as of adults, who have received Sunday School instructions; we find almost all the Parkhurst boys

acquainted more or less with the Church Catechism,
all familiar with the Lord's Prayer; while other
data in the similar tables, and particularly in Mr.
Clay's, show that this appearance of knowledge was
not even that of the understanding, for very few out
of hundreds knew the meaning of common words,
and when some attempted to write down the Lord's
Prayer, they not only showed that they had attached
incorrect ideas to it, but many had associated with
it the most absurd ones, and evidently could have
repeated it only as a sort of charm—unintelligible
words strung together. " I asked my class," says a
teacher, " the meaning of the first clause in the
Lord's Prayer. Not one could give me any idea of
it. X. said he had learnt an explanation in the
Catholic Catechism, and repeated fluently a long
paragraph, but could attach no meaning to it."
This gives a clue to the method too frequently
adopted in teaching, from which no fruit ought to
be expected. But a small proportion of the prisoners
were, however, acquainted with even the leading
features of the Gospel history, and even if they were,
did not understand it. This is easily explained. In
too many Schools the Scriptures are made an
ordinary reading lesson; familiarity with the words,
without attaching any interesting meaning to the
sense, only deadens the heart to the holy truths
contained in them, and is a great hindrance rather
than help to subsequent benefit being derived from
the Scriptures. Nor even is a full acquaintance

with the Bible, and understanding the meaning of it, sufficient to influence the heart and conduct. "The most thoroughly unprincipled and unimpressible boy I ever taught in the Ragged School," says the same teacher, "was one who had been long taught in a Church of England Sunday School, and was thoroughly acquainted with all the facts of Scripture, together with various points of theology, which he would willingly have discussed, had I permitted him. He gloried in having been mentioned in the newspaper as the head of a gang of thieves, and is now in prison. Several boys have come to my class for a few times on leaving gaol, and I have been quite astonished at the full and accurate Scripture knowledge they had acquired while there; but in only one or two cases out of many has any permanent good effect seemed to arise from this; they had read the Bible only, as a Catholic boy said, 'to pass away the time,' and it had not entered their hearts." But should such experience discourage us, or make us doubt the value of that "Holy Scripture which is able to make us wise unto salvation?" Shall we no longer believe the pearl to be of great price to these children, because they cannot discern its lustre and feel its beauty when presented to them under a hard casing of words, to them without meaning, their own eyes being dim with ignorance, and a veil being over their hearts? Let us rather, believing as we do, that religion is essential to all reformation, strive to find out how it may be so communicated as really to engage the affections and influence the conduct. A few suggestions founded on experience, may be useful.

With those who are totally ignorant and uninformed, formal religious lessons will seldom be advisable, though as the School improves they may be made most interested in regular religious instruction; reliance must not, however, be placed in these alone, but the teacher, whose heart is thoroughly awakened to the importance of his work, will be ready to seize every opportunity presented by passing events, or the ordinary teaching, of impressing on the child's heart some valuable lesson. The affections must be roused, and a love of virtue and holiness excited.

"I addressed my class," says a teacher's journal, "on the crucifixion, entering into minute details respecting the sufferings of our Saviour, and his heavenly forgiveness. The little ragged U., who has now some decent clothing, came for the first time, and it was all new to him; G., wild, and as yet apparently untouched by our teaching, was by him. The little imperturbable inert face was soon fixed on me with a look of earnest attention, and I saw almost a tear in G.'s eyes as I realized to their minds the agony of Christ; it seemed the first awakening in them of a spiritual sentiment, and I felt the greatest reward a teacher can have, my soul in real commune with theirs." * * "I took the younger ones apart, and showed them the picture of the youthful Christ in the temple; it was beautiful to see how those little faces were at once transformed, and fixing their delighted looks on that holy child, there was the same quiet sweetness diffused over theirs; I hardly needed to add a word."

The mere presence of goodness in others has a

tendency to soften and purify the most obdurate, on whom its spirit is exercised. We have seen the picture of the infant Samuel, in his holy innocence and child-like waiting on God, and the likeness of the Saviour standing in heavenly humility and meekness amidst his persecutors, transform even rough and wild faces into a gentle calmness, and infuse for a time a spirit of love unfelt before. It may be said that such feelings were transient; yet who can tell what would be their influence if frequently called forth;—who can say that even that short vision of the holy and beautiful may not, though long hidden in the hearts of those children, some day shine forth with great power in their souls, and help them to subdue the evil? Love of the Saviour, and of the narratives of his life on earth, will be thus cherished.

"Jesus going to the synagogue on the Sabbath, as his custom was :—Z. asked, with a tone of love, ' Why do not *we* keep Saturday as our Sabbath, if our Saviour did?' After teaching my class of older boys the parable of the Good Samaritan, and of the Talents, I showed them what a treasure they possessed, and told them of a little Jewish pupil I had to whom I was not permitted to speak of Jesus. They seemed very sorry for him, and E. asked if he could read. I said he could. ' Then,' he exclaimed, ' depend upon it when he grows up he'll get hold of a Testament, and when he once begins, he'll not be able to stop, and he'll find many things in it that you have said to him.' They could not think how I could teach him without teaching him Christianity.— ' Go and do thou likewise.' ' This,' I said, ' has originated all our infirmaries and institutions for the distressed ;—there were none before Christ came.' ' Without the infirmary,' said M'A., ' I should have been dead.' ' So would E.'s brother,' I added :

'see some of the fruits of Christianity.' Hardly one of the class knew anything of the Gospel before he entered the School."

Scripture narratives must be related to the children in such a manner as not only to excite their interest, but to create a firm belief in their reality. Those who, nurtured under happier auspices, have yielded an undoubting credence to the religious teaching of their parents, can hardly imagine the difficulties felt by those who now for the first time hear these as they would any other strange and wonderful story. " This is so extraordinary that I cannot believe it," said a little boy, on first hearing from his teacher of the passage of the Red Sea. " I asked an intelligent boy," said a master, " where he imagined that the circumstances respecting our Saviour occurred, which I had been detailing to the class;" he replied, " I suppose in heaven!" Let us again refer to the teacher's journal :—

" The History of Joseph :—Those who had not been present at the previous readings, were quite unacquainted with it. They all found a difficulty in realizing that this had really occurred. One asked if Egypt existed now, and if people lived in it. When I told them that buildings now stood which had been erected about the time of Joseph, one said that it was impossible, as they must have fallen down before this. I showed them the form of a pyramid and they were satisfied. One asked if *all* books were true."

Again :—

" The Cup found in Benjamin's Bag :—When they had read the account, and understood the particulars, they had not the least idea of the intention of Joseph in having it put in, or of the motives of the brothers in their conduct. They were much interested in Joseph's conduct, but have still difficulty in realising that these events really happened. One asked if Egypt was still standing? I showed them engravings of Egyptian buildings, being desirous of giving reality to the Scripture histories as a groundwork for their faith."

It will be then peculiarly important to show the scholars not only good prints of the events narrated, but also, as much as possible, drawings of the country where they occurred. The common feeling of the ignorant, "It must have happened, for I saw the very place," may thus be turned to good account; and when the Jordan, the Sea of Galilee, the Garden of Gethsemane, &c., are thus so familiar to the child's eye and fixed in his imagination, the events that occurred there will have a touching reality to his heart. This reality must also be given by bringing the scripture records as much as possible home to the daily experience and needs of the scholars, and encouraging them to ask questions, and express in their own words their impressions, which will often be found to have in them a freshness and truth, quite unknown to those children who have lost their relish for narratives with which their minds have been crammed. Here are a few illustrations :—

"The Crucifixion :—'Children, why was not Peter at the foot of the cross?' several answered, 'Because he was afraid.' 'Of what?' some, 'Of the soldiers?' 'But what was he afraid of more than of the soldiers?' '*Lest Jesus should look at him!*'"

Again :—

"Gethsemane :—I let my class read in each Gospel the narrative of the events, making them remark the additional incidents recorded by each evangelist, afterwards reading to them one connected narration from the four. They quite entered into the spirit of it, and I was able to address my remarks to their own consciousness. 'Why did the officers fall to the ground?' C.—'Because they were afraid!' 'But why were they afraid?' C.—'*They were afraid not to see him afraid!*' How much is revealed in this! Questioning my class on the last Sunday's reading, I asked, 'How did Ananias address Paul—did he reproach him for his past conduct?' H. answered—'*No, he patted him on the back!*' I could hardly repress a smile, but I was pleased to see that he had engrafted the idea on his mind, and expressed it to me in language which the class evidently felt to be appropriate."

Examples might easily be multiplied, but space forbids. The experienced teacher will learn to make such a commencement the foundation of high spiritual truths, and will watch for moments when the heart is softened or opened, to present to them the realities of another world, and to make them in some measure comprehend the spiritual existence of man, and the grounds on which alone he can hope for salvation.

Religious instruction almost necessarily includes moral teaching, yet with a class possessing as yet so little distinct notions of right, direct moral instruction, as well as training, must be made a distinct and frequent subject of lessons. It has been remarked by one well qualified to judge, by his high legal position, and by his long acquaintance with the juvenile nature, that a large proportion of young criminals are absolutely unacquainted with the "science of morals." The experienced teacher in a Ragged School will confirm this:—

"When encouraging little G. who has lately come out of prison, to behave well in place of work I have fortunately obtained for him, I begged him to be *honest*. With the greatest simplicity he looked inquiringly at me, and said 'Honest,— what's that?' 'To remember, G.' I answered,' what things are yours, and what are other people's.' 'O yes, I understand,' he said at once. Yet he had been for some years irregularly at school, and had had many months' instruction from the prison chaplain! At the next lesson I gave, when speaking to a class of fifty boys and girls, of Noah being a just man, I took occasion to ask what 'honest' meant. Not one could tell! Some said it meant 'good,' a vague answer which has seldom any definite meaning in their minds;—others, 'speaking the truth.' When I explained the real signification of the term, they all seemed to enter into it, especially the young thieves."

"What is the meaning of being naughty," said a mistress to an Infant School of such children. She could elicit from them no greater idea of sin than "To make a noise." A master dwelling, to his school, on the perfection of Jesus, which was shared by none of us, one remarked aside, "I am sure I tell plenty of lies every day of my life." On his teacher's expostulating with him, he said he did not tell lies to his master or to his parents, but seemed quite unconscious that he was doing wrong by telling lies to his companions. To these untaught boys, the announcement of a robbery or murder is one which rather calls forth their curiosity or sympathy, than excites horror ; and it is of great importance to lose no-opportunity of enlisting their feelings on the side of virtue, and showing them that godliness hath the promise of the life that now is, as well as of that which is to come. This may often be done not only by the scripture narratives, but by the reading of stories having a direct moral bearing, which may be so conveyed as have a far stronger influence on their hearts than any more direct lesson. We have seen the wild idle thieving boys of an evening Ragged School absorbed in deep interest by Miss Edgeworth's inimitable story of Lazy Laurence, every one warmly sympathizing with the honest and diligent Jem; and though we know well, that with children, even more than with adults, opinions and professions far outstrip practice, and that good emotions are very transitory; yet these are most valuable to appeal to, and work on, in support of more direct lessons; and a public opinion, so to speak, having been once thoroughly established in a School in favour of right conduct, the great difficulties arising from the bad influence of the ill-disposed will be much diminished, and the master will find the School co-operate with him in the support of a moral standard. No opportunity should be lost, afforded by passing events of which the scholars are cognizant, of showing them the evil consequences of bad actions, and bringing scripture injunctions strongly to bear on them. The *Teachers' Journal* may furnish an illustration :—

"March 30th, 1849.—I learnt, to my surprise and sorrow, that K. who had left prison only the preceding week, was again confined for stealing bacon ; and that Q. had been with him, but had escaped. He was in my class. Pharoah's heart hardened ; his repentance not sincere ; worse plagues came upon him, and he perished miserably. I endeavoured to make the lesson forcible, but did not address Q. individually. At the close of the evening the conversation turned on temptation to evil, which must be strongly resisted, and Divine aid invoked when evil thoughts present themselves. Q. and his brother looked earnestly attentive. When the others were gone, I detained Q., and brought the lesson home to him ; he said that he and K. had been tempted by another to commit the theft ; that he had been as much to blame as K., and bursting into tears, he exclaimed—' I am resolved that this shall be the last time ! I wish I could get some work !' I felt truly grieved for him !"

Again :—

" March 21st, 1849.—Reading Cain and Abel :—I referred to the murder of a lady by her servant which had been lately committed. Covetousness of the property of others the great incentive to crime, and hardener of the heart. The infatuation usually attending crime ; habits of falsehood shown in the witnesses. Cain wandering over the world with a branded forehead more wretched than if he had been deprived of life. ' My punishment is greater than I can bear.' The mark of a murderess on M. T. would make her miserable even if at liberty."

" Sunday, January 20th, 1850.—The Rev. Mr. —— this evening addressed the school on the transportation of P., and the imprisonment of their poor little schoolfellow ; he spoke for above half an hour to them in an earnest and solemn manner, and though what he said was not so much calculated to excite their feelings as to impress principles of action on them, one could often have heard a pin drop. They sang gently and well, and Mr. —— was able to conclude with·prayer."

The foregoing remarks may suggest some hints for moral training ; but more will be done in this by the exhibition in the master of a high moral tone, and by

his constant watchfulness to excite and strengthen all
good feelings and principles in the minds of his
scholars, to make them *desire* to do right and resist
temptation to evil, to detect and punish what is
wrong, yet to observe and encourage every virtuous
effort and sign of repentance,—than by any system
of rules, or strong machinery of law. The effect of
such a course will be hereafter exhibited.

Most persons will probably assent to the necessity
of making religious and moral instruction a main
object in Reformatory Schools; there will be greater
difference of opinion on the degree of *intellectual
training* which should be given. It is a popular
notion that giving a small amount of knowledge of
reading, with a little writing perhaps, and some
figures, is quite sufficient for these " low children ;"
and that any additional knowledge is a sort of
luxury which it is unjust to bestow upon these
degraded children, while so many of the labouring
classes are without it. The fallacy of the first part
of this statement, even if supported by the opinion
of many in high places, must be obvious to all who
have perused with any degree of care the preceding
pages. Of what avail to most of the young prisoners
who could read had been their power to do so? The
eyes of their understanding had not been opened—
they had read the words, but attached no ideas to
them ; thus it was not wonderful that even the
gospel histories, which they did not understand, had
taken no hold of them, while words without meaning

had fallen on their ear. It is beginning to be un-derstood and acknowledged by all enlightened and practical persons, that the Scriptures are best under-stood by those to whom secular knowledge has been imparted, and whose minds have been not only in-formed but enlightened by it. But again, Mr. Clay informs us that almost the only books with which the criminals as a class are acquainted, are of a character directly to stimulate to vice. " I found," he says, " that though the boy was utterly ignorant of everything which he ought to know, he *was, like other children of his class,* quite familiar with the history of Dick Turpin and Jack Sheppard. I asked the poor child, ' Who told you about Turpin and Sheppard ?' ' My father.' ' What did he tell you about them ?' ' Why he told me they robbed the rich for the poor.'" A similar testimony is borne by one who ascer-tained from seven venders of popular publications in a large city, the comparative number sold of different classes of periodicals. Of works of a moral and elevating tendency, such as *Chambers'* and the *People's Journal,* there are sold in proportion to those below only *seven.* Of works neither elevating nor immoral, such as the *London Journal,* &c., 384. Of works of a decidedly immoral tendency, such as Turpin and Sheppard, 234. Of periodicals of an atheistical and deistical kind, which circulate ex-clusively among the intelligent of the working classes, 55. Now it is impossible that children should be drawn away from enjoyment of this kind

of reading while they have no knowledge of any
state of society higher than is pourtrayed in these
immoral books, with which alone they have as
yet sympathized, and while they have no acquaintance with any objects of thought beyond those immediately surrounding them in their own degraded
sphere. Present to the children of the labouring
classes educated in a good British School, a book of
travels, the history of heroic adventurers, or narratives
of inventions and discoveries, they will devour them
with eagerness, and when their minds have been fed
on this wholesome food will turn with loathing from
poisonous trash.   But offer similar books to such as
can read among the degraded orders we are considering, they will throw them aside with apathy, or
listen to them with a listless vacant look.   Words,
names of places, of things with which they are utterly
unacquainted, stop them at every line, and the book
is to them in an unknown tongue. If only to aid them
in their religious and moral instruction, it is needful
to make the communication of useful and entertaining knowledge an important object, and not less so to
enable them to enjoy higher pleasures which may
take the place of the debasing ones to which they
have hitherto had recourse.   And if it be admitted
that this is likely to be the effect of such knowledge,
if it be allowed that our Reformatory Schools are
not merely to withdraw the young from temptation,
and deter them from the commission of crime, but
also so to develope their powers and regulate their

springs of action, as to enable them, if they use the opportunities afforded them, to become useful members of society,—are we to deny such knowledge because it is not within the reach of a large portion of the children of the labouring part of the community? Assuredly not ;—rather let all who feel and know that such need exists, labour earnestly to supply it ; and the more earnestly, from the very fact that the need is being more clearly revealed by the utter destitution of these perishing ones.

The fuller development of these views will be found in the practical illustrations of them which will be hereafter given ; and we will only, before concluding this chapter, say something respecting the kind of instructors who should be selected to carry out such plans and principles in Reformatory Schools. To do so effectually, a very high character, very peculiar powers of teaching, and patient persevering endurance are necessary. Too low a standard at present exists of the requisites for this office, which we deem a very high and honourable one. The salaries too often offered to such an instructor, would be rejected with scorn by a skilful mechanic ; and yet the one is to mould into beauty and utility material nature only, the other to fashion the spirit of man, God's noblest work. The master of a School for these children is not only to communicate that mental culture which is needed in all Schools, but to aim particularly at the eradication of those spiritual evils which have already made frightful progress.

" They that are whole need not a physician, but they that are sick ;" in proportion to the danger and inveteracy of the disease, we seek out the most skilful medical aid; so to heal the deep-seated mental malady of these poor children, we must seek the most excellent master. To find such as are suited to these Schools is difficult, partly from the smallness of the remuneration generally offered, and the low estimation in which this office is held ;—partly because there are really few who are qualified to fill it. There are many who are admirable masters of the ordinary public Schools, who could not, even if they would, efficiently conduct these.

So important did the admirable founder of Mettrai feel the character and qualifications of his masters to be, that, before commencing his plans, he spent some time in personally superintending the preparation for their work of those who were to carry it on, and it ever afterwards formed a part of the system of the establishment, to have a supply of teachers constantly training under his own eye for this express object, forming a most admirable Normal School. A master adapted for such a charge as this, must, in the first place, have a strong desire to serve God in all that he does, and a warm love to these poor children as heirs with him of immortality. We have dwelt already on the importance of the religious element being made a primary one in these Schools; it must therefore have deep root in the master; without it he cannot find out and enter the " holy place" in the

hearts of the children : and he will constantly sink
under his work, unless he does it " as ever in his
Great Taskmaster's eye." The deep love he has for his
charge must, if possible, manifest itself to them by
an affectionate manner, which will win, not coax
them,—which will draw, not force them into the right
way. " I quite envied that master," said a missionary,
" his power over the hearts of his fellow-creatures ;
as I walked with him through some of the most
miserable streets, children came flocking round him,
even from the very gutters, clinging to him, and desiring to share his smile." It is not always that the
warmest love can so manifest itself as to be thus
attractive, but the possessor of this power has a valuable gift. Having found an individual endowed with
these first requisites, and who desires to devote himself heart and soul to this work, who is armed with
patience, perseverance, self-control, and evenness of
temper, to meet and surmount the discouragements
and difficulties that will constantly surround him,—
we would desire that he should be thoroughly experienced and trained in the *art* of school-keeping. It
is not, indeed, necessary that he should be acquainted
with the higher branches of knowledge, which it would
be useless to attempt to teach in such a School, though
the possession of them may enrich and strengthen
his own mind : but it is quite needful that he should
thoroughly understand the methods by which order
and discipline are most readily introduced among the
unruly and wild, and the most· skilful way of so im-

parting knowledge, as to make it an agreeable rather
than an irksome exercise.   It is wonderful how soon
a master who is well trained in the art of teaching
will introduce discipline in the most disorderly assemblage of children, and quicken into intelligence those
who before seemed dead to all but animal pleasures.
Yet it is not sufficient thoroughly to understand the
ordinary school routine; it is necessary to know how
and when to relax it, as circumstances appear to
require;   to adapt the method to peculiar circumstances; to loosen the rein to the wild and hitherto
uncurbed creature, and yet make him feel, almost
without his knowing it, that there is a bound which
he must not pass; to unite the greatest kindness
with firmness.

It has been well said that education, above all
reformatory education, is a tentative process, a process
of experience and ever fresh discovery, demanding
sagacity in the application of the general principles
which experience has accumulated.   Minds are as
unlike as faces and constitutions.   The successful
physician must be more than well-read in his profession,—he must not be entirely unable to discover the
precise form of disease in every case, a form it may
be, which has never before been presented; and the
successful teacher must have the discernment to
detect the precise variety of human nature which
comes under his eye in any given scholar, a variety
it may be, which has never before been noticed;—
no easy matter in either case.

"Who," it may be asked, "is sufficient for such a work?—one requiring the utmost devotion of the highest powers, yet apparently so repulsive, so disheartening!" Let none undertake it who do not feel within themselves a Divine strength to quicken and encourage, who cannot discern the "image of his Maker" in each of these miserable outcasts. With this spirit weakness will be made strong, and we shall become more than conquerors;—under its guidance let us now pursue our inquiries.

CHAPTER II.

EVENING "RAGGED SCHOOLS."

THE only organized movement that has been made in the present century to carry education to the lowest depths of society, to seek out in their hiding-places the most wretched and deserted children, to shed over them the light of knowledge and of Christianity, and thus if possible to raise them from their hopeless condition, has been made by the promoters of Ragged Schools. The enterprise was prompted by religious faith and love;—it has made discoveries of waste places of the earth which none but a Christian would have had courage to penetrate, and has awakened public attention to a work which is of God, and cannot come to nought.

It will be the object of the present chapter to consider these Schools in their objects, their working, and the principles by which they should be guided; to point out the errors into which they have fallen, and the dangers to which they are necessarily exposed;—to exhibit some of the good results which have arisen from them;—to show what they can do, and what is beyond their scope and power.

Though in the present century the Ragged School movement is the only one which has been directed professedly to the elevation of the most degraded of the population, it must not be forgotten that, long before its commencement, a similar need was felt, a similar undertaking was attempted. In 1781 the Sunday School was first founded by Robert Raikes at Gloucester, which, small as a mustard seed in its origin, has now spread wide its branches, and overshadows the land. The idea of imparting religious instruction to poor children was even then not a new one. Many private and individual efforts had already been made, before Raikes commenced his attempt to collect together the "wretchedly ragged little heathens," the children of parents "themselves totally abandoned," and to instruct them on the Lord's day. The difficulties encountered by the first teachers in Sunday Schools, were precisely similar to those which have awakened so much zeal and excited so much sympathy in our own day.

In the middle of the seventeenth century the eloquent and pious Joseph Alleine, the well known author of the *Alarm to the Unconverted*, used, with the assistance of his beloved wife, who has recorded the fact, on every Sabbath day to gather from sixty to seventy children together, to teach them the religion of Jesus. Similar efforts were afterwards made by Bishop Frampton, by Rev. Theophilus Lindsey, Mrs. Catherine Cappe, Miss Hannah Ball, a humble bobbin-winder near Bolton, James Heyes, and doubtless others, who were preparing the way for the great movement. Raikes was trained for his work by a long practised habit of visiting the Bridewell, and endeavouring to impart Christian principles, with instruction in reading and writing, to the unhappy inmates. Observations here made rooted important convictions deeply in his mind. As this may be considered the *first Ragged School,* a short account of Mr. Raikes's plan and object may be instructive; it is extracted from a letter addressed by himself in 1783 to Colonel Townley.

"Some business leading me one morning into the suburbs of the city, where the lowest of the people (who are principally employed in the pin manufactory) chiefly reside, I was struck with concern at seeing *a group of children wretchedly ragged, at play in the street.* I asked an inhabitant whether those children belonged to that part of the town, and lamented their misery and idleness. ' Ah ! sir,' said the woman to whom I was speaking, ' could you take a view of this part of the town on a Sunday, you would be shocked indeed ; for then the *street is filled with multitudes of these wretches,* who, released on that day from employment, spend their time in noise and riot, playing at chuck, and cursing and swearing in a manner so horrid, as to convey to any serious mind an idea of hell rather than any other place. We have a worthy clergyman, minister of our parish, who has put some of them to school ; but upon the Sabbath day they are all given up to follow their inclinations without restraint, as their parents, *totally abandoned themselves, have no idea of instilling into the minds of their children principles to which they themselves are total strangers.*' ' Can nothing be done ?' he asked himself, as it is elsewhere related, ' for these poor children ? Is there any one who will take them to a school on Sunday ?' "

At this moment the word " TRY," suggested itself

to him, and was so powerfully impressed on him as to decide him at once for action; and well indeed might he remark to another labourer, who visited him in his old age, Joseph Lancaster, "I can never pass by the spot where the word 'TRY,' came so powerfully into my mind, without lifting up my hands and my heart to heaven, in gratitude to God, for having put such a thought into my heart." He immediately agreed with four well-disposed women, at a shilling a day, to take charge of a number of destitute children on the Sabbath, and engaged the co-operation of the clergyman before mentioned, (Rev. Thomas Stock), who promised

"To go round to the schools on a Sunday afternoon," we again quote his letter, "to examine the progress that was made, and *to enforce order and decorum among such a set of little heathens.* This, sir, was the commencement of the plan; it is now about three years since we began, and I wish you were here to make inquiry into the effect. A woman who lives in a lane where I had fixed a school, told me, some time ago, that the place was quite a heaven upon Sundays compared to what it used to be. The numbers who have learnt to read and say their Catechism are so great, that I am quite astonished at it. Upon the Sunday afternoon, the mistresses take their scholars to church, a place into which neither they nor their ancestors ever entered with a view to the glory of God. But, what is yet more extraordinary, within this month, these little ragamuffins have, in great numbers, taken it into their heads to frequent the early morning prayers, which are held every morning at the cathedral at seven o'clock. I believe there were nearly fifty this morning. They assemble at the house of one of the mistresses, and walk before her to church, two and two, in as much order as a company of soldiers. I am generally at church, and after service they all come round me to make their bows, and, if any animosities have arisen, to make their complaints. *The great principle I inculcate is, to be kind and good-natured to each other; not to provoke one another; to be dutiful to their parents; not to offend God by cursing and swearing;* and such little plain precepts as all may comprehend. I cannot express to you the pleasure I often receive in discovering genius and innate good dispositions among this little multitude. It is botanizing in human nature. I have often, too, the satisfaction of receiving thanks from parents for the information they perceive in their children. Often have I given them kind admonitions, which I always do in the mildest and gentlest manner. The going among them, doing them little kindnesses, distributing trifling rewards, and ingratiating myself with them, I hear have given me an ascendancy greater than ever I could have imagined, for I am told by their mistresses that they are very much afraid of my displeasure."

The first Sunday School celebration, held at Painswick, Gloucestershire, September, 1786, even more strikingly exhibits the wonderful and rapid change effected by this agency. It was under the direction of Mr. Raikes.

" He selected for the purpose a Sunday which from time immemorial had been devoted to a festival that would have disgraced the most heathenish nations. Drunkenness, and every species of clamour, noise, and disorder, formerly filled the town on that occasion. On the day selected for the celebration it was filled with the usual crowds who attended the feast ; but instead of repairing to the alehouses, as heretofore, they all hastened to the church, which was filled in such a manner as I never remember to have seen in any church in this country before ; the galleries, the aisles were thronged like a playhouse. Drawn up in a rank round the churchyard, appeared the children belonging to the different Schools, to the number of three hundred and thirty-one. The gentlemen walked round to view them ; it was a sight truly interesting and truly affecting. Young people, lately more neglected than the cattle in the field, ignorant, profane, filthy, clamorous, im-

patient of every restraint, were here seen cleanly, quiet, obser-
vant of order, submissive, courteous in conversation and in behaviour, free from that vileness which marks the wretched
vulgar. The inhabitants of the town bear testimony to this
change in their manners." *

Such were the immediate and striking results of
this first organized attempt to carry Christian knowledge and extend Christian sympathy to the morally
forsaken. The objects aimed at were to introduce
order and some degree of decency of deportment, to
give simple moral teaching, and to implant the seeds
of religion; and this was done through the medium of
love, which made the rebuke of the teacher far more
effective than corporal chastisement. How this work
has flourished, it needs not to tell. If the sceptical
point to the prison records, and show as they may do
[vide. p. 26] that a large proportion of the criminals
have been Sunday scholars,—the answer is simply
this : " Sunday Schools have a distinct object, and
must be added to, not *made to supersede* the Day
School, where a regular education should be imparted; a few hours on the Sunday cannot do the
work of the whole week, and those children who
have attended only a Sunday School, will generally
be found irregular and inattentive in their attendance
there." That Sunday Schools have failed to do
what they could not do, and that teachers have often
been inadequate to their work, can be regarded as
no reproach to the cause; that very many who have

* " History of Sunday Schools," by Lewis G. Pray, Boston,
United States.

had the benefit of such instruction have fallen into vice, should only be a stimulus to teachers to labour more abundantly, while they are encouraged by the concurring testimony of thousands, or even myriads, who have greatly owed an honest life and a happy death to this agency.

But the Sunday School is no longer the refuge of little "ragged children;" the poor little thief, who, released from prison, seeks an entrance into one, is looked coldly on by those who, poor as they are, feel themselves still "respectable." We go into the narrow streets of a manufacturing town as Raikes did, and no longer find there "multitudes of these wretches, the children of parents themselves totally abandoned," but we find them filling the Schools instead of the alleys, delighting to learn of him, their master during the week, who, for more than forty years, has been on the Sabbath the kind and willing teacher of their fathers and themselves. Yet still there are abundance of ragged children to be found, if we will seek them out, and discover some of the dens of vice undreamt of until lately,—unrealized even now by any who have not witnessed them.

As in the original idea of Sunday Schools, so also in the present attempt to carry the blessings of knowledge and of Christianity to hitherto unexplored depths, one of the earliest and most persevering workers was a labouring man. Though many efforts had probably been made in the same direction of

which the world knew nothing, before Ragged Schools
assumed the character of a distinct movement,—yet
the name of John Pounds, the poor shoemaker of
Portsmouth, deserves to be ever remembered as
their first originator. He was a cripple, but managed
by his own industry to maintain not only himself
but a nephew, who was similarly afflicted.

" It was in thinking over the best way of educating this boy,
[Vide *Philosophy of Ragged Schools*, p. 42,] that the thought
struck him that the companionship of another child would
render learning easier and pleasanter to him than if he had to
study alone ; he accordingly found a companion for his nephew
in the son of a poor woman, his neighbour. The experiment
was successful ; so successful that in a short time two or three
others were added to the class. But even when the boy, for
whose sake he first became a teacher, no longer stood in need
of his instructions, the good shoemaker did not abandon the
class he had thus formed ; on the contrary, he added to its
numbers, until it consisted of upwards of forty scholars, including twelve little girls. The pupils he taught were the
destitute and neglected, ' the little blackguards,' as he called
them, and many a time has he been known to go out upon the
public quay, and tempt such as these by the offer of a roasted
potato, or some such simple thing, to enter his School. There
is something in the voice and manner of an earnest, truthful
man, which is irresistible ; it is an appeal made to that divine
image of which there is some trace still left in the most corrupted heart ; and it was seldom, therefore, that the summons
of John Pounds passed unheeded : and when once in the
School, his scholars seldom needed urging to come a second
time ; for their master taught them not only ' book learning,'
as he called it, but his trade ; if they were hungry he gave
them food ; if ragged, he clothed them as best he could ; and
added to all this, he joined in their sports. What wonder that
they loved him, or that when he died, [in 1839,] and his death
was sudden, at the age of 72, the poor children who then

formed his class wept, and some of them fainted on hearing the news."

Here was a true Ragged School, where the earnest christian spirit first prompted to work, and then taught how to proceed in ways which the highest experience has proved to be the best.

This, however, was an individual effort:—the movement itself was commenced by some Sunday-school teachers in our great metropolis. The first organized attempt to concentrate their efforts was made in April, 1844, by a meeting held at the St. Giles's Ragged School. "These teachers," says the Report, "having often observed with regret the many children that are excluded from the regular Sunday or Day School, in consequence of their *ragged and filthy condition*, and also the great numbers who constantly infest our streets and alleys, to idle, to steal, or to do mischief,—resolved to establish Schools expressly for that destitute and depraved class, in the very localities, courts, and alleys where they abound." The result of their determination was, that from time to time Schools had been opened; the rent and other expenses being generally paid by the teachers themselves—sometimes by one or more benevolent individuals in the locality of the Schools. There was no lack of pupils; numbers very often could not be admitted for want of room, or want of teachers, and a policeman, in some cases, was kept at the door to drive away those who wished to force themselves in. These Schools then originated, as Sunday Schools had done, in an earnest desire to do something for those who were perishing for lack of knowledge, and, like their precursors, they have continued to be mainly carried on by unpaid labourers. It was soon found advisable, in order to give strength and unity of purpose to the efforts made, to organize a society, and a "Ragged School Union" was formed to encourage and aid those who engaged in the work, and "to collect and diffuse information respecting the more efficient management of such Schools, and the education of the poor generally." The first circular issued by the Committee states, that "the main object of the Association shall be to teach the children of the lowest poor to read the Word of God, and to understand its simple truths." The first occasional paper declares the object of the society to be, "to bring destitute and neglected children under some moral and religious influence, by means of Schools, where such children could receive, once or twice a-week, or oftener, *some simple knowledge of their duties as responsible beings, and as creatures born to live for ever*." It is then simply as *Evening Schools*, intended to carry some light and knowledge to the lowest depths of society, that we shall at present consider them.

Now it will be at once evident, that to attempt to reform, by the teaching of a few hours in the week, children whose daily life is wild and reckless,—who have no inducement but to steal for every natural desire prompts them to it, and no law but that of force, so often successfully eluded,—who cannot obey the "first commandment with promise," without violating almost every other which God has given,— that these should be thus changed in their very natures by a few hours of better influences, *is not to be expected.* It was not anticipated by the supporters of these Schools. They believed that the Word of God is very powerful, sharper than any two-edged sword; but they were aware that to introduce that Word with quickening force into hearts so hardened, so corrupted, was no easy enterprise, and they cautioned the public "against imagining that any vast educational effort was being made for the diminution of juvenile delinquency, or all being done that might be and ought to be done, for the destitute and depraved masses of our overcrowded metropolitan population." [*Sixth Annual Report of the Ragged School Union,* p. 6.] But they determined to do what they could ;—to bring devoted hearts, earnest persevering efforts, Christian love, to bear upon these children, and watching the effect of the seed sown, to strive if possible for something better.

It is important, at the outset of our inquiry, to understand the real ground occupied by this movement ;—to perceive what it cannot do, and to ascertain wherein it has failed in the object it aimed at. Surely it must be a want of accurate understanding of their true position which has rendered the support given to the cause so inadequate to its necessities, and has directed against it so many unjust accusations.

Since these Schools are conducted solely through the medium of moral and religious influence, it is clearly necessary to secure a large enough amount of this to obtain absolute control over the hitherto unsubdued material that is to be wrought upon. We have not here the aids, so important in all other Schools, of an established discipline, which of itself imposes considerable check on children ; nor is there any of that feeling of sanctity which in the Sunday School, as it now exists, would at once rouse the co-operation of all the scholars to check any outrageous breach of discipline. There is not even existing that desire for knowledge which would lead the bulk of them to repress the noise and tumult, which would prove a hindrance to their acquiring it. A number of wild and generally vicious children assemble together, for an object which many of them cannot understand, without any effective curb on their wildness and violence, without any authority, as yet acknowledged and established, to subdue them. To attempt such a work, zeal and qualifications of no common order are required. The spirit that should animate these labourers is well described in the report of the committee of a recently established School.

" Who are they upon whom the committee can depend that through evil and through good report, through calm and through tempest, through discouragement and through success, the School shall remain faithfully worked, opening its door as an asylum for wretched and sinful youth ? It is not the teacher who at first willingly pledges himself to take a share in the work, and then as soon as it loses its novelty loses his zeal ; it is not the teacher who considers it a matter of indifference whether he is punctual or not at the appointed hour of commencement, or even whether he is present at all ; it is not the teacher who takes his seat and goes through the round of duties mechanically and grudgingly ; this is not the teacher upon whom the Christian public can rely for carrying out their philanthropic designs.

"We want teachers who will take upon their shoulders a heavy burden, and will, for the sake of their Saviour, esteem it light ; who will not grudge their time, and the expenditure of their strength, or the sacrifice of their comfort ; who will feel the responsibility of the work as much as if it rested entirely on themselves ; and who will be anxious to be at their post at the appointed times, as though the whole machinery would stop if they were not present. Teachers, whose hearts are bathed in Divine love, and who, in the Spirit of Christ, will set about the work of Christ ; teachers who will not count their comforts, their convenience, aye, their lives, dear to them for the sake of their work ; and who, after their utmost efforts, and their utmost self-sacrifice, will yet remain ashamed of their slothfulness, and will exclaim, ' We are un- profitable servants.' "—*Ipswich Express*, Oct. 29, 1850.

Yet even this is not sufficient. It is not enough ardently to desire to do this work, and to bring a per- severing and devoted heart to it ;—it is needful also to know how to teach, and how to adapt one's language and manner to these children, so as to make oneself really intelligible to them. The want of such power has often been felt an insuperable diffi- culty to many, especially of the higher classes of society, who have truly wished to lend their aid. "There are only one or two gentlemen," says the experienced superintendent of a London School,

" who can stoop low enough to reach these poor ignorant wretches." Thus, though it may be hoped that in all ranks of society there are hearts sufficiently warm towards these outcasts to stimulate them to the work, yet a perfect inability to perform it has been felt by them, and it is in general found that the bulk of the teachers are from the ranks of those who are less separated from the children by conventional refinements, and superiority of intellectual culture. The close engagements of most of these during the day will, however, absolutely prevent many, who are both willing and able to work, from doing so, except on the Sabbath. Female teachers are often found to possess peculiar power of subduing by force of gentleness the very wildest, and their ordinary modes of life prepare them better than those of men to communicate knowledge in a simple intelligible manner;—but very great difficulties must constantly exist to prevent even those ladies who are able and willing to work, from detaching themselves from the domestic circle and social engagements, penetrating at night the districts which, from their very degradation, are usually selected for Ragged Schools. It is not, then, a matter for wonder that the inadequate numbers, and the irregular attendance of teachers, has always been, and continues to be, a matter for deep regret to the supporters of the Schools. Yet on the power of these uncertain voluntary teachers depend the results of the undertaking, whether for good or evil.

That Ragged Schools may be productive of the good effects contemplated by them, the following conditions must be fulfilled :—

General order and obedience must be established throughout the School. A superintendent or master must have ultimate and undisputed authority, and must infuse a moral and religious tone into the whole School.

Each teacher must have entire control over his or her class; he must be regarded by the scholars as their friend, yet able, at the same time, to obtain from them a ready and willing obedience.

The instruction should all be given in a simple and familiar manner, adapted to the comprehension and wants of the scholars. The awakening of moral and religious principle, and the communication of scriptural instruction, should always be the leading object of the teacher; while he should, even with the view of obtaining this, seek opportunities of giving such useful and entertaining knowledge as may raise the minds of the scholars, and lead them to seek better things.

Christian love must be the controlling principle; and the teacher should, as far as practicable, become acquainted with the individual circumstances and homes of his scholars, thus extending his influence into their daily lives.

In proportion as these conditions have been fulfilled, good, unspeakable good, has been effected by Ragged Schools ; but where the moral force has been insufficient to establish that degree of control which is necessary to prevent the contamination of the good by the bad, and that degree of quiet and order which are indispensable to the communication of instruction ;—where the teaching is of a kind rather to inform the mind than to touch the heart, or, still worse, to give the form of religion without the spirit of it ;—where the teacher has been satisfied with merely placing in his pupils' hands such power of reading and writing as may make them only more skilful in doing evil,—there Ragged Schools have been absolutely injurious in their effects on the majority, however much good may have been wrought on individuals.

The perception of the existence of such evils in many of the London Ragged Schools, led to the publication of a letter in the *Morning Chronicle*, [March 25th, 1850,] which produced a strong impression unfavourable to Ragged Schools, on those who had no means of judging for themselves. The facts alleged in that letter in support of the objections made to Ragged Schools were afterwards so clearly proved to be absolutely false, on the testimony of the very individuals whose assertions were professedly quoted, and so satisfactory a refutation of the charges was made by the Secretary of the Ragged School Union, in a letter which appeared in the same journal, on the 22nd of the next month, that it would be unnecessary here to do more than refer the reader to the *Ragged School Magazine* for

May, 1850,—the substance of which has been re-
published in a pamphlet, *Crime and its Causes*
But the dangers spoken of in the letter, do, we
believe, really exist, and ought to be most watchfully guarded against; instead of closing our eyes to
the evil, we should strive to remove it.   Those who
believe most firmly in the importance of such
Schools, and the beneficial influence which they
may and do exert when well conducted, should be
most anxious to listen to the objections raised both
by friends and enemies, and profiting by the suggestions offered, endeavour to place them on a
better footing.   We shall therefore consider the
actual state of some of the Schools, and pointing
out the faults existing in their management, offer
some suggestions respecting their increased efficiency.   In doing so it will be unnecessary to make
more direct allusion to the letter above alluded to,
than to notice one of those perversions of statistical statements which so often deceive those who
have not the means of detecting their fallacy.   The
statement in the letter is as follows:—

Increase of Ragged Schools in the Metropolis since 1844.					Increase of Juvenile Offenders in the Metropolis since 1844.	
Year.	Schools.	Teachers.	Children.	Amount Collected.	Number of Juvenile offenders taken into custody.	Number of population under 20 to 1 juvenile offender.
1844	20	200	2,000	£61 0 0	13,600	One in 56
1845	26	250	2,600	320 0 0	15,128	„ 51
1846	44	454	4,776	824 6 10	15,552	„ 50
1847	62	902	12,823	1,174 4 1	15,698	„ 50
1848	82	1,053	17,249	4,142 16 8	16,917	„ 47

" Hence it appears," says the writer, " that the increase in the number of Ragged Schools throughout the metropolis, since 1844, has been 62 ; of Ragged School teachers 853 ; of Ragged School pupils, 15,249 ; and of Ragged School funds, upwards of £4,000. And yet, in spite of all this vast educational machinery, the number of offenders under twenty years of age has increased in the same period no less than 3,317—or very nearly one for each guinea that had been subscribed in the hope of diminishing juvenile depravity."

This statement certainly does at first sight appear irrefutable, and very disheartening to the supporters of the movement. Yet are we to consider only the co-existence of Ragged Schools, and an increase of juvenile crime, without inquiring whether other concomitant circumstances may not have had considerable effect ?

" May not," asks Mr. Anderson, in his reply to Mr. Mayhew, " the ' alarming increase' of juvenile offenders in 1848 be more reasonably ascribed to the above and similar causes, than to the operations of Ragged Schools ? Is it necessary to remind him that, in 1848, the streets of the metropolis were swarming with destitute Irish, driven by famine from their own country ; that, from January 1st to 31st of that year, the number of Irish applicants to the Mendicity Society, who had been *less* than twelve months in London, were no fewer than 18,589 ; and that the number of vagrants committed to the Houses of Correction at Coldbath Fields and Westminster, was 1200 more than in 1847 ? Is no account to be taken of the severe privations to which very many of the working population were exposed, by the commercial panic in 1847 and 1848, to the effects of which—if I am not mistaken—your correspondent refers in his previous articles. Is 'the ever-memorable 10th of April,' and the riotous meetings which occurred for several weeks before and after it, to be entirely exonerated from having any connection with this 'alarming increase ;' when, according to the accounts of the *Morning Chronicle*, 'Scotland Yard grew pale,' and the metropolis had to be guarded by 'three hundred thousand men, including a formidable vanguard of regular troops ?' The same authority states, that, 'the new recruits were for the most part young lads, filthy and ragged in their appearance, and that in others, 'the insurgent patriots were dirty boys, with a sprinkling of professional thieves,' and that 'prigging was carried on throughout on the very largest scale that circumstances permitted.' On another occasion, I find that 'scenes of the most indescribable blackguardism were enacted by those wretched boys, who evidently represented the lowest scum of the metropolis, and hoped to reap a rich harvest in picking pockets ;' and that, in addition to this, 'a band of blackguard boys, amounting to several hundreds, and not having a full-grown man amongst them,' paraded the streets until midnight, smashing in windows, and stealing where they could ; and that next day, *the principal station-houses of the West End were filled with prisoners.*' May not these transactions have more to do with the 'alarming increase' of juvenile offenders in 1848, than the 'guineas' subscribed to the Ragged School Union ?"

Let us, however, as we should in all fairness, take the five years preceding those in which Ragged Schools were established, placing them side by side with the five years succeeding, and we shall at once see the subject in a very different light :—

Metropolitan Juvenile Offenders.			
Taken into Custody.	Number of persons under twenty years taken into custody during the five years preceding the establishment of the Ragged School Union, in 1844.	Taken into Custody.	Number of persons under twenty years taken into custody during five years since the establishment of the Ragged School Union, in 1844.
In 1839	13,587	In 1844	13,600
1840	14,031	1845	15,128
1841	17,425	1846	15,552
1842	16,987	1847	15,698
1843	16,316	1848	16,917
Total . .	78,346	Total . .	76,895
Average .	15,669	Average .	15,379

" Thus it appears," continues Mr. Anderson, " that, regardless of the increase of the population, the *average* number of juvenile offenders, during the latter period, is less than the former by 290. Surely this does not look like an alarming increase. The difference will appear still greater when the increase of the population is taken into account."

Proportion of Criminals under Twenty Years, to the Population of the Metropolis under the same Age.			
Years.	Number of persons under twenty years to one taken into custody, from the years 1839 to 1843, inclusive.	Years.	Number of persons under twenty years to one taken into custody, from the years 1844 to 1848, inclusive.
1839	One in 53	1844	One in 56
1840	52	1845	„ 51
1841	„ 42	1846	„ 50
1842	„ 44	1847	„ 50
1843	„ 46	1848	„ 47
Average .	One in 47	Average .	One in 50

" By the above, the matter will be seen in its true character, so far as it can be seen from the returns of the last ten years. During the five years that preceded the establishment of Ragged Schools, the total number of juvenile offenders committed in the metropolis was 78,346, giving an average for each of those years of 15,669. Whereas, during the five years that succeeded the establishment of the Schools, the total number of committals was 76,895, giving an average for each year of 15,379; thus showing an average *decrease* of 590. If we attend to the proportion of juvenile offenders to the estimated increase of the population, the case will appear still more evident. It will be seen by the above tables, that during the five years *preceding* the Ragged Schools, there was, on an average, one youth taken into custody in every forty-seven; and during the five years succeeding the commencement of the Schools, there has only been *one youth committed in every fifty.*"

That among these young criminals a large proportion had not even been occasional attendants at Ragged Schools, is attested by the chaplains of some of the London houses of correction, to whom the Union applied for information on the subject:—

"The testimonies of these gentlemen," says Mr. Anderson, "have been invariably in favour of Ragged Schools, and some of them regard the accusations of the *Morning Chronicle* as neither honourable nor just."

Feeling thus satisfied that the *principle* of Ragged Schools has not been in any degree undermined by the public attacks which have been made on them, let us consider the different dangers to which they are liable.

We have already stated the importance of establishing order in these Schools; until indeed this can be done, no good influence can be hoped for. A more vivid idea can be hardly presented of the difficulties to be overcome in effecting this, than the narrative of a teacher, recorded in the *Philosophy of Ragged Schools* (p. 58).

" I was invited on the 1st of October, 1843, to assist in establishing a School of the kind, by the City Missionary. It appears that the missionary had given out that this School was to be opened on the Sunday, for boys who had no shoes or clothes to go to other Schools. About six or seven of us met in the little room in B——— Street, on the Sunday afternoon, little expecting what we should have to contend with. We opened our School this first Sunday afternoon with about twenty lads, from twelve to twenty years of age ; their object, as I afterwards found, was to have a lark. We attempted to teach them, but they immediately wished to leave the School ; this we opposed : the boys got resolute, so did some of the teachers. This very soon broke out into open rebellion, and had the teachers been *all* as resolute as some were, we should all have had our heads broken. Some of the *teachers used great violence, and when the boys saw the blood flowing from one of the boys, in consequence of one of the teachers holding him so tight by the neck, I could see and hear that they were urging one another to the attack.* I stood a calm spectator, but I at once saw the necessity of breaking up the conspiracy by diverting their minds to a new object, and holding out a prospect of some reward to those who were not so forward in the rebellion ; and thus we managed to divide them. We soon got some of the bigger boys on our side, and such a scene followed as I shall never forget : some swearing, some dancing, some whistling, and the teachers looking some of them as pale as death, and some quite exhausted : and thus we got over our first afternoon. Some of the teachers I have never seen since : most of the boys were reformed. Some short time after this, one Sunday evening, I was left to manage the School with one timid little man, when about seventy boys came in, and literally crammed the place : and seeing no physical force capable of resisting them, they at once put out the lights, and attempted to carry off every thing worth a penny in the place, such as

the candlesticks, boys' caps, &c. I at once authorized some
of the bigger boys, whom I knew something of, to defend the
rights and property of the School.   I set four of the best and
stoutest round the book-desk, which they defended like men ;
others I got to help me to clear the room and get lights, &c.,
and I found myself at last with sixteen, who all took part more
or less in restoring order, and who begged of me to let them
stay to the prayer meeting which we used to hold every Sunday
night after the School ; and it was a sight to see these sixteen
boys on their knees before God, listening silently to the prayers
that were offered up to God for the salvation of their rebel
companions, who had caused so much confusion. Not that
these sixteen were so much better than the rest, for they were
nearly all of the same sort ; but the fact is, that you may always
divide the interests of a mob of poor people, *if you know how
to go to work.*"

It is here evident that *moral force alone must be
employed,* and that unless that is sufficient to preserve
order *no teaching can be available.*   A subsequent
extract from the same journal of a teacher, shows how
powerful that became after five years had passed in
the work.   "There is," he says, "the greatest confidence between us : they are all convinced that I
would make any sacrifices to make them happy, *and
all they study is to know my will, and that is their
law.*"

Here is, however, a picture of the state of the Field-
lane Ragged School, one of the very first established,
after the lapse of several years, as narrated by a correspondent of the *Daily News* (April 12, 1850). After
describing the tumult at the entrance of the School,
he continues :—

"The remainder of the scene varies according to the day of

the week and the hour of the day. Let us suppose it to be Sunday night.

"At this period the appearance of the place unites with its railway-terminus aspect a slight dash of the tavern coffee-rooms. It is partitioned off on either side, into small boxes, or compartments, in each of which there is a class of scholars, presided over by a teacher. There are classes also in the middle of the room, divided from one another by screens. On a kind of platform at the upper end sits the superintendent, Mr. Mountstephen, at his desk. The scholars are of all ages, from manhood downwards, yet none of them seem young. As some men are always children, so some children are always men. Misery and misfortune have more than done the work of time. Out of the 300 children who are here assembled, there are probably few who know the *comforts* of a home, and many who know no home at all, however wretched. How they live, and what their resources are, one can scarcely venture to imagine. As the visitor walks round the school—being cautioned beforehand to 'take care of his pockets'—and surveys the various groups, he looks in vain for the regular features and open countenances common to other classes of children. Sunken eyes lighting up sallow cheeks, coarse and misshapen features, matted hair, and melancholy, despairing glances, these are the substitutes : varied occasionally by faces of such obvious and unmistakeable villainy as turns one's pity into something like alarm.

"The instruction on Sunday evening is entirely religious. The teachers—whose voluntary and unrewarded exertions entitle them to the highest praise—read portions of scripture to their respective classes, those who choose repeating the words after them—many of the boys having bibles, which are supplied to them on some small payment little more than nominal. There is a great buzz of voices, caused equally by the zeal of the attentive and the follies of the idle. The latter are numerous enough, and specimens may be seen in almost every class. These may be called the 'fast boys' of the school. Their amusements consist of contemptuous gestures, winking at visitors, putting their tongues into their cheeks in a knowing manner, kicking upon the ground with their heels, punching, and pulling one another's hair, and so forth. Occasionally a shrill whistle, such as may be heard any night in the gallery of the theatre, or a popular song, is struck up, and occasionally the smoke of a short pipe may be seen wreathing above some refractory group; but such amusements are promptly suppressed, and the latter enormity I believe is now of rare occurrence.

" If any extra confusion is observed in any part of the room the superintendent taps his desk with his cane—an instrument which I believe is seldom employed for any other purpose—and makes the usual demand for 'silence;' if silence is not restored after two or three appeals, he goes himself to the scene of disorder, and drags its principal authors from among their companions. A little admonition, and perhaps temporary banishment to a corner, will generally keep them quiet—if not, there are always numbers of faithful boys at hand, who are ready—perhaps a little too ready—to expel the mutineer, who, in the event of matters coming to this extremity, is generally tolerably well kicked when he gets outside by his dutiful companions. These young gentlemen then help to people the steps, as I have before stated. Such a scene, however, is not of nightly occurrence, and it is as well that it should not be. I have seen a boy look like a young demon when he is being turned out, changing on a sudden, and bursting into a wild derisive laugh. Yet this is perhaps the most harmless punishment that can be administered; at any rate it prevents a general and successful rebellion, which, according to a legend afloat in this establishment did once occur in its very early days, when the lamps were extinguished and the masters and teachers expelled by the boys, who held the place for a couple of hours. It is not a little amusing to see—as may be seen even now—the delight of the pupils when the master crosses the room for the purpose of quelling an insurrection amidst the banging of crackers, which have been industriously scattered upon the floor for his reception. The familiar 'crack, crack,' is by no means unfrequently heard even on Sunday evening; but as the culprits are not often caught in the fact, and it being a well-known and valuable maxim among boys, that it is impossible 'to thrash the whole school,' the masters very wisely take no notice of such impropriety, but pocket the affront with as much gravity as may be."

Now it certainly is evident that if the School is generally conducted as is here described, after an experience of seven or eight years, it must be doing *more harm than good*. No moral tone has been established which would prevent attempts at robbery even in the School-room;—there is an open defiance of the master's authority which he does not dare to vindicate; the teachers cannot so control their classes, even by the sacred lesson they are giving, as to prevent many from contemptuous gestures, and from derisive interruptions. The numbers collected are indeed far too many to prevent any likelihood of effective discipline being established. The excitement of the presence of multitudes is very great, especially among such young persons as these, and if they assemble with the feeling here manifested that they *cannot* be controlled, the worst evils must arise from the association. It is to be feared, from the testimony of eye witnesses, that many of the London Ragged Schools present similar spectacles; in as far as they do so, they are doing harm : the contrary may doubtless be affirmed of others, where the conditions above stated have been fulfilled.

The communication of religious knowledge cannot be advantageously made until some degree of discipline is introduced. Such a lesson as the following, given in the same School, must produce anything but a good effect, even on the attentive.

" The religious teaching of the Sunday evenings seems to be appreciated by the majority of the boys, and many are doubtless considerably influenced by it. Upon some, however, it seems impossible to produce any effect. A few Sundays since, a gentleman—a visitor from another School—delivered a short discourse to the Field-lane boys upon some scriptural text. In the course of his address he was explaining to them, in familiar language, the vast and all-seeing power of the Deity, saying, ' At this present time, my dear children, the Lord is looking upon you : He is there above you' (motioning upwards with his hands.)   On this one young boy in the centre of the room put on a most ludicrous expression of in- credulity, and, standing up, proceeded to scrutinize the ceiling with a mock-critical air, saying at the same time, ' Blest if I see Him ;' a remark which seemed to give inexpressible de- light in his immediate neighbourhood, and which was doubt- less considered a very satisfactory refutation of the argument. At the conclusion of the address the first words I heard were in the form of a complaint addressed by one boy to another to the effect that ' Bill somebody would'nt give him the ha'penny that he had lost by his toss.' "

It is evidently impossible that the best disposed youths can avoid ludicrous impressions in connection with religious services when such remarks are made ; the very incongruity with the time and place must strike the youthful mind as irresistibly comic, and produce an effect decidedly adverse to religious in- fluence.   It may be supposed that this is an unfor- tunate example, the very large number of the children rendering it impossible that control should be exercised over them, and the tension on which their minds had been previously, rendering a rebound inevitable.   Here is, however, another example of a similar kind, where there is not the same excuse, for

there are only about fifty children and their minds
have just been pleasingly interested. It is extracted
from an account of a visit to the Brook-street School,
recorded in the *Daily News*, May 23, 1850.

" The scientific discourse having been concluded, a prayer
followed, after which the School was dismissed. Here I cannot help stating it as my opinion, that the latter portion of
the proceedings was far from satisfactory. The indifference
and levity displayed by the majority of the boys during the
prayer, and a hymn in which they all made a show of joining,
was a most repulsive exhibition. Indeed, several boys were
expelled during the ceremony for noisy interruption. Though
I am bound to admit that this is the worst case of the kind
that ever came under my observation, yet it convinced me of
the necessity—which has struck me upon more than one
occasion—for some effectual check to such demoralising scenes.
The system of teaching boys *en masse* is a very excellent and
convenient system to a certain extent. Arithmetic, reading,
&c., may be taught by means of a piece of chalk and a large
black board ; history, whether sacred or otherwise, may be
implanted by a single teacher addressing a large class. It is
a mere question of time. Every boy has the same opportunity
of learning ; and the cleverest and quickest will learn first,
while others may perhaps make very slow progress. As long
as mere matters of fact are concerned, the dull boys, who require more exclusive attention on the part of a teacher, are
at any rate not receiving positive harm. But go a step beyond, suppose religion and morals to be the subject of instruction, and the case becomes more grave. The boys who are
not deriving good from the instructor *are effecting injury to
themselves and others, at his expense. They are ridiculing his
precepts, and inducing their companions—for everybody, great
or little, high or low, has his circle of admirers—to do the same ;
and their ultimate conversion becomes a matter of the more difficulty.* A wandering vagabond—a thief, perhaps, whose short
life has been one long battle with society, in which he has
been the losing party—who feels no veneration, because he

has never experienced any beneficence—and who believes law and authority to be his natural enemies, because he has never benefited by their protection—is suddenly required to join in prayer. Without food, he is told to return thanks for precious gifts; without hope, he is instructed to ask for apparently impossible blessings. The whole system seems to him ridiculous, and the chances are that he acts accordingly. It is evident, then, that public prayer is worse than useless in an utterly ignorant and unprepared assembly, or in an assembly containing any portion of the utterly ignorant and unprepared. The question then arises, how are these children to be taught the necessary truths of religion and morality? It appears to me that the work should be commenced individually and in privacy; that worship should be offered—not in the public School-room, which in most Ragged Schools is open to all comers, but in a separate apartment, where only those are to be admitted who are believed to be qualified to understand and participate in the proceedings. Under this system I firmly believe that the latter class would be continually increasing in number, and would not be long in including the whole School; after which only the new comers, who might arrive from time to time, would have to undergo this temporary seclusion. I believe, too, that the system would lead to honourable emulation among the boys to rank with the privileged class; and it certainly would tend to remove the fears which have of late been expressed with regard to the evils of contamination in such institutions. As for any pecuniary objections which may be made to such a mode of working, I cannot think that they can be very material. A very slight addition to the number of teachers and masters would be sufficient; and the urgency of the case is, I am convinced, quite sufficient to warrant even a greater sacrifice. It must, indeed, be quite plain to all reasonable persons that a boy who can scarcely address his teacher without a gibe or a sneer is scarcely in a condition to approach his Creator."

Yet, when order has been thoroughly established, the highest spiritual truths may be brought home to these poor forsaken children; but to attempt this, considerable experience and power of utterance, as well as a deep conviction of their importance, are needed to put them into such a form as most easily to find entrance into their hearts. We have seen an assembly of those who were among the most degraded in a large city, awed into stillness, and many of them enthralled with absorbed attention, by the striking and touching address of one who loved them, and who understood how to speak to their hearts. As he told them of the " throne of grace, the throne of judgment, and the throne of glory," and showed them that without holiness no man can see the Lord, they seemed deeply to feel his meaning, and were able to listen with stillness to the words of prayer. Frequent visits to the same School, though not of course always equally interesting, will yet *never* disclose scenes such as have been just described. It is a touching sight to enter the School-room on a wet Sunday evening in the winter, and see the gallery filled, before the School hour, with wild ragged little fellows, besides the older boys and girls, who, but for the agency of this School, would have been in the streets in gross ignorance. They are singing hymns quietly and thoughtfully, and the others who come in, often full of gaiety and spirits, sit down quietly, and soon join seriously. As the greater number cannot read, the master recites each verse to them, while they follow him gently; frequently he stops to explain the verse, to lead them to realize the meaning of it, and to apply it to their own circumstances; for he endeavours to gain as much knowledge as possible of them, and frequently brings the events passing in their little world home to their consciences in a forcible manner; then their voices rise with true harmony, and none can doubt that these holy words are borne by the sweet strains deeply into their hearts. Here is a sample of the lessons given:—

"Good Friday, April 6th.—A truly happy evening with my class, who were with me for nearly two hours, dwelling on the scenes of the 'last day of the Saviour's mortal life,' without appearing in the least wearied. Indeed I had to make no effort to control them, or to keep up their attention. *A year and a half ago there was scarcely one of these boys with whom I could have ventured to have read this sacred narrative, so wild were they, and untouched by religion;* yet now they delight to understand every incident, and to realise the whole scene to themselves: by this means the living character of Jesus will, I trust, take hold of their hearts, and his commands and blessed promises be a guide and support to them. * * * Joined the School for the master's address. The man with the withered hand. The true observance of the Sabbath as taught by Christ. The severe punishment inflicted under the Mosaic law for Sabbath breaking. Christ has brought a new law, the law of love; but this should be equally binding. Christ is not now here to heal our withered limbs, we must pray to God to heal our withered hearts. Drunkenness, stealing, lying, Sabbath breaking, &c., signs of a withered heart. He developed his subject very simply and clearly, and the assembled scholars, 139, were generally attentive and orderly. Then singing of hymns for half an hour, which they much enjoyed, and they learnt two new tunes, Creation and Calvary, very quickly and well."

We doubt not, then, that Ragged Schools may be

made, as is the hope of their supporters, " one of
the most successful means at work for the elevation
of the most degraded portion of the youthful population," but that they may become so, they must
be *wisely and efficiently conducted.* But when large
numbers of children, of these wild and lawless habits,
are collected together without sufficient moral force
to control them,—when year after year passes, and
finds the School still ungovernable, unsubdued by
the voice of religion, we cannot doubt that the very
fact of so assembling is highly injurious, and that
the evils which have been publicly attributed to
these Schools exist in great force,—that the bad
gain strength by union, that the good are in im-
minent danger of being drawn aside, and that the
Word of God, instead of coming with power, becomes a subject for scoffing. How, indeed, can any
permanent good influence be anticipated when the
attendance is so fluctuating, and for so short a
period, as it must be if we judge by the printed
reports of numbers. The London teacher above
quoted states that at least 2,000 children have passed
through the School in five years ! The last *Report
of the Union Mews Ragged School*, states that in
1848, 928 names were on the books, with an average
attendance of 99, giving about six weeks schooling
for each child ;—in 1849, there are 824, with an
average attendance of 146, giving the lengthened
schooling of two months to each child. Now it may
be that these are extreme cases, and that even in

these, there has been more power of doing real good
than would at first appear;—were it possible to
analyze these statistics it would most probably appear that a large number of children whose names
were entered, were mere wanderers who staid only a
few weeks at the School, and that a few remained
steadily under its influence, thus obtaining great
benefit. Of the 2,000 above alluded to, the history
of about 100 only can be in any way traced; some
of these are dead; some have become soldiers; some
boys and girls are in places of service; seven are in
the industrial class; two or three have emigrated
and are doing well; others are transported; but
"from these," says the Teacher already quoted, " I
have had letters to show that what they were taught
in the School fastened on their memory. Shall I
stay to tell you what we have heard from the lips of
the young immortal spirit, about to wing its way to
the celestial regions, there to show by its appearance
the effects of Ragged Schools? Shall I tell you how
the happy soul expressed its gratitude in a thousand
ways to the teacher, or the effect on the bereaved
parent?" Such effects, even on a few, will well reward the devoted teacher for years of apparently
unrequited toil, and make him bless God that he has
engaged in the work; for he will probably be assured
that without this instrumentality they must have
remained in deep ignorance, probably sunk into
vice;—now they feel that they have the power of
rising from their degraded condition, and that they

EVENING " RAGGED SCHOOLS."   **143**

have friends to whom they are bound by some of the
closest ties that can unite human beings, a spiritual
relation which will be eternal! Such an influence,
when steadily exerted, must do good. A more
striking instance of it cannot be found than in
a small School near Bristol, commenced for the
poor quarrymen and boys, and the wild donkey-
drivers who frequented that neighbourhood, many of
whom were in the habit of passing their nights in
the kilns or other holes. They had been notoriously
more rough and vulgar in their deportment even
than the same class in the city; their language was
offensive beyond description, and unchecked by the
presence of the superior classes of society. The
change after a year's kind and persevering instruction
by a gentleman who devoted to them his evenings
after a day's toil, mixing with them as *their friend,*
is almost incredible; they are orderly and respectful
in their demeanour, and evidently prize the opportunity afforded them of gaining knowledge; a blind
gentleman who gave them a lecture on the formation
of coal, declared that he had never had a more interesting and intelligent audience, and that it was
touching to hear their expressions of simple gratitude
to their kind instructors. "Before," they said, "we
did not know that any one in the world cared for
us." Great indeed is the change that the being
" cared for" has wrought on them. A similar improvement, if not so striking a one, has generally
been noticed in districts where Ragged Schools have

been established, and has been attested in numerous cases, by the policemen in whose beat they were situated. An interesting testimony to the good actually done has been already before the public, in the records of meetings held to receive the opinions of the parents of the children attending these Schools, after the attacks made upon them in the *Morning Chronicle.* At these meetings 450 parents were present, and " the gratitude expressed by these poor, and in many instances poverty stricken mothers, was," as is stated by those who were present, "sufficient to convince any one of the immense benefits conferred by the Schools, and prove an ample reward for years of anxious labour in the good work."

We may however gain a more definite idea of the kind of good done by these Schools, when a *personal* interest in the welfare of the scholars, is superadded to the general benefit conferred by the School, from a review made by a teacher of between three and four years' engagement in this work.

"During the four years that I have been teaching in the Evening Ragged School, I have had in my class at different times 42 boys from 12 to 18 years of age, besides occasional stragglers. As mine is the oldest class, it has not been so subject to fluctuations as the others, it has varied in the numbers present from 6 to 14, 10 being now the ordinary average, which is indeed as large a class of such boys as I think it useful to teach at once.—Of the 42, 1 has enlisted :—4 have left from the nature of their work preventing their attendance :— 8 were of a class above those for whom the School was intended, and had other opportunities of gaining instruction ; they staid

but a short time :—about 7 were too irregular and inattentive
to derive benefit, and do not now attend ; 2 of these have been
in prison, and there seems no possibility of reclaiming them :—
3 are dead :—17 may be considered as now belonging to my
class when they come to School ; of the present attendants 7
are quite regular, and manifest an interest in the class and an
intelligent attention to my instructions, which are very encouraging ; 2 of these have been in prison, but are now, I have
every reason to hope, reforming ; one of them having been
since in the Workhouse School for a year ; the other I removed
from his drunken mother, with her consent, when he came
out of prison, and he is now doing well as a shoemaker's apprentice, neither was in my class when he fell into thieving
habits. The 10 others are merely occasional attendants, but I
always encourage them to come when they can, hoping that
the good spirit which moves them to attend, may enable a word
spoken in season to sink into their hearts ; of these 4 are in
regular employment, 2 get occasional work as labourers, 1 is
actually in prison, 4 have been in prison, and are, with the
remaining 1, of that class, who, if Mr. M. D. Hill's recently
proposed plan were acted on, would be immediately arrested
to prove that they had some lawful means of maintaining
themselves, which I am sure they could not. Yet every one
of these 17 I have seen at times seriously affected, and manifesting a desire, at the moment, I doubt not, truly sincere, to
lead a better life, to be 'born again.' But what can a few hours'
instruction during the week do to lead them right, when they
have daily temptations of the worst kind constantly around
them ? A few of those who have been in my class, I have lost
sight of ; but in general I feel that I have acquired an influence
over every one whom I have taught, which none but a Ragged
School Teacher can comprehend, still less gain ; and that every
one feels me his friend. Some have been certainly rescued by
the agency of the School from utter degradation ; one who was
when I first knew him an idle ragged lad, has now been nearly
two years in a respectable chemist's shop, and is highly valued
by him ; many others are at work who would certainly have
been loitering in the streets if not in prison. On a Sunday
evening, my boys usually are so respectable in appearance, so

well behaved, so intelligent and seriously interested in their
scripture lessons, that a stranger would hardly imagine that
we have seen nearly all of them ragged and wild, and that
scarcely any one of them had the slightest knowledge of
scripture before coming to the School. The three who have
departed were, I trust, better prepared for their great change
by the instruction they had had. One died suddenly ; he had
said to his mother a little before that he wished he were like
his teacher, for then he thought that he should go to heaven.
Another had been very wild, but the hand of consumption
subdued him, and he smiled happily when I told him, a few
days before he died, that I hoped I should meet him in heaven ;
—he was a Catholic, but said I talked to him just like
the priest. The last was one of the most pure and childlike
spirits I have ever known ; the chapter I had read him on the
death of his sister, and the hymn he had learnt at School, were
almost all he knew, for he was a Catholic, and had not long
joined my Sunday class ; but he 'tried to love God' and be
resigned to His will. I did not fear for him, for I remembered
'Of *such* is the kingdom of heaven ;' I mourned to lose him,
but shall ever feel thankful that I helped to train heavenward
that pure young spirit, which the Heavenly Father removed
from the misery and wickedness that surrounded it, to his
everlasting garden."

Such is a specimen of the disappointments to be
anticipated when engaging in this work, and the
benefit which may not unreasonably be hoped to
arise from patient, earnest teaching in a Ragged
School. The good done will always be greatly increased by visits to the homes of the scholars ; and
here the influence of women who dare to penetrate
these miserable abodes has often been found peculiarly valuable. " I am told," says the correspondent
of the *Daily News,* " that the most valuable teachers
in Ragged Schools are of the female sex ; their in-

fluence upon even the most abandoned boys is something extraordinary. This was especially mentioned to me with reference to the Field Lane School," the unruly one above described.

The movement has already proved a most important one; it has doubtless conferred great benefit on multitudes of children, and shed an indirect influence for good on many more. Yet its most beneficial results will probably prove to be of a different kind. Before its commencement the "perishing and dangerous" classes were separated by an immense and apparently impassable gulf, from those who are commonly regarded as the more favoured classes of society. They saw each other from a distant and distorted point of view. If the benevolent rich wished to do something for the miserable children they saw around them, they knew not how to effect anything, or even what to do. A way has been opened—a means has been shown of reaching these outcasts. Many hearts have responded to a call for aid which they could understand. The rich and titled have felt their human sympathies awakened by coming into actual contact with the wanderers of the highways and byeways; and high-born children have been pleased to serve the tables of the lowest in the land. There may have been much that was unnecessary, much that was unwise in what has been done, and in the manner of doing it; but it has tended to establish the practical conviction that we are *all* of one human family, and that, as such, the strong ought to try to help the weak; that we have all common sympathies, common destinies; and that the givers of the most precious gifts will be even more blessed than the receivers of them. An active stimulus has, by this movement, been given to exertion in the right direction, which requires only to be wisely guided to do great good.

Another excellent result has arisen from the experiment which has been made, in the attempt to instruct these children. *It has proved that if right means are adopted, much can be done, and, therefore, ought to be done, towards raising a class, hitherto regarded as hopelessly sunk in ignorance and vice;* and that efforts *judiciously made* in their behalf are most abundantly rewarded by success, if we do not expect from them what they cannot possibly effect.

The Ragged School movement, weak and inefficient as it was in its origin, and likely to continue so if limited to the original plan of giving one or two evenings' instruction during the week to these untaught creatures, has already led the way to something better;—we trust that its onward progress will not cease until there shall be no ignorant, destitute, or criminal child throughout our realm, for whom Christian effort is not made to enable it to become a usefu' member of society—an heir of eternal blessedness.

CHAPTER III.

THE last Report of the Ragged School Union, referring only to the metropolis, states that there are now in existence 95 Schools; the number of voluntary teachers being 1,392; of children on week evenings, 5,352, on Sunday, 10,439. How little we can gather from this statement the actual amount of real instruction efficiently given, the reader is now prepared to estimate. The supporters of the various Schools soon began to feel the necessity of doing something more effective to raise the class they wished to work on; industrial training was added in many on certain evenings, attendance on which was regarded as a privilege; yet, even now, some of the Evening Schools are open only on one evening in the week; several only two, and but a fourth part are open every evening. The attendance of voluntary teachers having been proved to be little reliable, in almost every School there is at least one paid teacher. Another agency has now been found needful, and has been added—*Free Day Schools.* To the consideration of the actual position and character of these the present chapter will be devoted.

These Schools have hitherto still retained the name of Ragged Schools, which was originally applied only to Evening Schools; they are also of very different kinds, some being merely Day Schools for free instruction; others Feeding Industrial Schools; while others again are a species of refuge for the destitute and vicious. Our attention · will be now confined to the *Free Day School for the classes for whom Ragged Schools were established.*

The mere establishment of such Schools, without right plans and sufficient moral force, is in these, as in the Evening Schools, *worse than useless.*

We cannot have a more striking illustration of the evil of such Schools, carried on without the establishment of sound moral discipline, and a firm influence established over the scholars, than subsequent passages in the diary of the master of a London Ragged School, quoted in p. 59.

"To compose the children, if possible, I proposed that we should have a little music, and ―――― sang very sweetly the first verse of the Evening Hymn. We then invited the children to follow us, and we got through the first line or two very well,—but a blackguard youth thought proper to set up on his own account, and he led off a song in this strain. * * I need scarcely add that every boy followed this leader, ay, girls and all, and I could not check them. After some time, I spoke to them very gently and sadly, and having gained attention to some degree, I ventured to close the School with a very short prayer. I did so. Fearful to relate, in the midst of the Lord's Prayer, several shrill cries of 'Cat's meat !' and 'Mew, mew,' added another fact to the history of this School.

So by the help of God we must both work harder. It is a post of honour. *It is a forlorn hope!*"

Here we see a teacher, zealous and earnest, but injudicious or inexperienced, or he would not have run the risk of such desecration of sacred offices with a School in so excited a state; with boys and girls together, which certainly should never be allowed unless control can be maintained over them, the latter under the care of a "*poor old woman*, who looks after the sewing," but cannot prevail on them to do anything but "*sampler work*. They have no notions of thrift or of useful work." "All our copy-books," he says, on the second day of his work, "have been stolen, and proofs exist that the school is used at night as a sleeping room." We sympathise in his exclamation, "May God help us! What a solemn charge is this!" yet have little hope that with such machinery much good will be effected. But, to our surprise, we find in the course of the diary that these children had already had much instruction, and were accustomed to the presence of persons of a superior class; but what influence had been exercised by them for good? Knowing, indeed, the length of time required to instruct the totally ignorant, we perceive from the following extracts that they must have had much teaching; and being aware how much good may be effected by kind and judicious visitors, we feel indignant that any should go, as these appear to have done, from mere curiosity.

"In scripture history, I got a series of answers that are above the average in point of information of those which could be obtained in some National Schools. *But of what use that kind of knowledge can possibly be, unless it is brought to bear on the moral training and conduct of the possessor, I am at a loss to determine.* It is a very easy thing to stuff these boys with scripture history, or with anything indeed which is or can be made interesting ; but it is a sad desecration of the subject, and a sinful waste of time, to give them mere facts. * * Without one exception, these boys are precocious· *They require more training than teaching.* The great city has been their book, and they have read men as such boys alone can do." Several clergymen called on the first day ; on the third, " great noise, turbulence and confusion, but no serious outbreak. The reverend the rector called, and left without saying anything. A lady visited us this afternoon, and waited for some time. I am at a loss to ascertain the motives which induce ladies to visit such a place. * * We should get on much better without visitors. *The children are so accustomed to be shewn off,* that they fire their witticisms with more impudence than when no strangers are present."

The effect of *mere teaching,* even of the holiest things, is strikingly shown in this concluding paragraph :—

" The fact is being constantly forced on my notice that these children are not so deficient in mere *religious wordiness,* if that is the word, as might be supposed. They have had a great deal of good schooling in a certain sense, or rather much labour has been expended in teaching them to read, write, and cipher well. *But I cannot believe that any attention has been bestowed in making this knowledge useful.* They are utterly destitute of feeling or propriety ; *and their technical education, such as it has been, has not made them civilised or better children.* After all, the school must be looked upon as secondary to home teaching. It is apparently worse than useless to expect a man to be made better by merely learning to read and write. *Those of our scholars who can do so best are decidedly the most depraved.*

One boy, who is quite as well schooled as the average number of boys at his age are schooled—(say twelve years of age)—said to me to-day, ' Please sir, I'll go down on my knees, and say The Lord Jesus Christ, and the Fellowship of the Holy Ghost, for a halfpenny !' Another, as we went along the lane from School, called after us, ' Glory be to the Father, &c.' All this is very monstrous, and I am puzzled to find the cause for such impiety—*there must be a cause*—*and until I can come to some conclusion upon the subject, I am at a loss to apply a remedy*. I have prohibited the use of the words, ' Praise the Lord, Hallelujah !' which they are very fond of shouting, and I have resolved to make their religious lessons as impressive as I can : I use the Lord's Prayer only in opening or closing School ; and in the lessons generally I have attempted to introduce a sober solemn tone, for that flippant, irreverent, thoughtless, gabbling manner, to which they are very prone. We have almost shed tears to-day when we pondered over our work—Sursum corda !"

The foregoing extract must convincingly prove to all, that it is not sufficient to found Schools, to communicate knowledge, or even to impart religious " wordiness" as it is aptly called, without wisdom to direct, and power to guide and control these wild beings. These children were absolutely in a worse condition, one far more dangerous to society, than if they had been left alone to their own ignorance. What had they gained ? Such knowledge only as was to them power for evil. What had they learnt ? Holy words to be a subject for their ribald mirth, pearls to be trampled under foot. What influence had the presence of the more educated had over them ? The master was powerless, and the visits of clergymen and ladies were only an incitement to insolence and vulgar jesting. And when we read that a "poor old woman" is set to control these violent, lawless girls, we are transported in imagination to the secluded village of Waldbach, where the good Pastor Oberlin found that the village School was kept by an old man, whom the parishioners had appointed to that office because he was too infirm to keep the pigs! Schools such as these not only discourage the efforts of the wisely benevolent, by the positive harm they do, but they are a direct injury to society. The Free or Ragged Day School, to effect its object, must, as we have already shown, be founded on high principles, and bring to bear on the difficult materials on which they have to act, the highest powers.

"It is a grievous error," says Mr. Fletcher (in his general Report to the Committee of Council on Education, 1850, p. 297), "to suppose that because the children are ragged, the institution should be ragged also. *To bring such children together in numbers on this principle, is to do a direct and serious injury to society.* 'The sympathy of numbers,' if there be not power to direct it to what is good, does but fortify the evil. It is no mean power which is required to deal with such materials; and though a devoted Christian spirit only can labour with success in such an atmosphere, yet surely the labourer is worthy of his hire; and if acquired tact and skill be required any where, it is demanded in dealing in numbers with the little vagrants assembled in a Ragged School, not divided among many teachers, as in the Sunday Schools, but dependent upon one for every influence. Every proposal, therefore, to form such assemblies, *without placing them under a qualified and therefore a fairly paid teacher, is one to establish a dangerous moral nuisance*, a new class of pauper Schools, worse than those which disgrace our workhouses. * * Schools to which children may come for nothing in dirt and rags, are essential to the present state of society; and these Schools being for children who live in *holes*, not in *homes*, should, besides exhibiting every moral and intellectual power which a trained Christian teacher can exert, have some means of cultivating domestic habits and habits of industry." This Mr. Fletcher considers well exemplified in the Ragged Day School, in St James's Back, Bristol, which had been brought under his notice by having applied for Government aid, and had undergone his inspection. "The fair capacities and attainments of the teachers of this School," he says, "combined with their unaffected devotion to a duty which has completely enlisted their hearts, render this School, in regard to its *powers*, and the industry and accuracy with which they are employed, equal to the average of Day Schools generally; and the good order, pleasing manners, and gentle tone of the School, extending as it does to that ready expression of sympathy in the countenance, which only wise and good treatment awakens or preserves, are ample testimony, independent of technical progress, to the

good produced by such a labour even among the
dregs of an old commercial metropolis like Bristol."
This being the only Ragged or Free Day School
which is alluded to in his Report, as at all fulfilling
the conditions requisite for such a work, we shall proceed to give some details of its actual position and
working, its success and its failures, its struggles, its
hopes, its encouragements and its disappointments,
for all these will be valuable to any who undertake a
similar work, in which experience is essential to
guide the wisest theories.

" A walk through Bristol," says Mr. Fletcher,
" will leave upon the mind of any one the indelible
impression that no other city in England contains
the like proportion of the destitute classes contemplated by Ragged Schools." Nearly five years ago,
a small number of persons, strongly moved by pity
for the miserable children, who in groups of twenty
or thirty may often be seen swarming in its streets,
determined to make an attempt, as yet unheard of in
this city, to open a Free School for them, and selected
a locality strongly exhibiting in its crowded population the " antique poverty, dirt, ignorance and
disorder, which characterize the poorer parts of that
old capital of the west." In Lewin's Mead and its
adjacent courts and alleys, the Sunday games of the
children but seldom meet with interruption from a
policeman, and the passengers to a neighbouring
place of worship who venture through it, must frequently choose the middle of the street rather than

penetrate through the clusters of dissolute half dressed men and women, who have possession of the footpath, unmolested;—they are probably talking over the midnight brawls and drinking bouts which are now almost unchecked; for within no long memory two policemen were killed in an attempt to interfere, and others have received warnings which have left, as is believed by the inhabitants, a salutary dread in the minds of these functionaries; it is now a matter of wonder to see one here or in the adjacent White and Blackfriars, Christmas-street, Host-street, places once—as their names import— the scene of sacred rights, now of drunkenness, quarrelling, theft. Into such scenes a master was sent, a man who had received no training as a schoolmaster, and had had but a defective education, but who was possessed of untiring kindness, as well as a strong desire to benefit his fellow-creatures, and to fulfil his duty to God, and who, from his having been frequently engaged as a temperance agent, was well acquainted with the habits of this class, and with the means of exciting their attention, and in-fluencing them.

Did space permit, we should gladly trace the effect of this first experiment in the diary of the master. With graphic, because truthful simplicity, he there pourtrays the characters of his scholars, as developed in various striking incidents,—the success or failure of different attempts to influence them,—his ardent love for them, and strong faith in the immortal spirit, prompting his appeals to their inner consciousness, which, combined with ready tact and strong determination, seldom failed to affect them powerfully. At the end of six months he had so far reduced them to obedience, that he was able to conduct nearly 100 boys and girls to a public exhibition of dissolving views, their orderly mode of walking through the streets eliciting much surprise and sympathy in the passengers, and their conduct while there being "truly praiseworthy." He thus concludes his journal:— " Nothing but *firmness of purpose and untiring love; yes, a love that nothing can repress, will do for these long neglected sons and daughters.* I feel an increasing love for them and the work, and pray that the Father of all my mercies will bless me in this glorious, holy, and fearful work."

Yet energy, faith and love, though indispensable, are not sufficient for such a work. This master was admirably calculated to break up the fallow ground, but he knew not good modes of sowing and watering; he had not any acquaintance with the best methods of communicating instruction, or with that well-organized system of School discipline, which are essential in all education, most of all in this. Before the expiration of a year he felt his health and spirits unequal to his arduous task, and resigned. The committee saw that they must now seek a master who had been *regularly trained to tuition,* possessing at the same time such earnest religious purpose and qualities of heart as would lead him to devote his powers earnestly and faithfully to his work; they were fortunate in meeting with the master and mistress alluded to by Mr. Fletcher as now conducting the School. They found it, as was to be expected, entirely deficient in any technical organization, and it is through their efforts, aided by the warm sympathy and cordial co-operation of friends of the School, that it has arrived at the condition in which we shall now describe it.*

The School-room (formerly a chapel) is large, airy and light, well warmed and ventilated, with three smaller rooms for classes ; it is supplied with washing apparatus, and has a bath-house adjacent. There is a playground, small indeed in reality, but large to those inhabiting a crowded locality, provided with swings, leaping poles, &c., and a spacious airy play-room, where the younger children may remain during the interval between the morning and afternoon School, besides going for occasional recreation during School hours. The premises are in a narrow court surrounded with small dwelling houses; this was formerly damp and close, the tenements being in a state of the utmost dilapidation, and inhabited by

* Those who desire to see further particulars respecting the early history of the School, may find them in *Howitt's Journal*, Nos. 11, 21, and 40, in articles headed " Bristol Ragged School;" in the *Appendix to Mr. Fletcher's Report to the Committee of Council on Education*, (1850, vol. ii.) ; and in *Ragged Schools, their Principles and Modes of Operation*, by a Worker : Partridge and Oakey, Paternoster Row ; from which, here and elsewhere, extracts have been made.

incredible numbers of the lowest Irish, whose drunken brawls often disturbed the School. Having recently come under the control of one of the members of the committee, the whole aspect of the place is changed; the application of sanitary measures has made the court comparatively clean, dry, and airy, and the complete repair of the houses has rendered them comfortable residences for decent people of respectable character, who alone are admitted into them, thus providing for the children a healthy moral atmosphere, and making them feel the superior comfort of good habits; an opportunity is besides afforded to the master of locating under his own eye, boys whom he desires to have under his more immediate moral influence.

The following rules were framed with great care at the commencement of the School, and have since been fully acted on, with increasing conviction of their importance :—

"1. The School is intended for the gratuitous instruction of such young persons only as cannot attend the other Schools in Bristol, owing to the poverty of their parents, or their own want of character or necessary clothing.

"2. The fundamental principles of religion, in which all professed Christian; agree, shall form the basis of the instruction given. All sectarian theology shall be carefully avoided.

"3. The business of the School shall include the most common branches of useful knowledge, instruction in some industrial occupation, and the inculcation of cleanly and orderly habits. The routine shall be left to the discretion of the Master, subject to the approval of the Committee.

"4. No corporal punishment, or holding up to public

shame or ridicule, shall be made use of; but discipline must be maintained by the Master's own firmness, order and kindness.

" 5. The hours of attendance shall be regulated by the Committee, according to circumstances.

" 6. Scholars shall be admitted and dismissed at the discretion of the Master, subject to the approval of the Committee. A register of their names and attendance shall be kept.

" 7. The Master shall make himself acquainted, as much as he is able, with the parents and homes of the scholars, both as a means of greater influence and usefulness, and as a check upon the admission of those who might be otherwise taught.

" 8. No books or other publications shall be introduced into the School, or distributed to the scholars, which have not received the sanction of the Committee.

" 9. No gifts shall be made to the scholars, at the School, unless under peculiar circumstances, and when sanctioned by the Committee.

From the different reports of the committee, we may select the following passages, as giving an idea of their plans and intentions, and the actual condition of the School:—

" The committee have seconded the efforts of the master and mistress as far as their limited funds would permit. They have been desirous that nothing should be omitted which appeared essential to the development of the purposes of the School and which was within their reach, having in view, *physically, intellectually, socially and spiritually, to raise the children out of their debasement, and prepare them to become better members of society than they could be if left only to the miserable training of the streets.*

"Throughout the year which has just closed, (1850), the School has not only been maintained in its former efficiency, but has continually increased in good discipline, regularity, and attention to the instruction given. Through the indefatigable exertions of the master and mistress, the wild elements with which they have to deal,—the juvenile frequenters of the streets for amusement, and because they have no comfortable homes in which to remain, some sorely tempted by want, others by covetousness, others by the seductions of older persons to become criminals, some actually criminals,—have been reduced to order, made capable of regular instruction, and taught to consider the School-room as a place of refuge from the numerous evils by which they are surrounded. Books, maps, pictures, lessons, lectures, all are made use of with greater advantage than formerly ; and the influence of the teachers seems to grow with every passing month.

"This obedience and order, and their necessary correlative self-restraint, are not only of immeasurable value in themselves, as the foundation of a religious life, to be laid with all care and diligence, with watchfulness and prayer,—but being laid also with all patience and tenderness, not through corporal punishments and severities, constraining the outward manifestations of the inwardly rebellious will, but through that love which is the fulfilling of the law,—they lead to another most gratifying and important result,—they prepare the minds of the scholars for listening willingly and attentively to those Scriptural lessons by which it is sought to awaken their minds to a perception of the relation in which they stand to God, to Christ, and to the everlasting world. The seed is continually sowed, in whom it shall strike deep root, spring up, come to perfection, and bring forth thirty, sixty, and a hundred fold, can be known only to Him who blesses the efforts of his servants as it seemeth to him good. The morning lesson from the Scriptures, given by the master, and the subdued and reverential repetition of our Lord's Prayer, cannot fail to leave some impression upon minds and hearts which are, at least for the time, submissive."

The system and plans pursued in the School are so similar to those adopted in a good British and Infant School, that the ordinary visitor at first hardly imagines this to be a Ragged School. Cleanliness and order produce a surprising change in the ap-

pearance of children; fresh, happy, well regulated
faces in the young are always interesting, often
beautiful, and draw away the attention from the
rags that cover the body; yet even these are made,
after a little time, externally neat, by increased attention to personal decency; and it is only the more
frequent visitor who has seen the same children little
dirty truants in the streets, or visited them in the
bath, and observed the miserable fragments of clothing that half cover their poor little limbs, carelessly
pinned on, or even *sewed* on the child, as if never to
be removed till they dropped off,—that can form
some idea of their real condition. Thus much for
the infants and girls; the boys' division of the School
is more unequivocal in its first aspect; there the
most casual glance will at once observe the wild,
sturdy, barefooted little fellow, joyous and careless of
his rags, which seem likely soon to drop off him;
some listless, half-starved miserable looking boys
near him form a striking contrast to him; many
wild-looking ragged urchins excite one's astonishment that they *can* sit tolerably still during a
scripture lesson; the bare feet of that manly little
fellow of nine, are a contrast to the clean brown
pinafore which covers his raggedness; he is standing by the master, with an evident pleased consciousness of being an object of interest, not of partiality;
he is one of the wildest and most experienced in
thieving in the School, and has resisted all entreaties
to come here even when shivering in the snow;—he

was in prison twice last year, and the earnest interest expressed in him to his parents, with the conviction on their part that the master was "particularly fond of him," have at last induced them to send him to School;—the change wrought *in him* by six weeks' training is wonderful, and shows what may be done if only the co-operation of the parents can be obtained. We notice, however, several who seem rather superior to the School; among them two of about twelve, decently dressed, and who appear so well informed that it is difficult to prevent them from answering for the whole School; these were two of the first scholars in the little room; one of these has to fight a very hard battle of life, his parents being drunken and quarrelsome, and often subjecting him to cruel usage and privation; to him the School, when he can get to it is indeed a refuge;—the other, now sweet and serious looking, was last year quite wild and given up to pilfering, accompanied by his younger brothers; his mother seems utterly regardless of her duty to them; on coming out of prison for the second time, about a month ago, he was placed to lodge in the court, and occupied in the School; he is thankful for the kindness shown him, and seems likely to do well. Now it is evident, that though the general system pursued may be similar to that in ordinary Day Schools, yet that much judicious adaptation is needed, and in many respects a completely different *mode* of teaching. Any one who carefully observes that adopted by the master, will perceive that he combines a great degree of individual freedom in the boys, with an imperative sense of duty. Each one feels that he is under a firm discipline, yet such as to stimulate rather than check his intellectual powers ;—that his own personal existence is recognized ;—that he is not a part of a complex machinery which must all go on in a certain way,—but that he is a *being* who must submit to certain laws if he would obtain the benefits conferred by the School, and that any infringements of these laws must deprive him of some of these benefits. The effect of such treatment is evident in the friendly confidence, combined with absolute obedience, exhibited by the boys to the master ; there is a perceptible desire not to elude, but to support his authority ; and an avoidance of all intentional mischief. An instance of this will be appreciated by those who know the proneness of most boys to mischievous destruction. During the repairing and painting of the premises, no finger-mark was ever observed in the wet paint, though the freshly coloured doors offered a singular temptation; and when some creepers were planted against the play-ground wall, contrary to augury, not only was no injury offered to them intentionally, but there was an evident effort to avoid doing it accidentally. The same principles, modified to their respective conditions, pervade the School for girls and infants, which is under the direction of the mistress ; and the sense of duty, of submission to regular discipline, and obedience to teachers which has been imparted to these poor little creatures may be gathered from the fact that a visitor going to the School one morning, and observing its different departments going on as usual, learnt after a time that the mistress was ill at home; thus the whole School of infants and girls was being carried on by the two head monitors, as the master was in another part of the building with his own boys.

The branches of knowledge taught are much the same as those in an ordinary British and Infant School, viz., such as will be likely to be useful to them in their position in life;—but there is another kind of teaching peculiar to this School, one which we believe ought to form a part of all similar ones, industrial training. Two hours are occupied every afternoon by the girls in sewing, by the boys in learning shoemaking and tailoring. These occupations were selected, not with any expectation of making the boys proficients in these trades, but because it was conceived that they might be made available in improving the dress of the children, and would be useful to them in after life, whatever may be their mode of gaining their living. This industrial occupation has been found most valuable both for boys and girls; it has aided in forming habits of industry which are of essential importance for these children, and has given an opportunity of leading them to feel the good effects of diligence, as they received small payments for work done, which are laid out in the purchase of the articles made. A desire is also excited for an improved appearance; this stimulates many to bring halfpence and farthings which would otherwise have been wasted, and which are placed in the master's hands, to accumulate, generally for the purchase of clothing. During 1850, we learn from the last Report,—

	£.	s.	d.
The amount earned by the industrial classes, has been	5	16	3½
Saved by these classes for clothing	4	7	0½
Deposited by all the scholars in the Savings Fund.	14	1	3¼
	£24	4	7¼

The scholars have, therefore, been £24. the richer owing to their own diligence and economy, and that improvement in their clothing has taken place, which has a great influence in creating and cherishing self-respect. During the year, 120 articles of clothing have been made by the girls, and 8 pairs of stockings knit; besides this, they have made, at their own desire, a handsome table-cover, from a number of cloth patterns sent to the School, for an anti-slavery bazaar; this work has called for much neatness of execution, and has excited much good feeling, by leading them to feel the duty of doing something for others. The boys have made, in the tailoring class, 40 articles of clothing, and repaired 27; in the shoemaking, 38 have been made, and 26 repaired. Great obstacles to improvement of course exist in all these classes from the irregular attendance of the scholars, universal in such Schools; but it is gratifying to observe that the privilege of attending them is greatly prized both by the children and their parents; and that both boys and girls, who have discontinued coming from getting work, are glad to return to their classes when not employed.

It will be anticipated from the principles laid down, that much stress is laid in this School on personal neatness and cleanliness, which have so great an influence on the moral character. Arrangements are made to facilitate this, by the introduction of a good supply of water, and convenient apparatus for washing the children who come dirty to School; they are stimulated, however to desire to come clean, and this is now the case with a large number of them; many parents who were at first utterly regardless of the appearance of their children, now make some effort to improve it, and thus a regard for cleanliness is introduced into their homes. Provision is also made, with a similar object in view, for bathing and hair-cutting, &c.; these are represented to them as privileges, which they are thankful to be permitted to enjoy, and as such are appreciated far more highly than if they were compulsory.

A respectful and courteous demeanour is adopted towards themselves by their teachers, and this insensibly creates in the School that true courteous-ness which can spring only from a correct sense of our real relation to those around us. Those who are disgusted with the cringing civility of the children in many of our Charity and Union Schools, will perhaps object to the requirement of any external mark of respect in a Free School, such as this ;— those, on the other hand, who are accustomed to receive as their due, constant servile attention from their inferiors, will conceive that such ought to be required from those low, mean children, towards persons of a higher rank in this world who may condescend to notice them. But the Christian, who views himself and all others under the same relation to one Heavenly Father, however in external circumstances they may differ, will behold in each one of these poor ragged children a young immortal being, entitled, in proportion to his needs, to affectionate consideration. While, he will neither desire nor accept those hollow external forms which are co-existent with but little real respect, he will strive, by his own conduct towards them, to awaken in them that true self-respect which leads to a respectful demeanour towards others. Such a course has, we believe, invariably been successful; true politeness in those whom Christian feeling leads to mingle with these forsaken ones, excites a similar return ; it has been adopted with happy results in this School. Nowhere can be witnessed more respectful or even graceful salutation to a visitor with whom the children are on terms of affectionate and friendly intercourse, and to a mistress whom they love, and whose manners to them show that she not only loves, but respects them. The master having been requested to ascertain how many of them had been in prison, for the purpose of making a statistical statement, replied "that his own feelings would not permit him to do so—he could not bear to hurt theirs by such an inquiry." This answer gives a clue to his ordinary deportment with the scholars.

"I have always treated my class with courtesy," says a teacher, "and have always received from them respectful courtesy in return. Although some of them have been in prison, and I have seen many of them in the lowest condition in the streets, yet there is now little in their deportment, when in class, to remind one that they are not intelligent scholars in an ordinary Sunday School. I have never but once heard a word which they knew to be vulgar, and then there was a cry of 'shame' from the others. One Sunday night a boy came in quite intoxicated ; the fact of his being so under any circumstances, seemed to make no impression on their minds, or even of his being in that state on the Sabbath ; but they said 'he ought to have been ashamed to come into the class so ;' the next time he came to school, he did not dare to enter the class-room until encouraged to do so by his teacher, and then came in with downcast looks. When a new scholar is introduced, even from a higher grade of society, he soon requires to be told that here '*perfect politeness is expected*,' and that he must learn the manners of the class. If I arrive at the School before the door is opened, and find it surrounded by wild and rather tumultuous boys, they at once open a passage for me, and push back any who may be in the way."

This is said especially in reference to the Evening

School, which forms a part of the system, and to which many of the day scholars come; but the master expresses his belief that among them all there is not one who would be intentionally rude to any one of the teachers.

It may be thought that too much stress is laid on this point, but it is one which we deem of great importance, and in which a very different system is necessary from that usually adopted in the ordinary Schools. The same may be said of the last topic to which we shall advert in the general management of this Free School, namely, amusements.

As in these Schools we have in view not merely to give instruction, but education; not merely to teach, but to train; it is peculiarly needful that the principles of human nature should here be carefully studied and allowed to guide us. Refreshment of spirit, and repose of body and mind, are needful to all;—they were especially provided by the Great Father for the children of Israel, in the Sabbaths and fasts which He appointed for them, which were not solemn days of religious gloom, but of rest from labour, social intercourse, and rejoicing in the presence of the Lord, music and even dancing lending their exhilarating aid, and being thus consecrated, by being performed under the very shadow of the law, for "David danced before the ark." We believe that the necessity of the human mind for refreshment, if not for actual amusement, has not, in general, been taken sufficiently into account in philanthropic efforts for the elevation of the poorer classes. In pro-portion as the mental resources are low, will be the necessity of direct recreation; the young artisan, with such degree of culture as he may acquire by attendance at a good British School, and his own reading, will find his spirit greatly awakened and refreshed by an evening lecture, which would be perfectly unintelligible to a common labourer, and inevitably give him only repose for the body, instead of food for the mind. If for this class pleasures are not provided which are, while innocent, real enjoy-ments to them, they will seek them, and do seek them, in the most degrading animal gratifications. Now this must be borne in mind in the management of all children, especially of these. This necessity of amusement is in some measure provided for in the infant system, but is not carried out in the Schools for the more advanced in age. *Steady ap-plication* to any thing, especially to such unusual mechanical processes as are necessary parts of School teaching, is irksome to these untaught creatures, and will not be endured by them unless rendered in some way agreeable. They are not sent to School, willingly or unwillingly, by their parents; for the most part their attendance is completely optional, and must be secured by the actual pleasure and evident benefit they derive from it. Knowledge must be made attractive to them by the em-ployment of pictures and varied illustrations, and by communicating it so skilfully that the actual exercise of their faculties shall be a pleasure to them. The master must also carefully watch the effect of his lessons, and give the children such variations in them, and short periods of recreation, as will prepare them for renewed efforts. Besides this, the play-ground should be open to them during the intervals between school-hours, and there they should be encouraged in active exercise, and the free development of their dispositions and tastes in play. Dr. Howe, of Boston, U. S., in his recent admirable report on the institution for idiots lately established under his direction, dwells much on the importance of active sports as a means of strengthening and calling out the intellectual powers; he has found them the most useful of lessons. The master of the School under our consideration finds this most true. The play-ground not only affords a much-prized refuge for the children in play hours, which otherwise would be passed in the streets, under influences calculated only to destroy the good effects of the morning's lessons; but, by mingling familiarly in their sports with them, he greatly increases their attachment to him, without in any way lessening his authority, and has a valuable opportunity of observing the free development of their characters, and checking what is wrong more effectually than by a formal lesson. More direct efforts are also made from time to time both to gratify the children and prove to them, *in a way that they can understand,* the

interest felt in their welfare, and also to draw them
away from injurious amusements by gratifying in a
healthy manner their ravenous appetite for pleasure.
How strong this appetite is, can only be understood
by those who have personally observed it. " A piece
of bread they gave me was the only food I had
tasted for eighteen hours," says the ' London thief,'
(*Ragged School Magazine*, February, 1840) *" though
I could spend sixpence to go to the theatre !"* The
children of this School having been offered permission to go to the panorama of the Mississippi on
payment of one penny each, to the master's great
surprise almost all brought it, though he knew that
they often had not a farthing to spend in bread.

Feeling the importance to the School in many
ways of such innocent recreations, those interested
in it have endeavoured occasionally to provide them,
selecting, if possible, such seasons as would most
probably be otherwise occupied less innocently.
Christmas is one of such periods, and every year at
this time the poor children's hearts are rejoiced with
luxuries never tasted but then, while their eyes are
delighted with the tasteful decorations of the room,
gaily adorned with abundance of evergreens by the
ungrudging toil of their teachers; and over all is
shed that spirit of Christian love, the benign influence of which the children cannot but feel, and
it is by direct allusion associated in their young
minds with Him who came to bring "peace on
earth, and good will among men."

The following account of some others of these anniversaries appeared in a local paper :—

"Gratuitous admission has been kindly granted to the School by the committee of the Zoological Gardens, on two successive May Days, and not only did the children abstain from doing any injury, but their conduct was pronounced, by officials on the spot, to be much more orderly than that of some Charity Schools in the City, who had received a similar favour. On the last two May Days, a gentleman of the neighbourhood kindly invited the School to his grounds, where a plentiful supply of bread and cheese was provided for them. Though allowed to indulge in active exercise on the lawn, they showed no disposition to commit any mischief or depredation, and all who witnessed the scene felt their best sympathies excited. This day was selected as a festival to withdraw the children from the practice of begging, dressed up tawdrily, on May Day, and the plan had the desired effect. The oldest classes, both of boys and of girls, have been several times conducted by their teachers over the Museum of the Scientific Institution ; and an annual exhibition of the magic lantern gives both instruction and amusement."

The experience of these exhibitions shows however, that great caution should be exercised in the selection of the subjects of the slides. Instructive slides, *adapted to their actual progress in knowledge,* will be interesting, and may be varied by amusing subjects ; *but all representations of vice, under any form, especially of the effects of drunkenness,* instead of exciting disgust and repugnance, as they would in children of a higher grade, give rise only to expressions of low mirth, and familiar as they already are with such scenes, merely render the children more callous to them. Here, as in every fresh experiment, effects must be carefully watched and referred to guiding principles.

Among innocent recreations music will hold a prominent place in all good Schools; it has also a higher mission, especially in such as these. We need only observe the attraction presented by a street singer to the children that crowd around, to be fully assured that music may have a most powerful influence over the wild and refractory. Its value has been attested already by so many that we need not here dwell on it, only stating that in this School most sensible benefit has been derived from it. The children are taught to sing in a well-regulated manner, with great attention to time, and even to written notes; hence a singing-lesson is one which exercises moral and intellectual qualities;—a most softening and subduing effect is also produced by melody, and this, associated in their minds with some useful or pleasant songs and beautiful hymns, blends good sentiments in their minds with sweet sounds, and carries refinement even into their homes.

With the employment of all these varied agencies, the intellectual progress is quite as great as can reasonably be expected; the boys exhibit great quickness of apprehension, eagerness for interesting knowledge, and retention of instruction given, which render the office of teaching them, when once under complete control, very agreeable to one who loves his work; the girls, on the contrary, generally manifest

dulness of intellect, want of desire to learn, and care-
lessness of instruction, which make efforts to teach
them very disheartening.   The infants also are in a
very low condition of intellectual development, and
contrast painfully with a good Infant School; still
they reward skilful efforts to instruct them.

" Of the moral improvement," says a recent report, " produced upon the objects of their solicitude, the Committee
desire to speak with hesitation and diffidence, but not without hope.   To the Great Searcher of hearts alone can be
known the depth to which any seeds of holiness and virtue
they have attempted to sow may have taken root ; but when
from one to two hundred of the most destitute and most
neglected children of this large city are seen coming voluntarily and with considerable regularity to School,—exhibiting
a great change for the better in the cleanliness of their
persons,—acquiring habits of neatness and industry by learning to make and repair their clothes,—improving rapidly
in reading, writing, figures, and general knowledge,—manifesting increasing familiarity with the scriptures, and interest
in them,—and exercising, in general, sufficient self-control to
behave in an orderly manner, unawed by the fear of punishment,—those who have watched this process trust they may
discard the fear that their labours and their prayers will be
unblest in those higher aims to which all education, whether
secular or religious, should tend,—the training of immortal
beings for a future existence."

It is the constantly repeated injunction of the
Committee to the master to admit no children into
the School but such as come directly under its rules,
viz., such as are virtually excluded by their condition or character from other Schools, and the
inquiry is frequently made whether this rule is

strictly observed. The superficial glance of an inexperienced eye, would lead to the belief that a large portion of the day scholars, in their present state, ought to be attendants at some of the numerous pay Schools in the city;—but the more penetrating observation of respectable labouring persons, whose children attend such Schools, at once detects the very different circumstances of these, from their own, and they have often been heard to express warm sympathy in the work, and gratitude to the Giver of all good, who has put the desire to accomplish it into Christian hearts;—a visit to a good British and Infant School in the vicinity, will at once convince the most sceptical that these two establishments are·filled with beings in distinct spheres of existence;—while a still more important testimony is borne by the keen, detective perception of the government inspector, that these little ones, evidently the offspring of parents from different parts of the kingdom, who all congregate in Bristol, though differing in circumstances, habits, and manners, all have on them the general stamp of depressing poverty or vice. The master makes himself more or less acquainted with the families of all his scholars, and states his conviction that, as a general rule, all the children in his School would, if not there, be either wandering in the streets, or neglected at home, at any rate without any education but to evil. A large proportion are decidedly of the perishing class, in the lowest condition of abject poverty, uncertain of every meal, careless therefore of everything but of obtaining the bread that perisheth;—a smaller proportion are of the dangerous class, themselves, or those connected with them, being known to be engaged in practices directly or indirectly injurious to society; while a smaller portion still are members of families who should be in a different position, but who have been sunk by circumstances which may or may not have been under their own control, but from which they cannot free themselves without a helping hand. To none more than to these last has the School proved valuable; it has, in many cases, been the means, with the co-operation of Christian friends, of improving the whole family, and putting the children in a position in which they could attend higher Schools. The reputation for good teaching which the School has now acquired has led many parents of a superior grade to wish to place their children in it, but they have generally acquiesced with readiness in the refusal of the master, when it has been explained to them what is the object of the School. *No begging children have ever been induced to attend the School,* even though inducements have been privately held out to them by friends to do so; many who were already well known as thieves, have for a longer or a shorter time come steadily to School, and *while under its influence have exhibited no inclination to pursue their unlawful calling,* but when the vigilance has relaxed which led them to attend regularly, they have again fallen into evil, and the gaol has been their place of instruction.

An Evening Ragged School is under the care of the same master, his attendance not being required at the afternoon Industrial School. Here will be found a much larger proportion of those who may be considered as vagrants, who are professing to gain their livelihood during the day, who are hawking, or jobbing, or, to use their own expression, "looking about for a bit of bread," honestly or dishonestly, as the case may be. The attendance of these is, of course, most irregular, and a fine night, or an excitement of any kind, such as a fire, or a show, or a fight, as well as innumerable other hindrances, will keep them away;—it has been already shown how little a few hours in the week of good influence can be expected to counteract their hourly temptation to evil. There are, besides, many who are really at work, some youths and girls, or even young women, who ought to have had earlier imparted to them the rudiments of useful knowledge, but who now thankfully avail themselves of opportunities they have learnt to value; these, if not at School, would probably be under contaminating influences, and their attendance is encouraged. The Evening School, then, is *evidently* a Ragged School, and though the rags of many of them have disappeared under the stimulating influence of education, yet here, as in the Day School no child is ever made to feel by the conduct of the other scholars, or of the teachers, that his miserable and tattered condition renders him in any way an object of contempt or aversion, or that what *he has* draws the attention from what *he is*.

It may be feared by many, from the foregoing statements, that much moral contamination must be anticipated from the association of such children; the master and mistress feel confident, from most careful observation and watchfulness, that such is not the case, but that the *moral tone pervading the School*, and the *constant occupation of the time and attention of the children*, prevents any such evil influence. Yet as the thoughtless and unfounded assertions made by persons who are supposed to have the means of forming a judgment, have been continually repeated in the public prints, and influence a large class of persons who have themselves no means of ascertaining the truth, we may copy from a local paper one of those attacks made not unfrequently by the chief magistrate, with a portion of the justly indignant reply of the secretary of the School, himself well acquainted with its workings :—

" Sir—In the *Bristol Gazette*, of December 26th last, (1850), under the head of 'Bristol Police—Monday,' some young criminals having been arraigned before you, I find the following report :—

" The Mayor supposed they all went to a Ragged School ?

" One of the boys said he went to one—to Mr. Andrews's.

" The Mayor—' There is nothing taught at that school but roguery, thieving, and mischief ; the intention of the schools might be good, but they do a vast deal of evil.'

    *   *   *   *   *   *

" If you said, as you are reported to have said, that at the Ragged School, whose master is Mr. Andrews, in St. James's Back, 'nothing is taught but roguery, thieving, and mischief,' with all due respect to the high office which you are permitted to hold, I must inform you that the accusation is altogether unfounded, or founded upon total ignorance of what is doing there.

       *   *   *   *   *   *

" But, sir, I have the authority of the master for saying that of all the juvenile rogues, thieves, and mischief-workers connected with the School, who have been brought before you and your brother magistrates during the past year, *not one has begun his career of crime after his introduction to the School; but that, on the contrary, several boys have been redeemed from a course of idleness, vice, and crime by its influence,* who are now conducting themselves with a degree of respectability that promises fair to save them from the ignominy to which they were fast hastening, of being brought before you, to be committed to your prison, and perhaps punished by your sentence.

" With regard to the boy who gave occasion to the reported remarks,—when he first entered the School, now some years ago, the master and managers were warned that he was an habitual vagabond and thief, and that any efforts bestowed upon him would be utterly fruitless. They resolved, however, to try what they could do ; they bore with his waywardness, his insubordination, his irregular attendance, his thorough impracticability in every way, in hope that in time some impression might be made upon him. They have altogether failed. He is now most justly in durance. In other instances of attempted dealing with criminal propensities, developed before the boys came to the School, they have also failed. But is it, sir, one of the duties of your office to make these individual failures the ground of a sweeping charge against the teaching of the whole three hundred children who compose the School ?"

When the accusation of the mayor was communicated to the tea-meeting of the parents already alluded to, loud cries of "Shame, shame!" "No such thing!" &c., resounded from all parts of the room; and a proposal was afterwards earnestly made by one parent, that an address to the mayor should be prepared and signed by them all, to convince him of his error, and of the strong personal conviction they felt of the beneficial influence of the instruction given.

With respect to the parents themselves, an examination of the School register will probably at first lead to the conclusion that these are not of the class for whom such Schools are intended. A large proportion of them have ostensibly some trade or calling; the greater part are professedly day labourers; many are tailors or shoemakers, very few assign no means of living;—some have even shops by which they might easily earn enough to pay for their children's schooling. Few, comparatively, of the children have but one parent, scarcely any are without either. But frequent visits to the homes, and acquaintance with the habits of the parents, will sufficiently reveal the sad moral destitution of the children. This old man who is working diligently as a shoemaker, and rejoices that he has never been in the hands of the police, had two boys in prison last year, one of them twice. His wife has the reputation of being a receiver of stolen goods. We should not enter this well-stocked shop to find our scholars, until we learn that the second son gloried in being mentioned in the newspaper police report by name, as the head of the St. James's gang of juvenile thieves, and that the mother's heart is often half broken by the excesses of her husband. We have known many widows support their children by their own exertions, even without parish aid; the mother of those three little fellows has a small parish allowance for each, and can earn something by washing; but two were in prison last year, one twice;—she is seldom at home to check them, the public-house has greater attractions for her, and her two daughters live in an adjoining brothel. Similar revelations would be made of many were we to inquire into the home histories, and we should not wonder that during the last year twenty-five of the children of such parents were in prison, several of them twice. Now it is distinctly stated by the master, that *not one of these boys was in regular attendance at the School, at the time of committing his offence,* and that very few of them had ever been steadily at the Day School. The fact, therefore, proves only two things, that the School is frequented by children of the class intended, and that there are cases which such a School *utterly fails to influence.* What should be done for such children will be the subject of future inquiry. In pleasing contrast to such painful failures very many individual instances might be adduced of the striking change produced by even a few months of regular attendance; but it is hoped that such are not needed, for that the reader is already fully convinced that a very beneficial influence is being exerted, and that it is directed to the class intended. Its full value can be proved only when the lapse of years shows, as it is firmly believed it will, the younger members of families growing up under steady and good influence from beginning *early* to be trained in the way they should go.

From the daily register which is kept of the attendance of each child, some important results may be derived.

		Morning		Afternoon.		Evening.	
		Girls and Infants.	Juvenile Boys.	Boys.	Girls.	Boys.	Girls.
Numbers on the Books . .	1848	137	86	Included in the Morning School.		—	308
	1849	360	120			—	486
	1850	444	127			228	106
Attendance for 1 month only	1848	50	51	24	36	12	35
	1849	64	47	14	43	42	8
	1850	105	18	17	42	45	26
Attendance from 6 to 11 months	1848	31	14	5	8	46	15
	1849	41	16	15	14	39	18
	1850	44	23	12	28	24	14
Attendance the whole year, 11 months.	1848	4	3	0	0	4	0
	1849	7	10	3	9	17	21
	1850	24	14	5	11	15	12
Numbers on the books, both in January and December. .	1848	19	6	0	0	22	7
	1849	25	18	17	11	27	14
	1850	44	11	11	8	39	8

In a School of this kind, as accidental circumstances thinning the School for a few days, affect the registration for the whole year, we give both the average as derived from the registration papers, and the ordinary average.

| | | Morning. | | Afternoon. | | | | Evening.* | |
| | | | | | Industrial. | | | | |
		Girls and Infants.	Juvenile Boys.	Infants.	Tailoring.	Shoemaking.	Girls.	Boys.	Girls.
Average from the	1849	112	31	69	14	6	17	33	22
Registration papers	1850	118	26	90	13	6	26	32	22
Ordinary average...	1849	100	30	70	15	8	30	40	20
	1850	130	30	100	15	8	30	40	25
Numbers occasionally at School at once in	1850	200	40	170	25	10	40	70	30

It will be observed that the numbers on the books
are very large in proportion to the attendance; and
that the numbers who attend only a few months are
greater than those who are at School during the
whole year. Such must be anticipated to be the
case in this School, even more than in others of the
same class, because the district in which it is situated
is particularly the resort of the Irish population,
some of them stationary, but most of them of migra-
tory habits, and passing the summer in the rural
districts. It is pleasing to observe, however, that
even these usually send their children again to the
School, after their temporary absence. This is,
indeed, generally the case with families who have
moved, or children who have obtained temporary
employment, when circumstances permit them to
return, and a majority of those now attending may

* In this table, many of the evening scholars are included
in the Day School.

be considered as more or less under the influence of
the School.   It will also be observed that there is a
steady increase, during the three years, of those who
appear to avail themselves of the advantages of the
School as much as they are able.   The infants form
a large proportion of the Day School, and it would
not be difficult greatly to increase it, did the agencies
in operation permit that to be done; and though
little creatures, too young for direct instruction, are
sometimes admitted with the older ones, who would
otherwise be kept from School to take care of them,
yet it is found impossible at present to receive these
very young infants, who might, however, be most advantageously withdrawn from the neglect and exposure they suffer in their homes.

Let us now consider a few of the obstacles which
prevent this School from being as effective as it
might be.

The first and fundamental one arises from *the want
of pecuniary resources*.   The expenses of the School
during the past year were £244. 19*s.* 6½*d.*; the annual subscriptions amounted only to £129. 12*s.* 6*d.*,
and there is a balance, &c., of £9. 5*s.* 5*d.* due to the
Treasurer.   The Committee feel that, to carry on the
School in its present state, no reduction on the year's
outlay can be made; for strict economy has always
been exercised, and they would desire to increase,
rather than diminish, the salaries of a master and
mistress, who devote all their energies to a work
requiring more than ordinary educational powers.

Having made, then, every effort to increase their settled income, and finding that it does not amount to more than half the necessary outlay of the School, they dare not make any alterations which, while greatly augmenting its usefulness, would increase the annual expense, unless they have any certain means of meeting it.

The second originates in the very nature of the School, and must always exist in similar ones, requiring peculiar arrangements to remove it,—*the want of an effective body of monitors in each department of the School.* Those who can realize to themselves the nature of the scholars, will easily perceive that but a small number of them can be in any way adapted to act as monitors, that these must require considerable training to enable them to do so, and that when they are thus trained and improved, the older boys and girls will most likely leave to gain their livelihood. This is exactly the state of the case in the School under consideration. The mistress has the sole charge of the Infant School, in which the girls are included for want of any separate instructor for them, and for a number of children varying from 130 to 200, she has no aid on which she can rely except from one boy and one older girl, trained by herself, who are now receiving a small stipend from the committee to secure their services; of the girls whom she is obliged to employ principally as monitors, and to whom she has no time to give special instruction, only from 8 to 10 can read at all tolerably, and these are scarcely equal in general culture of mind or actual attainment to the highest class of a good Infant School. Yet of these she cannot be secure, as their family needs often detain them from School, and she has been left sometimes without the help of a single girl that can read. Some of the girls show good promise, and might soon become very useful, but, as soon as they are so, the offer of a low place of service where they can earn only 1s. per week, without food, will take them away. As the School then at present stands, there is no prospect at any material progress in the instruction given; the girls have no means of making much improvement themselves, and of course the infants cannot be expected to be trained as they ought to be by such teachers. The same difficulty exists in the boys' department, though to a less degree, because here the master has only from 25 to 40 under his care, the room at present occupied being too small to contain more; as long as they are receiving collective instruction from the master, order is preserved, and the minds of most are actively working;—but no sooner are they divided into their reading classes, than the scene is changed; the most intelligent often show themselves the most pugnacious, the quieter spirits become quite listless, and it is evident that very little can be done, until some monitors are trained to the mechanical art of teaching, and to the power of self-control. Until these are provided, *which the finances*

of the School prevent being done by the Committee,
and which the low condition of the scholars pre-
cludes from the power of obtaining from the aid of
the Council on Education under the existing regulations, it is impossible that the "active and
essentially collective instruction of the School,
should," says Mr. Fletcher, "become a subject of
fair criterion, *which as yet it is not,* all that is
possible, and far more than could have been hoped
or expected, having been accomplished by teachers
literally yearning over their flock, in their endeavours
to lead them aright."

The third great obstacle to the improvement of
the School is one which only magisterial vigilance
can remove, viz., *the very neglected state of the neighbourhood in regard to police surveillance.* None who
have not witnessed it, can realize the injurious
effect which this has on the moral influence of
the School. When, on Sunday morning, a zealous
teacher walks through these degraded streets and
alleys, striving by force of loving entreaty to compel
some ragged urchins to come in, how can he be
successful, while they are allowed, as they are now,
to continue their game of tops or marbles unmolested, and would have not only to lose this pleasure,
but to bear the ridicule of their companions if they
yielded. And when the master sees a lad of fine
promise, but with whom Satan seems playing a
fearful game for mastery, join, now covertly, then
openly the group of known thieves, who stand on

the very footpath to the house of God, plotting wickedness,—how can he withdraw from such contamination the object of his anxiety, while he is alone against a host, unless the frequent passing of the policeman, and his faithful discharge of duty, prevents such meetings for evil. How, again, can parents or teachers restrain youths who are already old in sin from spending their evenings and nights in the lowest public-houses and eating-houses, while such resorts are secure from official intrusion, and remain open to all comers many hours after midnight. Yet such is the state of this locality, as all who pass frequently through it, and the inhabitants themselves, can testify. Most seldom is a policeman seen here, notwithstanding repeated complaints on the subject, and when he does go, his walks are so little effective, that he has been seen to pass a group of women fighting on the footpath, without remonstrance.

Let us now compare the actual position of such a School as we have been describing, with that of a series of Schools under one general management, and placed under government inspection. Such a series, comprising a large Infant School, a Boys' British School, a Girls' School, exists within five minutes walk of the Ragged School, giving to about 350 children an excellent education, adapted to their condition in life, and besides training for domestic service 20 of the girls, 17 of whom are also clothed. Two masters and three mistresses devote the whole of

their energies to those Schools, aided by six well
trained and effective pupil teachers, whose regular
and continued services are secured by indentures
and salaries from government. The efforts and
interest of the masters and mistresses, three of
whom have obtained government certificates, are
sustained, stimulated, and directed, by the sympathy
and personal efforts of the religious body by which
the Schools are supported; while the emulation of
the assistant monitors is excited by the advantages
possessed by the pupil teachers, and the examination
of the government inspector.   No expense is spared
which can conduce to the real advantage of the
Schools, and yet the whole, we learn from the last
report, including a Sunday School for about 160
children, and the support of a Dispensary and two
Libraries, amounts to no more than £259 17s. 5d.
per annum to the supporters of the Schools; the
payment of the pupil-teachers and additions to the
salaries of the masters and mistresses being made by
government.   Now this Ragged School, or Free
Day and Evening School, gives an education, as
much as possible on the British and Infant School
system, to between 300 and 400 children, about two
thirds of whom are receiving daily instruction and
some industrial training.   But the circumstances of
the children necessarily require much additional
devotement of time and effort on the part of the
teachers; the superintendence of a play-ground
between school hours, that the children may not

unlearn in the streets the good habits they have just been acquiring, of a washing apparatus and bath, &c., are necessary ; besides there are frequent calls on them for out-door aid and effort. But to carry on this School there are only one master and mistress, beside the Industrial teachers; reliance for the remainder of the staff of teachers is placed on gratuitous aid, and on such monitors as may be formed from the children themselves. The experience of five years or more in the Ragged Schools, has proved how little dependence can be placed in unpaid teachers, who, unless those few that are impelled by a deep and earnest zeal, will allow other engagements to interfere with what to be effective must be regular. It has been already shown that no reliance can be placed on monitors selected from the scholars, unless in peculiar cases ; and that where boys or girls do appear adapted to be useful as such, the very superiority which fits them for the office will enable them early to be withdrawn, to go into situations where they can maintain themselves. The master and mistress, then, are placed in a situation of peculiar difficulty, where they have to work upon most refractory material, without the instruments and machinery which are found necessary in good British Schools. Now with respect to funds ; the British Schools before mentioned are supported by a congregational body, who feel responsible to themselves and to each other for their maintenance in an efficient condition. If, therefore, from accidental

circumstances, subscriptions fall off, efforts are at
once made to raise others; if expensive alterations
are wanting to improve the School, it is not a question whether the committee can afford them, but
how they may be effected in the best possible way;
for *" of course the money must be raised."* The aid
given by government does not in any way diminish
the funds needed and raised for the regular expenses
of the School, but merely renders these funds more
efficient for the well-being of the Schools and the
position of the masters and mistresses, and thereby
gives stimulus and encouragement to the contri-
butors. The same will be probably more or less the
case with other Schools supported by religious or
other organized bodies. But this Ragged School, in
its greater needs, stands struggling alone; and with
but feeble aid from the religious bodies who profess
sympathy and interest in it. Those persons who are
charitably disposed have generally gone already to the
limits of their powers, in the support of institutions
connected with their own household of faith ;—those
who " care for none of these things," will not readily
exert themselves in the hopeless task of teaching
these " ragamuffins."   This School has, besides, suffered in its funds, from the very circumstance of
avoiding what Mr. Fletcher, in his Report, justly
reprobates, as the " very antagonism of class, which
it should be a prime object of this and every other
form of Christian effort to soften, if not eradicate."
Because on its Committee, and in its School-room,

members of the Established Church unite har-
moniously with dissenters of every shade, all for a
time forgetting their differences, and desirous only
to lead in the right way these little wanderers,—this
School is excluded from a participation in the general
interest in the work excited in the city, and can
gather around it only the faithful few who love
Christ better than sects,—who desire to do good
in the best, not in the cheapest way. Yet even the
parochial visitation of the whole city by zealous members of the Church of England, has raised, for their
own Ragged Schools, during the last year, by subscriptions and donations, only the sum of £367 3s. 5d.,
an amount evidently by no means adequate to the
effective maintenance of four Day Schools, and a
Feeding Industrial School for 40 or 50 boys.

Before proceeding to suggest remedies for these
evils, and stating the conclusions which appear
inevitable from the facts which have been brought
forward, it will be well to consider an objection
which exists in the minds of many against the establishment of good Free Day Schools ; especially
as it takes a somewhat different ground from those
which were answered in the introductory chapter.

A fear has been felt, and not without foundation,
that the establishment of Free Day Schools for the
class we are considering, would have an injurious
and lowering effect on the good pay Schools now in
existence,—injurious, because checking exertion and
fostering a dependent spirit ; lowering, because the

education given being necessarily of a lower intellectual grade, parents may be led to rest satisfied
with this instead of seeking a higher kind.   Such a
danger is alluded to by Mr. Fletcher, in his last
Report :—

"For an evidence of this lowering testimony," he says,
p. 297. "I need not go beyond the very city in which my
attention has been officially forced to the subject, that of
Bristol, where the Red Cross-street British School, though
largely supported by the Society of Friends, with every power
and appliance for giving to all the children who would attend
it a sound and vigorous system of instruction, was for a time
far from full, while that having a gratuitous admission, (not
a Ragged School,) expressly called the Friends' School, within
a few hundred yards, without any course of instruction or of
training worthy of mention in comparison, was crammed with
some 500 children, and regarded with popular admiration for
its *success ;* which was so far from being real, that the moment
it came into hands having any distinct perception of the
duties involved in their instruction, 200 of them were turned
away ; and the same pressure downward, not upward, into the
gratuitous School, will be testified by the promoters of Ragged
Day Schools generally." This may be counteracted, continues
Mr. Fletcher, " simply by the Committee, aided by the teacher,
and some system of visitation of which a city missionary will
be part, exercising a veto upon their *continuance* in it, which
would never be applied with the most exact nicety, but yet
with enough to accomplish the end desired ; and the economy
of one penny per week in the instruction of a child, is not
temptation enough to any sane man, however poor, to induce
him to affect a misery not his own, at the same time that he
can be made to tolerate the pity shown to the orphan, the
destitute, and the child of the helpless and hopeless, nay even
of the depraved."

That such checks are effective, and that the provision of real education for those now absolutely

without it will have a pressure *upwards* not downwards, is shown by the following extract from the
last report of the "Society for establishing Ragged
Schools in Bristol and its vicinity."*

" The attendance," says the report, " might be much more
numerous, but for the repeated revision of the lists of children, and the means adopted by the parochial Committees to
secure, by domiciliary or other investigation, the limitation of
the society's bounty to the really destitute. The committee
are aware of the difficulty of ascertaining the truth of the
statements made to them by the children and their parents,
but they believe that in general the object sought for has been
attained. Children are frequently admitted to the Schools
whose parents have for some time paid, but are no longer
able, through distress, to pay for their education, the committee regarding those as fit objects of their care. The
efforts to prevent infraction of the society's rules, in regard to
the admission of children, have happily been seconded, in no
inconsiderable degree, *by the parents themselves*, many of
whom, actuated by a proper spirit of independence, are very
anxious to contribute to the cost of their education. In
proof of the observance of the society's rules, the general
result of the inquiries respecting the attendance at the National Schools and others, in which payment is required of the
scholars, is, *that it has not been diminished, but on the contrary
increased*. And it is just that which might be anticipated, *as
the effect of the general stimulant to the education of the lower*

---

* This Society was established in 1847, subsequently to the
St. James's Back School, and on principles which prevented
that School from being included in its action, since it ex-
cludes from its management or teaching all persons who are
not members of the Established Church. The last report states
that four Day Schools are being carried on, in the morning
for boys under 8, and girls ; in the afternoon for girls only ;
a very few hours of withdrawal from the streets is thus
afforded.

classes, supplied by the Society's Schools ; and *the progressive improvement in the Schools in which payment is made will yet more effectually secure them from encroachment*."

A similar testimony to the stimulus given to the education of the labouring classes, by a *good* Free Day School for the destitute and depraved, is borne by the masters of the British and Infant Schools before alluded to, as being in the immediate vicinity of the St. James's Back School. It had been apprehended, particularly by the master of the Infant School, that many parents would avail themselves of this free schooling, to the prejudice of these Schools; nor was the fear groundless, for many of the parents now paying for their children were in the lowest depths of poverty, and residing in the very neighbourhood of the Free School, which offered equally good accommodations and comforts, and was taught by an equally kind and good master and mistress. But the contrary has been the result of four years' experience. Not only have no children been withdrawn from this Infant School to go to the Free School, but several parents have brought their children from that School to the pay School, feeling now stimulated *to make an effort* for their better education; and the master of the Infant School has found it an advantage to his own School, to draft off from it to the lower one those children whom no temporary aid in the payment induced to come regularly, and who were often kept at home for weeks together from want of suitable clothing;—such children have been found to attend much more regularly at the lower School. With respect to the British School, a single glance at this and at the juvenile department of the Free School, will convince the most casual observer that the two *cannot* interfere. The master of this School, who has greatly raised its educational standard and its general discipline during the last few years, has constantly a large number on his list waiting for admission, and was last year obliged to refuse thirty or forty from want of room.

Having, it is hoped, satisfactorily answered the objections which may be made to the Free Day School for the destitute and depraved, let us consider how the obstacles to their improvement can be removed.

The last-mentioned, the ineffective police agency in the neighbourhood of the School, may, of course, be only local negligence; where it exists, all those interested in the success of its working should, of course, make such representations to those in office, as will lead to greater vigilance, and, if necessary, to an increase of power to restrain. Wherever such neglect exists, it must seriously injure the School, and no effort should be omitted which might tend to remove the evil.

The second, which must, by the very nature of the School, exist in all similar establishments, requires more consideration. The government regulations, intended to meet the want in the higher Schools, are

not available in this, nor is the principle upon which
the arrangements for pupil teachers are founded at
all applicable here.   The great object in these is
to train up a set of young persons who will be well
prepared to enter in after life on the duties of
teachers, and, while so training them, to secure valuable assistance in teaching to the master and mistress, thus materially benefiting the School.   With
this view, a period of five years is secured by regular
indentures binding the young person to his instructor;
and high qualifications both of character and knowledge are required; the master devoting a certain
portion of time each day to give his pupil such instruction as may enable him to satisfy ·the inspector
at the yearly examination.   It is evident that it
would be quite undesirable to look for teachers who
may raise the perishing and dangerous classes from
among themselves; that it would be useless to expect
to find boys or girls among them who would be willing to devote five of the most important years of
their lives to the acquisition of a training which
would be of no direct aid to them in gaining their
livelihood, and that even could such be met with,
sufficiently unexceptionable in their own character,
and in that of their parents, to meet the government
requirements, yet that their deficiency in early instruction would render it almost impossible to prepare them to pass the necessary examinations.   Besides this, what has been said of the close and constant
occupation of the master and mistress of a School

carried on as this should be, would necessarily prevent the devotion of the required time to the instruction of pupil teachers. Difficulties almost as insurmountable as these prevent the aid offered to stipendiary monitors being available in such Schools. We learn from Mr. Fletcher's last report that similar obstacles exist to the improvement of a large class of Schools, in agricultural and other districts, where the very greatness of the necessity prevents the possibility of receiving aid, or of rising to a higher educational condition. The plan proposed to their lordships by Mr. Fletcher, is exactly that which the needs of this School would suggest. It is virtually this:—" The agency," he says, " of stipendiary monitors from 13 to 15 years of age is of a value infinitely beyond its cost, when in the hands of teachers of even moderate attainments, who both *understand and practise good methods of instruction,* and especially when combined with extended inspection and verified responsibility. * * It would be of great advantage to abandon altogether the standard required in the latter years of stipendiary monitors, unless it were *sustained for two years' engagements only,* with an express view to the *elevation of the Schools,* and with only a secondary regard to the training of teachers, as the local supporters of Schools, have generally contemplated that it would be; those few only who showed peculiar aptitude and inclination being permanently retained for the service." Such a plan, which he believes most im-

portant for a large class of Schools which now remain
hopelessly in a condition which is calculated rather
to deaden than to excite a desire for education
among the labouring classes, and is in perfect accordance with the opinion expressed by their lordships in the Circular of Instruction to Inspectors,
dated 25th of November, 1838, viz., that "their
claims to stipend, from the public funds, rest upon
the discharge of those duties, (the steady progress of
the classes which have been entrusted to their care),
rather than the cultivation of their own powers; for
the latter is of itself, if not quite, a sufficient reward
for any labour that may have been bestowed upon
it." Mr. Fletcher adds his conviction that "every
possible assistance should be rendered to the promoters of the Reformatory Ragged Day Schools of
our large towns, *on condition that they shall be as
good*, (in respect to the means employed rather than
the progress made,) as any of the pay Schools of
the humbler classes, by which they may be surrounded;" and suggests also that there should be
a double fee on the certificate of its teacher or
teachers, being an additional augmentation to each,
in lieu of *that proportion of their income generally
contributed by the pence of the children;* that the
grant for the cost of apparatus should be two-thirds
instead of one-third, in consideration of the excessive
wear and tear; and that an unusual proportion of the
costs of the premises should be given, on verification
of the fact of their being well adapted for the purpose.

A grant made in such proportion as is suggested by Mr. Fletcher, might enable a School similar to the one we have been contemplating to stand on a firm footing, instead of depending for its existence on the precarious hope of donations. As yet the utmost efforts made to fulfil the government requirements have enabled it to receive only the value of a couple of pounds towards the purchase of books; the premises, admirably adapted as they are for their purpose, are not such as can receive aid from the council;—no scholars can be produced likely to become qualified teachers for British Schools;—and the teachers, well-trained as they are, and highly qualified for their office, cannot devote that time and attention to branches of knowledge, utterly useless to them in this School, which would enable then to pass an examination, and thus to receive an addition to their income.

Such arrangements respecting stipendiary monitors, (the necessary term being shortened to two years, and the requirements only such are needed for the ordinary School routine), would infuse new vigour into the School and raise its status. Were there, as suggested in the Appendix to Mr. Fletcher's Report, six stipendiary monitors, four for the Infant, two for the Juvenile department, and were these selected for their advancement in knowledge and good character, and bound for two years, the engagement terminable at any time if the conditions were not fulfilled by the young person, sufficient payment being given them

to make their continuance desirable to them;—
the master and mistress would no longer have
the hopeless task of struggling against insurmountable difficulties, but would have a staff of
monitors who would really be capable of conducting
their classes;—a great stimulus would be held out
to the scholars to aspire to a post of real advantage
to them; great good would be done to the individuals themselves, who would afterwards go forth to
maintain themselves, much better prepared to do so
effectually and well than they would otherwise have
been, and most probably some of the six would remain
in the School preparing to be assistant teachers.

As yet we have considered the position and needs
of a single Free Day School for the destitute in a large
city,—one to which a large amount of personal effort
has been devoted to bring it to its present condition,
and on which its conductors have spared no needed
expense, because they felt that the experiment they
were trying was to benefit not only the children
there instructed, but many others, by eliciting important truths, and testing great principles. The
experience of this School has shown that true education may be brought to bear on that numerous
portion of our youthful population who are now
spiritually perishing for lack of knowledge, and that
the seed thus sown does spring up abundantly, and
brings forth immeasurably more fruit than its most
sanguine supporters anticipated;—it has proved, too,
that such Schools must be *good*, to produce these bene-

ficial effects. But can one such School sensibly affect a crowded city? Ten minutes' walk brings us to another of the "back slums" of the city, one totally differing in external appearances, and in the character of its inhabitants, similar only in utter degradation; a nest of close, filthy courts, the favourite resort of cholera, from which issue forth little half-dressed savages. "Is not the Red Cross Street British School in the immediate vicinity?" it is asked;—"was it not originally established in that very spot to gather in such children?" It has been already shown that Schools adapted to the respectable labouring classes in no way affect these. Yet what attempt has been made to gather them in, and render them civilised beings? The same question may be asked of numerous parts of every large city. A Liverpool Missionary to the poor states the following startling fact, which probably represents but too well the condition of a large number of the streets in our large cities. "I have ascertained the state," he says, "of two streets in my district; in one, Brick Street, there are 436 children under the age of 14, only 51 of whom go to any School, (or some of them only to an Evening Ragged School), leaving 385 who go to no School whatever; in the other, Crosbie Street, there are 484 children under 14, only 47 of whom go to School, leaving 437 who go to no School at all. As to religion, in Brick Street there are 717 professed Catholics, and 103 professed Protestants; in Crosbie Street 860 Catholics, and 37 Protestants. There are very many streets in the town equally destitute in an educational point of view. As to the cause of such wholesale neglect on the part of the parents, *poverty* has, no doubt, much to do with it; but *indifference* and the *want of appreciation of the value of education*, have, I am persuaded, infinitely more." Is it for the well-being of society that such multitudes of young children should be allowed to grow up in a depth of ignorance, which must be productive of an increasing and most *expensive* amount of pauperism and crime? Every free man in this country is at present taxed to support in idleness every pauper and every criminal. Will it not be a great saving to all, if a comparatively small amount were expended in preparing these children to pass through life neither as paupers nor as criminals? Considering the subject only in its economic point of view, it does appear most imperative for the good of society in general that *provision should be made for the education of those who cannot, from whatever reason, whether of vice or of poverty, obtain it in the existing educational establishments*. The experiment has been made sufficiently long of *doing nothing*, of leaving evils to remedy themselves, to work their cure, as some self-styled economists advise; this has not answered; ignorance kills good seed, fertilising only the bad, and its numerous progeny far outstrips the rapid increase of population. Another experiment has been made by the philanthropic, who believe that they have been guided by the soundest political economy, while obeying the Christian law;—that experiment has answered far better than any anticipated;—the sceptical have seen that something *can* be done;—the believing have rejoiced, and thanked God for such a stimulus to their future exertions. But the number of these is comparatively few, and they are not generally among the rich in this world's goods;—they cannot do alone what ought to be done. We have seen that in Bristol, which requires a large number of such Schools, only one exists whose modes of operation are so fully carried out as fairly to test the success of the undertaking, and that this is supported with great difficulty; while the utmost efforts of the Established Church have not, according to the last report, obtained for their Free Day Schools more than £400, with which *four* Schools are established, giving education during a very small portion of each day.

If, then, anything is to be effectively done to purify the corrupt mass that is diffusing its noxious influence around, all must be made to co-operate in furnishing the pecuniary means, either by a municipal rate in each town which is sufficiently large to stand in need of the agency, or by distinct government grants for the purpose, such inspection being always provided as will secure the establishment of such Schools in the localities where they are needed, and the management of them in an enlightened and efficient manner.

That the establishment of such free Schools as we
have been considering would be of the greatest
benefit to society, is strongly supported by the experience of New England.

"The provision for the elementary or district School by a
general tax," says an American writer [*Christian Examiner,*
Boston, U. S., January 1837, p. 39], "*is sufficiently justified by
the increased security of property and life in communities where
such Schools are sustained ;* they are as necessary as roads
and bridges, and if our villages are sometimes very bad with
them, they would be positively uninhabitable without them.
We suppose, however, that this argument could not be used
for anything beyond an elementary training, and fortunately
we do not need to make any such use of it. The increased
expenditure referred to may be justified, even when it is not
devoted to the erection of a barrier which ever waits at the door
of civilization, as *a wise economy, and as a wise charity,*—a wise
economy, because the practical talent which these high Schools
develope and train, must in the end enlarge the resources of
the whole community,—a wise charity, for what better use
can we make of the few dollars annually paid as a school tax,
than to bestow it upon the education of human minds ? Ought
we not to be willing, as public spirited citizens and as
Christians, to make sacrifices for such an òbject ? This is a
*gift which increases the independence and the capacity of the
receiver ;* at small cost it sets him free from hard and depressing circumstances, and makes him more truly a man. It
almost converts the poverty of a child into a blessing, for it
leaves just enough of difficulty to ward of the access of sloth.
But may we not go farther than this, and ask,—Is a generous
school-tax anything more than just, is it anything more
than a fair compensation due from capital to labour ? If
the ingenious and wealthy are making the very elements
and metals intelligent, and putting them into the places once
occupied by men, can they do anything less than educate those
who are to guide their machines ? Even where a generous
education is free to all, the interval between rich and poor

will be very wide, but without such a provision this interval must grow wider and wider. Can we afford this ? In a highly civilized age the value of uneducated labour tends constantly to decrease. For want of intellectual and moral culture, the new systems of industry, which are eulogized as the great improvements of our times, have depressed a great multitude to the very lowest depths of degradation and misery, below, sometimes, the last point at which life can be sustained. Paupers and thieves are multiplied, just in proportion as the wealth of a partially educated community is enlarged. The resources of Great Britain are known to all ; but it is not so well known as it should be, that a state which has provided the means of education for only one half of its children, was obliged in 1848 to support every eighth person as a pauper. There must be something very wrong in a system which issues in such a result as this."

Let us, then, no longer be a reproach to our neighbours; let them not point to our multitudes of ignorant and uncared-for children ;—let the philanthropist devote heart and soul to the work, let him go forth in the spirit of his great Master to the highways, and bring in the lost and ignorant ;—but let such arrangements be made by those who regulate the public finances that their labour shall not be in vain for want of means to carry it on, but that a wisely arranged plan shall oblige all to contribute to what is for the benefit of all.

CHAPTER IV.

In the preceding chapter some account has been
given of the two classes of Schools which are especially directed to the elevation of children utterly
unprovided for by other institutions. "And yet,"
says Mr. Fletcher, "when both classes of Ragged
Schools have done their utmost, it will be 'evident
to all men,' in the words of the Citizens' Memorial to
Edward VI., 'that beggary and thieving do abound;'
since there will still be a vagrant class selfishly raising
up their children merely as the companions and
instruments of their vagabondage; 'for there is as
great a difference,' says the First Ordinances of Bridewell, in 1557, in terms which three centuries have
not the least invalidated, 'between a poor man and
a beggar, as between a true man and a thief. The
poor man is he whom sickness and age oppresseth,
or by losses, or otherwise, is driven to the ground
with necessity; which doth labour willingly to gain
that which may be gotten, so long as power and
strength will serve. The beggar is the contrary;
one who never yieldeth himself to any good exercise,

but continually travaileth in idleness, *training such youth as cometh to his or their custody to the same wickedness of life!*' For these Bridewell was instituted, and our gaols must still provide ; but for 'the youth which cometh to their custody' *no sufficient provision ever was, nor is yet made ;* for though the Ragged Schools make a direct movement at this class, its very vagrancy eludes their influence. They will raise up the widows' children, and those of the poor, 'beaten down with necessity' to the lowest depths of physical privation and moral depression ; but will not reclaim the 'outer barbarians,' perpetually hanging and preying upon the lower frontiers of civilized society, to the injury of the honestly poor, quite as much as to the annoyance of the luxuriously rich. These will reject no help but that which the honest man often seeks in vain—education, to enable his child to do without help. *And it is the children of this class whom society is inevitably doomed to support, while it slowly grinds them down, by its gigantic and indiscriminating agency for the supposed suppression of crime.* This, obviously, is a subject of police, but not of police only ; and it becomes a question, which the Ragged School approaches only on one side, whether it would not be more economical, and infinitely more beneficial to society at large, to take all the children from 10 to 15 years of age found repeatedly begging or stealing, give them a brief training in 'some house of occupations,' on the plans of the Philanthropic Society, and then deport them to some of our colonies; *thus simply assuming the duty of parentage where natural parents showed their incompetency to its discharge.* If this privation of their children prove not to be punishment enough for them, while it is the salvation of the young people themselves, it will be time enough then *to impose some fine upon them, in part defrayal of their children's maintenance, or imprisonment on neglect of its payment,* especially if there should be any symptom of the plan encouraging vagabondage for the express purpose of getting rid of the children, which is not very likely, *because at this age they are ceasing to be burdensome, and beginning to be useful for honest as well as for dishonest purposes.* * * Your lordships' co-operation with the Home Office, (superintending the departments of justice and police) under a *sufficient legislative sanction, could alone accomplish such a work;* and I have ventured upon its suggestion merely because I am quite convinced that neither Ragged Schools nor courts of justice, *alone* and *severally,* can grapple with the rising flood of this disorder; but that *jointly they may accomplish a great and a saving work,* with sufficient moral security against mischief to the general economy of society, and in a manner consistent with the humanity of the age.   It would be easy to enlarge upon this plan, to show the numbers to which it would apply, to disprove the force of its economical objections, and to show the gain to the poor, as well as to the rich, by 'Ragged Schools' on such a plan and scale ; but this is not the place to do so without express permission." *

The children, then, whom the Free Day School fails to influence, are now to be the subject of our consideration. Of these there are some who have for a time come within its sphere of operation ; but the strong counteracting agencies of the home and the streets present temptations to evil and opposition to everything good, which no mere teaching, however excellent, can effectually oppose ;—others, again, *cannot,* either through the actual poverty of their parents, or the vicious tendencies they have already acquired, be in any way induced to attend School at all. All of these society is *inevitably* doomed to support *expensively* as paupers, the progenitors of a race of paupers ; or as criminals at large, luxuriously living on the spoil of the industrious ; or felons, carefully nurtured in gaols, and then provided with the means of free emigration to the penal colonies !

Let us observe individually a few of these children, belonging all of them to the class that cannot be touched by the Day School, yet differing much among themselves in character and condition. The records of a teacher in the School described in the last chapter, will furnish several examples, each of which may be regarded as the type of a distinct genus. It may appear to some that too many details of individual cases are made in various parts of this

* Mr. Fletcher's General Report to the Committee of Council on Education, p. 300.

work ; but remarks made by persons in influential
positions, and recorded in print, betray such utter
ignorance of the real condition of these children,
and their motives of action, that it is necessary to
place this in a clear point of view before a correct
judgment can be formed respecting the remedy to be
applied. C. B. Adderley, M.P., in a recently published pamphlet, entitled *Transportation not Necessary*, suggests that when magistrates have young
offenders brought before them they should *not* send
them to *Penal Schools*, but to *regular National
Schools*. Will such children stay there, or be benefited by them? A boy of 14, recently brought
before Alderman Humphries in the Guildhall, acknowledged, in answer to queries put to him by the
Alderman, that he did not know what an oath is,
what the testament is, what prayers are, what God
is, what the devil is ; that he had heard of the devil,
but did not know him. " I knows how to sweep the
crossing, that's all. I sweeps the crossing." The
Alderman said " that in his experience he had never
met with anything like the deplorable ignorance of
the unfortunate child in the witness box. He, of
course, could not take the evidence of a *creature*
who knew nothing whatever of the obligation to
speak the truth." Can those whose experience has
not led them to know even of the existence of this
class of " creatures," understand how to deal with
them? Lord Brougham, as chairman of the Lords'
Committee in 1847, asked a witness, (p. 363) " Do

you think that the people of Canada would like to have a convict of 12 years of age, or such a one as we heard of just now, (a homeless, destitute, little wanderer) who had been in prison three times at the age of 10, and *who was so wicked that he preferred remaining in prison to going out?"* This is the first time that we have heard of a child wishing to remain in prison from *wickedness!* But let us return to the teacher's Journal :

" A short time ago I met the bright black-eyed little S. looking wonderfully neat and well dressed ; he was just come from the Union Workhouse, where his mother had gone with him for a time ; before, when I had missed him once or twice, I had found that he had been in prison for begging ; I had frequently offered every inducement to him in my power to lead him to go to School, but in vain, and had begged my friends to abstain from giving any money or food to him and his little brother, which might encourage him in his vagrant habits ; I then tried again, but in vain, to get him to attend School, even promising to give him his dinner. *He now seems thoroughly established in his vagrant habits,* and with cunning enough to avoid apprehension. He looks very pleasantly at me when I meet him, for he knows I am his friend, though I give him nothing, *but I feel powerless to help him.* His little brother was happily removed by cholera from a career of vice. * * * As I went to School one morning I met a miserable little boy crying ; he said he felt ill from want of food, but that his mother beat him out of the house to go and sell oranges. I took him to the School, gave him some food, and promised to buy all his oranges, and to give him his dinner regularly, if he would come every day. The master called on his mother to induce her to agree to this, *but quite ineffectually ;* the neighbours said that she made this poor little fellow and his twin brother support her. I now see them in the streets idle and ragged, *but can do nothing.* * * * As I was going on Christmas morning to prepare the children's festival, I passed an Irish woman dragging along some miserable children who looked the picture of want and wretchedness. I told them to follow me to the School, and gave them some bread, desiring the woman to wash them, and bring them in two hours, when they should have a good dinner ;—she seemed grateful, and promised that they should attend the School. *They did not even appear for the dinner!* * * * The Irish children to whom we gave dinners and schooling all last winter when they were sick and starving, have been in the country during the summer, and are returned vigorous and wild for their winter's campaign. When I once saw the mother she looked like a wild savage, and could scarcely understand me, or I her ; these little fellows now seem quite independent, and *we cannot get them even within the walls of the School.*"

Some are become already such determined vagrants that even an attempt at parental control will not restrain them.

" One evening a boy came to the School looking more like a scarecrow, in dress and appearance, than anything else. The boys cried out that he was Irish, (many of them were really so themselves,) but he indignantly asserted that he was as good an Englishman as any one of them ! The master feared that his apparent quietness would soon break into insubordination, but he proved to be *quite a superior lad in education and manners, and had respectable relations at Bath.* He was an orphan ; had been apprenticed by the parish, and had run away, wandering over the country. We did what we could for him and sent him to his relations, but he soon came back ;—we put him into a situation and made every effort to settle him ;—but it was of no avail ;—he wandered away, and we have seen nothing of him since."

Here is a lad, actually placed in a School by his father, but preferring to engage in a vagrant life.

" A boy, named R. L., was charged with sleeping in an ash-house in D— street The case was proved by P. C. 59, and the prisoner, upon being asked what he had to say for himself, said he had run away from a Ragged School at Bath, in which he had been placed by his father. Mr. Phippen : ' What made you run away from a very good School ?' Prisoner : ' The boys used to make fun of me, and say, There goes one of the ragged ones.' The prisoner further said that he had travelled about the country, since he ran away, with some other boys. His father lived at * * * Bath, and *was a cabinet-maker*. The magistrates committed him for 3 days to hard labour, and directed the police in the meantime to communicate with his parents."—*Bristol Mercury*, January 11, 1851.

In this case there would appear to be some great fault in a father possessing a good trade, who should send his child to a Ragged School; yet otherwise we may say of this child, as of each one who has been mentioned, *ex uno disce multos*.

With such a juvenile population growing up around us, is it wonderful that " begging and thieving do abound." Soon they will serve their first apprenticeship to the prison life, and of such cases the following is an example, extracted from the memoranda of the Chaplain of the Bath Gaol.

January 13, 1851.—"Discharged this morning two Irish children, Margaret McCarthy, 15 years old, and James McCarthy, 9 years old, both committed for begging, for 5 days imprisonment. They appear to have a father and mother now lodging in Avon-street. Father sells oranges and mats ; —the mother makes the mats. They left Ireland 3 months ago ; ' 5 of us paid a crown to come on board the steamer to London.'—The eldest of these children is precocious. She says in a strong Irish accent, ' *We be put here for no reason*—we were only offering matches, and the peeler took us.' They have been wandering about the country *viâ* Southampton and Weymouth, and were directed to be in Bath a week after Christmas."

What can be hoped for such children under our existing institutions, deprived as they are of the power of.gaining what they consider an honest livelihood, and so uncared for by their parents? Yet the following example, extracted from a London paper, is even more touching. At a recent meeting, Mr. Rathbone, of Liverpool, is stated to have mentioned the following fact as a specimen of one of *frequent occurrence* :—

" He happened to be that day sitting on the bench with Mr. Rushton, and a child was put into the dock—a child of whose beautiful appearance any mother might be proud. She was placed in the dock for begging about the streets. A policeman had traced her mother to one of those low lodging houses, in which no fewer than 51 persons were found huddled together. He found her with 5 children, whom she was totally unable to support. What did she do ? She sent those children into the streets to beg ; to be punished if they did not bring home to her the means of subsistence. Now he appealed to every mother that was in that place—he appealed to every father that was present, what was the painful duty of Mr. Rushton ? He turned round to him and said, 'Good God ! what shall I do with this child ?' (a beautiful child, 6 *or* 7 *years old*, whom the officers had to raise up in the dock that she might be seen) 'Shall I return her to her savage mother ? ' (The woman was Irish) ' Now will you go home ; if you do, I'll send you.' She replied, ' No, Sir, I will not go home.' ' What then am I to do for this child ?' said Mr. Rushton ; ' I have either to commit her to prison, or to the tender mercies of her unfeeling and savage parent. *What a dreadful calamity is this, that I have no place to send this child to. I believe I must commit her to gaol for* 21 *days, as the safest place for the child, and removing her from the protection of her mother.*' And the child was accordingly sent to gaol."

Here even a tender-hearted magistrate is powerless

to rescue this little girl from her inevitable fate. Every one must feel his heart revolt at the idea of incarcerating a tender creature like this, who has done nothing but obey her mother;—yet it is the only place of safety; and then, when the three weeks are expired?—She will have learnt not to dread a place where she was more carefully tended than in her home; she has no hand to guide her, no law to restrain her;—what must she become with advancing years?

In the foregoing instances, actual crime has not yet commenced; we only perceive that such children must grow up to be of the "perishing," if not, as is most likely, of the "dangerous classes." Here are some other examples from the prison memoranda of the chaplain of the Bath Gaol, where the career of crime is begun in good earnest and early, for they are the children of parents who "train such youth as come within their custody to the same wickedness of life."

"*January* 13, 1851.—This morning there were two little boys, (Joseph and Henry Eades) twins, discharged from the gaol. Their history is remarkable. These children have appeared several times in gaol, and I would here trace their domestic and prison history. Their father works as a labourer on the railway; their mother is dead, but their father is married again. Joseph was first imprisoned, at the age of 10 years, for begging, and punished by 1 month's imprisonment. On inquiry of the child, it was evident that poverty was the immediate cause of the offence, but the neglect of the parents the real cause. He was found unable to tell a letter, and totally ignorant of everything religious, except that, when asked who came into the world to save sinners, he answered, 'Jesus

Christ.' *A month's imprisonment would do here but little good in this respect.* His account of himself and his domestic condition is as follows :—' His stepmother ties up wood ; father brings it home ; I sell it : it is deal wood. He got it from the railroad ; he brings it every night ; he works there now ; he earns 11s. a week. I sometimes get 6d. for what he brings home at night. I have been taken up 3 or 4 times by the police for begging, and let go again. I ran away from home, because father would beat me for being so long out selling the wood. Father and mother, and 3 brothers and sisters live and sleep in one room. My brother, who is of the same age, ran away because he could not sell his wood, and stopped away 2 or 3 months. I live about the streets all day, and go to lodgings at night ; pay 1½d. for night's lodgings, and get the money by begging. Brother went nearly up to London, begging all the way up and back with 2 or 3 others ; their names are ———. G., got no father ; was took up just before I was. *I sometimes get 5d. or 6d. a day by begging.* There are more than 12 boys or girls sleep at ——— every night. I went to a Sunday School that hadn't been open very long ; never went to a Day School ; 4 Sundays I went to Sunday School, until I ran away because I couldn't sell my wood. Father did use to go to public-houses on Sundays ; public-houses are shut up now till one o'clock, and now sometimes he goes to chapel. I can say the Lord's Prayer ; I learnt it in this gaol. Father and mother don't know I'm in gaol. When I go out, I shall go begging again, because father will beat me for being away so long—2 or 3 months—because I came to gaol. Father is kinder to me than mother-in-law ; she serves me worse than he do !' I visited this family, and found the child's account correct. *I offered to take the child into the Industrial School, but there appeared no willingness on the part of the step-mother that I should do so.* It will not be surprising that this child soon made his appearance again in the prison. His brother Henry, though not the first in the gaol, has exceeded his brother in the number of commitments. On February 27, 1849, he was committed for vagrancy, and punished with 4 months' separate confinement. His condition, as to education and religious knowledge was, if possible, worse than that of his brother. Again, for vagrancy for 7 days, July 2, 1850, when he had lately been living in Avon-street on his own account. Again, for a third committal, in company with his brother, for juvenile felony, December 24, 1850, and punished by 21 days and a whipping ; his crime being, on this occasion, one that would have sent him to Quarter Sessions prior to the operation of Sir John Packington's bill, as he was apprehended for stealing wood from the railway and from the Old Bridge."

Here, then, are children already so useful to their parents for dishonest, as well, it may be at times, as for honest purposes, that they will not part with them, even to be entirely relieved of their maintenance ; and it would not be felt by them to be " a bonus on vice," were the youth that are " being trained by them to the same wickedness of life " to be taken " from their custody."   These little twins are now discharged ; their utter ignorance (for 1 or 2 months' teaching in the prison could give them little more light than to reveal their darkness), their wild habits, their bad characters, now indelibly stamped on them by the prison brand—all utterly unfit them for gaining an honest livelihood ; besides, they have found that they can each obtain from the public 6d. a day, *which will comfortably maintain them* without work; and to this they may add by occasional thieving, as a safe opportunity presents itself to them ! We shall soon see whether, in such cases, the " children of this world," who, making Mammon their god, will do for these children nothing which would involve them in present expense, are as wise in their generation as "the chil-

dren of light," who think no sacrifice too great so
that they may win souls.

All of the cases which have been here considered
have been quite *beyond the pale* of any regular
School influence, and it is evident that *the establishment of any number of Free Day Schools would
have no possible effect on them.*   Scarcely less numerous are those children who have shown some desire
to gain instruction by occasional attendance at a
Free Day School, or an Evening Ragged School, but
for whom the counteracting agencies are too strong
to be resisted by the strength, as yet but very small,
of the good principles there imbibed.   A forcible instance of this is afforded by the records for the past
year of the Bristol Ragged School above-mentioned.
The statement is on the authority of the master, and
is the result of his daily observation of the character
and condition of his scholars.

"During the past year 25 attendants at the School have, to
my knowledge, been in prison, viz., 24 boys and 1 girl ; it is
probable that several others of those who may be called the
floating scholars have also been in Bridewell, but of these I
have no knowledge.   The girl is the only attendant whom I
have ever known of as in prison ; she was seldom at School,
and only in the evening.   Of the 24 boys, 5 are from 10 to
12 years of age ; 5 about 14 ; and 14 from 15 to 18 years
old.   12 of the 24 were attendants at the Evening School
only, but only 2 or 3 of them were ever regular for any
length of time, most of them appearing occasionally, perhaps
only once a month, so that though most of them had been
nominally in the School since I came to it, I could not
gain over them such an influence as would counteract the
wild habits they had already formed.   A few of these Evening

scholars showed real interest in the School, they had fine powers, good dispositions, manifested attachment to me and gratitude for my efforts for them, and would, I am persuaded, have made useful characters, could they have been withdrawn from the evil influences besetting them on every side; but most of them were wild, bad boys, with reckless parents, some with none. Of the day scholars, 3 only had professed attendance from the very first, but were always irregular, often staying away for months together; at times, especially during the winter, they would be regular for a few months, and it is remarkable what a change for the better was soon perceptible in them. The others were at School only a few months occasionally, but then the improvement was such as to make one greatly regret that they could not be induced to be always there; indeed, scarcely an instance *has ever occurred of a boy getting into prison while in the habit of attending School regularly.* On none of the 24 has any wise parental control ever been exercised;—the parents of some desire that they should do well, and are grieved at their fall, without exerting themselves to remove the causes of it; but in general they are of notoriously bad character. One of the boys only was without a home, another had been deserted by his parents;— these are the only cases in which *want* could be alleged as the incitement to crime;—both these boys were, through the influence of a friend, got into the Union after the imprisonment; one remains there and is likely to do well; the other soon ran away, and got into prison again; he had been there before several times. Seven are now in prison, four for the first time; one of these may do well if he can get into work when discharged; the others are notoriously bad already, and there is no chance of their getting into an honest way of living."

The mere fact, then, of a good Free Day School existing in the midst of a degraded population, can do but little to check crime in those who are already trained to it, or are so circumstanced that they must inevitably fall into it. Such an institution, conducted by teachers whose heart and soul are in the work, and aided by the co-operation of Christian friends, may, we have already seen, do very much for those who can be brought under its influence; but it can, of course, do little or nothing for those whose attendance is so irregular that they unlearn one week in the streets all that they have gained the preceding one in the School, or those who keep without its pale. These 24 boys whom the School has failed to influence will now be added to the criminal population of the city; it will be the subject of future inquiry how far their punishment has produced any salutary effect on them : here we need only add that the master states that several of them already form part of the notorious gangs of juvenile thieves, and that their influence is most injurious to the School. "I at once perceived a change for the worse in the School," he says, "when C., came out of prison; he has remarkable power over the others out of doors, and draws them after him most re- markably. I have noticed that many *are ashamed to behave well* in School when Z. comes in; I have been frequently obliged to forbid boys of this kind from attending; without behaving ill themselves, their very presence seems to excite to evil." The number of boys in prison from this School is not a large one in proportion to that from other parts of the city. The last Report of the Ragged School Society states that for "Temple Parish, which con- tains a very depraved population, more commitments are made out than for any two other parishes in Bristol." This city, though standing high in the amount of juvenile crime which it exhibits, is yet exceeded by other towns (vid. p. 12). Birmingham, Liverpool, and London can exhibit still larger multitudes of young uncared for, ignorant, unrestrained children, *who cannot be touched* by our existing educational establishments,—who are rising up to fill our gaols. What is to be done for these?

This question has of late years engaged the serious consideration of those who strongly felt the growing evil to the country of the fearful amount of juvenile crime; an amount dangerous and costly to the public in its actual existence, but still more so in its prospective consequences;—it has more deeply still affected those who thought of the future condition of these uncared-for creatures if no hand were stretched out to save them.

For the last ten years there has been an organized attempt to apply an effective remedy to this alarming and highly contagious moral disease in the town of Aberdeen. The experiment has been made under circumstances favourable to its having a fair trial; the sphere of operation was sufficiently limited to be subjected to direct influence from the plan adopted; the individuals most active in carrying it out were influential, and secured the co-operation of members of the different branches of municipal legislation and of charitable institutions; while the evident utility of the plan called forth such willing pecuniary co-operation throughout the town, that the proceedings of the committee were not shackled by want of money. Hence the experience of this School may now afford a fair test of what can, and what cannot be done by the adoption of similar agency, and a careful examination of it will materially aid in forming a judgment of the conditions necessary for the success of Industrial Feeding Schools, which are the subject of the present chapter. It will therefore be well to give some account of the Aberdeen Juvenile Vagrant and Industrial School. The general features of its management have been already sufficiently before the public; it is rather on the principles of its operation and their results that we shall now dwell.

"In the county of Aberdeen," said Sheriff Watson, who is well known to have been the mainspring of this School, [Vid. *Prevention better than Cure*, London, Nisbet and Co., from which, and from other pamphlets by the same author, the account of this School is derived.] "a committee appointed by the Commissioners of Supply, reported in 1840, 'that *not less than a thousand* persons were continually wandering about, preying upon the inhabitants; that every part of the country suffered more or less from these vagrants, but the more remote districts suffered most; that begging was followed as a regular profession, and was unfortunately more profitable than some more creditable pursuits, and that on every account such a state of things ought not to exist. *Vagrancy is, in every point of view, demoralizing to the country.* It has a bad effect on those who only witness it, and still worse on those whose trade it is. *It is the immediate cause of a great proportion of the petty offences committed, and not unfrequently leads to the commission of the most heinous crimes.* It has rapidly increased of late, and, if allowed to go on increasing for some time longer, will, to all appearance attain to such a height as to make it extremely difficult to deal with.' "

This is not a picture of one county only; to how many others may not a likeness be recognized? Of these 1000 vagrants, the rural police stated "that 328 children were vagabondizing the county;" the Superintendent of the City Police, "that upwards of 280 children were known to him as common beggars and common thieves;—the Governor of the prison "that 77 children under 14 years of age were annually in prison, a very few of whom could either read or write."

In the same year a Committee of the Managers of the Poor's Hospital, feeling "that it is a matter of deep importance, as well as a duty of the most sacred nature, *incumbent on the guardians of the poor*, that the religious and moral training of pauper children should be improved, and *that no effort should be left untried to accomplish this desirable end*," express their conviction that the palpable and growing evils now existing among the juvenile poor, can be remedied only by "bringing them under a proper system of moral and religious training, and superinducing upon their minds such habits of industry as will *make labour of some useful kind a pleasure;*—by showing them that they must gain their bread by the sweat of their brow, and that the property is most valuable which has been obtained by their own industry and careful frugality; *and if this is done, it is predicted that ere long a band of faithful and efficient servants of both sexes will be raised up, in place of so many pests of society as at present exist.'*

Would that all guardians of the poor held such views, *and acted on them.*

Influenced by such considerations, a few benevolent individuals determined to make the experiment of an Industrial School for these young " pests of society," at which a sufficiency of wholesome food should be given, and where they should be detained the whole day, returning to their parents at night. On the 1st of October, 1841, a dozen scholars were brought in by the police, and informed that here they would be fed and taught, and allowed to depart when they pleased, provided they did not again resort to begging. The School was opened for " the children of the poorest classes, and chiefly those who are found to infest the streets, begging and stealing;" of those who were admitted in the first six months, *half soon withdrew, unwilling to submit to the discipline of the School;* the average attendance during the first three years was about fifty, evidently a very small proportion of the juvenile vagrants and delinquents, even if they all belonged to that class. The *immediate* effect of the opening of the School, as attested by the Superintendent of the Police, was greatly to diminish petty offences and juvenile vagrancy, but this decrease was not permanent, for the number of children committed to prison in 1843 under 12 years of age, presented an increase of 31 over the preceding year. This was a startling fact. The School had already acquired considerable reputation; the system on which it was carried on seemed unexcep-

tionable ; the improvement of the children was most
satisfactory, both as regarded their physical condition
and their moral training ; yet the professed object
was not attained—for the vicious, the worthless, the
determined beggar despised the invitation ; they
begged, stole, and idled in spite of all endeavours to
prevent them. Sheriff Watson and his coadjutors
were, however, confident of their principle ; they
found only that it could *not be carried out without
the intervention of magisterial sanction and aid*. It
was proposed to the magistrates to authorize the
police to apprehend all begging children within the
city, and convey them to School. Their concurrence
was given, and instructions were communicated to
the police on the 19th May, 1845, to convey every
child found begging to the premises provided for this
new School. In the course of the day 75 were
collected, of whom only four could read ! The scene
which ensued was indescribably bad. The class of
children brought to this School were far below those
in the other and first established School ; they were
in the lowest condition of filth, disease and misery,
and manifested the most determined rebellion
against everything like order and regularity. They
were told that they may return or not as they
pleased, that if they did, they should be fed
and instructed, but that whether they did or not,
begging would not be tolerated. " Thus in a few
hours," says Sheriff Watson, " juvenile vagrancy was
finally extinguished in Aberdeen, and has never

raised its head again." Now, in the original Indus-trial Schools, the child was admitted on the appli-cation of the parents, or others interested in him, and there was little check on the admission of im-proper objects, or security of the continued attendance of the child. Some new course must be adopted in this. The police have introduced all such as sub-jected themselves to their interference, but may not those be admitted who would necessarily become vagrants if left to themselves? And what is to be done with the juvenile thieves, whom law obliges the police to carry to the council-house, not to the School? Here were great practical difficulties, and, in the hope of obviating them, a body was created which should decide on all cases brought before them, and grant admittance to the School without the applicant going through the ordeal of street begging. This body was composed of members of the Town Council, the Police Commissioner, and the Parochial Board, as well as of the committees of the other Schools. Now when children were brought before the magistrates, though they could not dismiss the case, they could adjourn it for inquiry into the child's circumstances; here the " Child's Asylum Committee" could investigate his circumstances, and place him, as seemed fit, in the Industrial School, or the Juvenile (vagrant) School; the charge of crime still remaining against him, to be made use of at once if he deserted from School, and returned to his old practices.

The success of the plan in checking juvenile vagrancy and crime has been most striking and satisfactory, as will be shown by the following table : —

Years.	Juvenile Vagrants apprehended by Rural Police.	Juvenile Delinquents committed to Prison under 12 years of age.
1841	328	61
1842	297	22
1843	397	53
1844	345	41
1845	105	49
1846	14	28
1847	6	27
1848	6	19
1849	1	16
1850	2	22*

The efficacy of these Schools, on their present system, in checking juvenile crime, is attested by those most qualified to judge. The County Prison Board, after speaking of the practicability and efficiency of the Industrial Schools, say, (Nov., 1848) "We would therefore recommend the establishment of such Schools, *and their support at the public expense.*" The Rural Police Committee, in their report for the year ending 1846, speak of the almost-complete disappearance of juvenile vagrants from the county, and add, " By the *activity of your police, the system of sending out children to beg has ceased to be*

* On examining into the committals, it will be found that the increase has not taken place at the Aberdeen prison, but at the prisons in the country, where, I believe, there are no Industrial Schools."—*Last Report of the Governor of Aberdeen Gaol.*

profitable, and has therefore been abandoned; and
farther, by the establishment of the admirable
Schools of Industry in Aberdeen, food and education having been provided for this unfortunate class
of our people, thus even the shadow of an excuse has
been taken away for sending out children to procure
subsistence by begging! A yet more valuable testimony is given by the governor of the prison, in his
report for the year 1848. "We have," he says,
"the number of criminals under 12 years of age
reduced, in the course of 6 years, from 1843 to 1848
inclusive, from 53 to 19; and if any one deems it
necessary to ask what has produced such a change, I
would just say, go to the Industrial Schools and you
will get a satisfactory answer imprinted on the happy
faces of the hundreds of children who are there receiving a moral, religious, and industrial education,
and who, but for these Schools, *would have been
training to be occupants of the prison cells, and pests
of society.*"

The following is the statement of the Child's
Asylum Committee, for the year ending 1st December, 1850 :—

"The Child's Asylum might justly be called the Juvenile
Vagrant and Juvenile Delinquent Prevention Office—Established in December, 1846, for the reception of vagrant and
delinquent youth, brought in by the police. Its committee
undertook the delicate and difficult duty of dealing with
these outcasts, sending such of them as were suitable to the
Juvenile School of Industry, and restoring the others to their
parents or the police.

" During the first year, the police brought in 95 children—56 boys and 39 girls. During the second year they brought in 46 children—30 boys and 16 girls. During the third year they brought in 28 children—22 boys and 6 girls. During the last year they brought in 12 children—10 boys and 2 girls. Of these last, 2 went to the House of Refuge, and 10 were delivered to their parents, chiefly at their own desire.

" If the Committee had confined its inquiries to the quasi-delinquent juvenile, brought up by the police, its operations would, before this, have been brought to a close—for it would not have been worth while maintaining a machinery, however simple and unexpensive, for the mere purpose of sending 2 children to the House of Refuge, and returning 10 back again to their worthless parents. But it soon became apparent that, to prevent juvenile delinquency, it was requisite also to prevent juvenile vagrancy, by anticipating the necessity of begging, and, therefore, after the first year, the committee considered the cases of children brought to the Asylum by destitute parents. During the first year's acting in this manner, it received applications on behalf of 149 children—92 boys and 57 girls ; second year, 135 children—103 boys and 32 girls ; last year, 112 children—82 boys and 30 girls—of whom

40 were sent to Boys' School ;

45 to Juvenile School ;

2 to House of Refuge ;

4 referred to Inspectors of Poor ;

21 refused as improper.

112

" These figures, carelessly read, may excite little attention, but they are deeply significant. Why, it may be asked, have the numbers of juvenile vagrants, apprehended by the police, diminished from 95 to 12 ? Have these functionaries become remiss in their duty, and allowed the plague spot of society to fester in our streets, instead of subjecting it by the discipline of the School. It is thought not,—it is believed that they have apprehended all the juvenile vagrants they could catch, and have not willingly allowed a single juvenile delinquent to escape. It is known that juvenile vagrants are still to be seen ; but it is supposed they are not the children of our native poor, but the vagrant children of stranger trampers, who, in their peregrinations, take a few days begging, stealing, and singing in our streets, and the neglected outcasts of worthless and abandoned parents who make a profit by their children's crimes. *With these classes, the Child's Asylum Committee cannot effectually deal. They require the exercise of a more powerful hand.* But their numbers are comparatively small, and a little more activity on the part of the police, excited by an intelligent and zealous magistracy, might render them considerably smaller. Though the Asylum Committee has not accomplished everything that could have been wished, yet, there can be no doubt that, with the instrumentality of the Industrial Schools, it has effected a social reformation altogether unexampled."

We perceive in the foregoing facts and statements a positive and incalculable advantage resulting to the people of Aberdeen from these institutions ; they are relieved from the constant annoyance and expense caused by young beggars; while, instead of maintaining a sufficient number of rural police to keep in check 328 young vagrants, only 2 are found in one year who required to be put in durance ; and the gaol, instead of having to furnish a living to 61 young culprits, now have had only 22 within its walls. There is, besides, a still greater prospective advantage ;—it will be shown in the next chapter that a first committal is nearly sure to bring on a second, and that these will be only the first in a long series, to terminate most probably with transportation,—a very costly kind of education. We need not go far to become assured of the fact that pauperism and vagrancy engender their like. Hence, the citizens of Aberdeen are relieved by their timely and wise exertions from the burden, both for the present and the future, of nearly 400 individuals. But to the children themselves how great has been the gain! They have been rescued from a condition at once physically wretched, degrading, and soul-crushing, from which they *could not have risen unaided;* they are placed in a position in which they can earn an honest livelihood, and have now not only the power but the desire to do so. Their very looks denote the wonderful change which has been wrought in them ; for the idle, ragged, mean, wicked-looking child, with matted hair, features disfigured by dirt, an object of disgust and loathing to the merely superficial observer, can now hardly be recognised in the diligent, open, intelligent boy, who may be poorly clad, but who yet is fresh and clean. Surely such considerations, affecting both the supporters of the Schools and those benefited by them, will be a sufficient answer to any who inquire why we, who are prudent and careful, should be charged with the support of children whom we had no concern in placing in their present baneful condition.

There is, however, a serious difficulty arising from the effect of such institutions on the parents, and this must be fairly met. It was shown in the introductory chapter that the giving of gratuitous education to the classes who neither can nor will procure it for themselves, rests on very different grounds from ordinary charitable institutions :—that it is in fact necessary as a safeguard to society. In these Industrial Feeding Schools it is found that education *cannot* be given without the food ; —shall we not now by supporting them be doing as much harm in one direction, as we do good in another ? Shall we not be increasing pauperism ? A sufficient answer is made to this objection by the following facts. In Aberdeen, *where alone the system has been fairly tried*, the average number of paupers on the roll of St. Nicholas, in 1844, was 1820. In 1845 the New Poor Law Act came into operation, and the following is the number to the present time :—

In 1845 the number was . . .	1750
1846	1753
1847	1796
1848	1502
1849	1219
1850	1009

While in 1844 the average amounts of *monthly payments* was £406. 14s., in 1850 it was £251. 7s. 11d. Now though, in the absence of further data, it would be unsafe to affirm that this wonderful diminution in the numbers of paupers, and in the amount of monthly payments, is solely owing to the establishment of Industrial Schools ; yet as we do not hear of such decrease taking place in other quarters, during the same period, and as it began when *vigilant police interference was exercised* in con-

junction with the School system, and has continued
to be even more striking from year to year, we
surely are justified in the assertion that the Industrial Schools have not increased pauperism, but
have most probably diminished it.   Nor do the
parents appear to have been encouraged by the
provision which has thus been made, to throw their
children upon the care of others, for the last report
states that the number of private applications has
diminished from 149 *to* 112.

While thus disposing of the children whose parents
cannot educate them, there is another class which
presents a still greater difficulty.   Sheriff Watson
states that of the 28 children brought up by the
police in 1849, 15 were delivered to their parents as
*quite able to maintain them, and, therefore, unfit
objects of charity*.   But in such cases the parents
are of worthless or vicious habits, who actually send
out the children to beg or steal, for which faults
they are brought up again and again.   Here nothing
can be done under the existing laws but to deliver
them up to the police, to experience the law's correction, or to give them up to their parents for
further instruction in vice.   This difficulty can only
be got rid of by an *act of the legislature authorising
the magistrate to send all such children to an Industrial School at the expense of the parents*.   Until
such provision is made, and until those exercising
magisterial functions actively co-operate with the
supporters of the Industrial Schools, *these will fail*

efficiently to perform the work contemplated by them.

Yet, were all these difficulties removed, another still remains in the minds of many benevolent economists, which perfectly alters the point of view from which they contemplate such establishments, and consequently renders all arguments in their favour perfectly futile in their apprehension. It is a beautiful fiction of the English law that no one shall be actually perishing from want of food. To give an appearance of truth to this law, another is made, inflicting pains and penalties on all such as shall show practical unbelief in the certain action of this law, or disobedience to it, and who solicit their fellow citizens to do that for them privately as a kindness, which they ought to have demanded as a right, from the legally authorised bodies. In other words, it is assumed that every individual who absolutely *cannot* support himself will be supported by the state; and, therefore, that all who beg or steal do so from criminal motives which deserve punishment, and that "Feeding Schools" are interfering with the duty of the government, and either relieve those who ought not to be relieved, or charge themselves with an unnecessary burden. How perfectly erroneous is the supposition that the Parish Union does relieve the wants of all who are absolutely destitute, it is hoped that those who have carefully perused the foregoing pages, will strongly feel;—how far it ought to do so is another question which will not be here considered. We need not now inquire whether the thousands of outcast children who infest our large cities cannot make their case known to the parochial authorities in the certainty of a kind and tender reception,—or why they do not dare to venture to solicit even temporary aid from the Cerberus of the dreaded Union. It is only the old and experienced thieves and vagabonds who employ such establishments as their inns on their peregrinations, demanding and obtaining there unpaid-for accommodation,—committing, if it is not according to their taste, such acts of mischief and insubordination as will entitle them to a week's lodging in a favourite gaol, where it is known that every attention will be paid them. It cannot be denied by any one that there are in our country multitudes of perishing children growing up in utter ignorance and depravity, *who would not receive any effectual relief* from the parish were they to apply. There are, besides, multitudes whose parents are receiving a weekly pittance for them from the Union, which barely supplies their necessities, and from which a farthing could not be spared for wants far more pressing in reality, but unknown by them. Before considering how the Industrial Feeding Schools and the Poor Law Act can be brought into harmonious action, let us observe the influence of the two agencies on each other at Aberdeen. Sheriff Watson mentions, in a lecture on the " State of Crime and Juvenile Delinquency in Aberdeenshire," (1847,) that "several paupers belonging to country parishes *have been sent to town, had their rents paid, and told that their children would be received into the School of Industry.* How has the last expectation been answered? On application for their children's admission into the School, they were informed that the parish whence they had come had not contributed to the School, and its paupers had no claim to share in its benefits." This is, indeed, a very significant fact, showing not only a high appreciation of the school on the part of the parish authorities, but their readiness to throw off a responsibility which really belonged to themselves. But the Child's Asylum Committee had another difficulty, which is stated in their last report :—

"One of the greatest difficulties the Committee has had to contend with arose from the circumstance of parties applying being at the time in receipt of parochial aid. There was an arrangement between the Parochial Board of St. Nicholas and the Managers of the Schools, by which the former were to be allowed to send pauper children to the Schools, paying at the rate of one shilling and sixpence a-week for each child. *But the arrangement has not been carried into practical effect,* and it is understood that it is now at an end, while a very considerable number of children attending the Schools *are confessedly the children of paupers in receipt of parochial aid.* Giving the matter the utmost consideration, the Committee resolved to act in all cases upon the principle of destitution,— admitting the child whenever actual destitution was proved, leaving it to the managers of the Schools to effect such arrangements with the Parochial Board, or other parties liable, as they thought fit. So far as the children were concerned, it was manifestly obvious that it was the same to them whether the inability of their parents to support them resulted from insufficiency of earnings or of parish allowance, and in order to prevent the evil consequences that must inevitably have ensued to the children, they were sent to the School. But it is clear that in doing so the parish authorities were enabled to effect a saving, either by diminishing or altogether withdrawing the allowances made to the parents on account of the children thus disposed of ;—*and there can be no doubt that the Parochial Boards are in equity bound to acknowledge, by a liberal allowance to these institutions, the good effected and the money saved to the public by the Industrial Schools.*"

Nor is the demand unreasonable, that the public, who reap the benefit of these Schools, should, either by a municipal rate, or by a direct parochial allowance for the support of each child who would otherwise have a claim to relief, take the main charge of the expense of such institutions, for, as the report most truly continues,—

" There can be as little doubt that the Police Board, the Rural Police Committee, the Magistrates, and the Prison Board, are in a similar manner bound to acknowledge their obligations to these Schools. As a preventive police their operation has been remarkable, but the Child's Asylum Committee has hitherto acted, and still acts, as a court of inquiry on the cases of delinquent children, dealing with them according to circumstances, and sending such of them as were suitable to the Industrial Schools, as houses of correction and reformation, for which they have proved infinitely more effective than either the whipping-post or the prison. Now, abolish the functions exercised by the committee, and shut up the Schools, and what would be the result? An immediate return to all the juvenile vagrancy and juvenile delinquency which formerly afflicted us, from which we are happily delivered, but which neither the police nor the prison could either abate or remove. *It is therefore most reasonable that the efforts of some hundred private individuals should be aided and encouraged by general*

public support, especially by those bodies whose sole existence is
for diminishing pauperism and preventing crime."

There will surely be found in every large town an
adequate number of benevolent persons, whose hearts
are sufficiently warmed by Christian love to give
their unbought services to the carrying out of such
plans for the rescuing of their fellow creatures;—but
such individuals frequently have not the pecuniary
means of doing so; and even if they had, it would
be really unjust that the burden of supporting the
poor should be transferred from the legal rate-payer
to the voluntary and benevolent subscriber; not to
say that the institution should be permanent and
efficiently supported, while voluntary contributions
would necessarily be fluctuating. Such provision
would be sufficiently made *if legislative sanction were*
given, to compel all such parents as can maintain
their children, but who by their criminal neglect allow
them to be injurious to society, to pay the cost of their
maintenance in the Industrial School; and to oblige
the Parochial Board, *in all cases where a claim can be*
established upon it, to transfer the sum allowed for the
maintenance of the child from the parent to the In-
dustrial School, where, as in the former case, it can
be shown that the moral training of the child is
neglected. Such an arrangement as this would not
appear to *require* legislative sanction; for we learn
from the Report of the Glasgow Industrial Schools
for 1849, that "the directors have much pleasure in
stating that a regular arrangement is now in oper-

ation with the City and Gorbals Parochial Boards, by which the pauper children having a claim upon those parishes, are received to the Schools for food and education, at the rate of 1s. 6d. per week. This arrangement is conceived to be of great benefit to these children, it being undeniable *that a large portion of the funds formerly granted for their maintenance and education, was misapplied through the vices of their parents or guardians.*" Yet if it should be deemed *essential,* as it certainly appears from the foregoing statements to be, that such an arrangement should be made, to secure needful and permanent support to the School, it must not be left to the *discretionary power of parochial boards, to make it or not as they please.* There are many Industrial Schools both in Scotland and England, yet Glasgow is the only place, as far as we can learn from the reports, where the parish authorities have been sufficiently clear-sighted to their true interests to contribute to the support of them ; and even here there is not unanimity of action. The same Report states, that "it is to be regretted that a similar arrangement has *not* yet been adopted by the Barony and Govan Parochial Boards, in reference to children alimented by them, whose education is in many cases altogether neglected. Instances have not unfrequently occurred in which boys and girls have been apprehended by the police for begging in the streets, whose parents, *while thus encouraging their children in habits of idleness and dishonesty, have been in the regular receipt of an allowance for their maintenance and education."*

Let, then, the existing regulations of the Poor Law Act be so far modified as to change into a *reality* its present fiction respecting the children of the perishing and dangerous classes, while the police vigorously enforce on all vagrant children the necessity of attending the School, under pain of severe punishment if again detected in misdemeanour; and let regulations be made to establish a sufficient number of such Industrial Schools to meet existing wants in every place where they are needed—and we shall soon find that the present rapid and increasing rate of demoralization will be arrested, that pauperism will be diminished, and that the public will in the course of a few years be taxed far less heavily than at present to support a vicious and dependent population. These results have now been demonstrated.

There is yet another view which may be taken of the relation of these Schools to the Parochial Unions. Should they be generally established, they might in a few years effect a *considerable saving to their respective parishes*. Many of the children now in our Union Workhouses have parents living, but unable to maintain them. In the Kirkdale Workhouse for children, near Liverpool, of 1119 inmates, 498 had parents; the annual expenditure of this noble institution is £10,000, exclusive of the interest of the cost of the building, which was £32,000; the actual expense then of each child, exclusive its share of the rent, is nearly £10; the cost of maintaining paupers in the Glasgow Town's Hospitals is upwards of £13 each per annum. But the annual cost of each child in the Glasgow Industrial School is £4; in the Aberdeen School it is even less. A large proportion, then, of the children in a workhouse who have parents living might be paid for in an Industrial School, care being of course taken to secure their attendance there, and thus, even with a small allowance for clothes, a saving of one-half might be effected !

Such an arrangement would, besides, probably be productive of great advantage to the children, to the parents, and ultimately to the parish, independently of the present saving. Even suppose all parish Schools were as admirable as those at Kirkdale, where, says Sheriff Watson, " Christian generosity has anticipated every wish, and nothing could be better arranged or better conducted,"—it still would be far more desirable, in ordinary circumstances, that the children should not be so completely cut off, as they must necessarily be, from all domestic ties and social affections ; that they should feel that they had *homes* to which they were bound by feelings implanted by nature. But no one can visit an ordinary Union School, without the painful sentiment that here the youthful faculties and affections are crippled and stunted, and that a race of paupers are being trained up to make the Union their final home.

Let, then, the children go to their own abodes at night, and they will carry to them the benign influence of the School, imparting to the parents a stimulus to renewed exertion, and to improved habits. This result has been continually observed, where the experiment has been fairly tried, especially in the Aberdeen Schools.

The success of the Aberdeen Schools has led to the establishment of similar ones, both in Scotland and in England; but in most of these the object has been, on the part of the benevolent individuals who projected them, simply to provide the most effective temporary remedy that suggested itself, to the juvenile vagrancy and crime that abounded. It was believed that destitution and ignorance were the main causes of this, and that such institutions were the most obvious way of removing them.

That the mere fact of providing food and education for a number of vagrant children will not stop vagrancy, is sufficiently proved by the table, p. 231, where juvenile vagrancy and crime are shown to have increased after the Industrial Feeding Schools were in active operation; it was not until Sheriff Watson induced the magistrates to exercise their restraining power, through the police, over the young beggars, and warmly to co-operate with the supporters of the Schools, that they had the desired effect. The exercise of Christian effort in behalf of hitherto uncared for children cannot fail to be productive of great individual benefit to those poor little creatures who could be brought and *retained* within its sphere of action; nor should such efforts be in any way checked, for the experience they will give may lead those who make them to seek out a more excellent way. But such Schools can be regarded only as palliatives, and do not strike at the root of the evil;—they may rescue many who would otherwise have fallen into vagrancy and crime, some even who have already entered on that career;—but the mass of young vagrants will remain untouched, until there shall be a general determination on the part of all magistrates to *apprehend every child who is vagabondizing through the country or the town,* and place him in such a position that he will learn to be an honest man. Until this is done universally, the Industrial School will fail in its avowed object, and will not touch effectually the really perishing and dangerous classes of children. Where they do co-operate with the workers in the Schools, the suppression of vagrancy will follow. "At this moment," (January 28, 1851,) says the secretary of the Industrial Schools at Glasgow, "our Industrial Schools contain hardly 200 children of both sexes, and it can scarcely be supposed that so small a number can have any great effect on the population of a city numbering about 400,000 souls. *It has, however, had this effect, that whereas formerly our streets were swarming with youthful beggars, these are now only to be found in localities where the police have failed to do their duty.*"

An examination of the reports of some of the best conducted Industrial Schools will show how large a proportion of the children are unwilling to avail themselves steadily of the great advantages there offered—how very few will stay a sufficiently long time to derive any permanent advantage from them. The Report of the "Edinburgh Original Ragged or Industrial Schools," states that in the year beginning March 3, 1848, and ending March 31, 1849, 379 had been in the Schools, with an average attendance of only 201; 163 of these had left during the year; 95 were entered in 1847; 109 had run away, but when brought back remained. Of the 163 who had left, 45 had got employment, and thus showed the benefit they had derived from the School; but 21 *left Edinburgh,* and 19 *deserted, being determined beggars;* these then are left to mature in vagrancy and vice. Of the 379 who had been in the Schools, 327 were "the offspring of drunken parents, that is, of parents who acquire means sufficient to enable them to indulge their degrading vice habitually. The children of such parents are almost invariably beggars, and accordingly we find that 271 of the children followed this course, and that 95 of them found their way to the gaol and police office." Should such parents *be permitted unchecked* to "train such youth as come to their custody to the same wickedness of life," and to throw so great a present and future burden on the public?

In Manchester there is only one such School; it

is situated, as such Schools should be, in the midst of a very low and degraded locality. The visitor, who finds the streets which lead to it swarming with children in a miserable condition, expects to learn that it is full to overflowing with those who are anxious to obtain sufficient food as well as instruction, and laments that there are not more such establishments in different parts of the town. The last report, however, informs us, that in the three years of its establishment 332 children have been received, and that the average attendance during the last year has been only 88, that being an improvement on former years; and this improvement has doubtless been obtained by the strict investigations that have been made by the master and mistress in case of absence. Now when it is known that the larger proportion of these children were beggars and the children of beggars, who threw every hindrance in the way of their little ones being removed from a profitable calling; it is evident both that a positive and incalculable good has been effected for these children who have remained a couple of years in the School, and have now risen to a position in which they can and do get regular employment;—but that the agency of a single School of this kind, is less than a drop in a bucket, when compared with the surrounding flood of vice, and that its influence to check vagrancy must be next to nothing, unaided as it is by the vigilance of the police.

There are in Liverpool a number of Evening

Ragged Schools, where many hundreds of miserable and ignorant children gain the only instruction they have ever received. It has already been shown in Chapter II. how inadequate such Schools are to produce any permanent change in the condition of these children, valuable as they are, when well conducted, in bringing them under some degree of Christian influence, and awakening in those of a higher class an interest in them and desire to benefit them. Such an effect the Ragged Schools have had in Liverpool. In March, 1849, an Industrial School was opened for the most destitute evening scholars : to this, in the first 10 months of its establishment, 228 boys were admitted ; of these 18 were dismissed as unfit objects; 83 left of their own accord ; 23 obtained situations; 1 died; 1 was taken to the workhouse; leaving on the roll 102 ; with an increasing monthly attendance of from 51 to 89. Those boys who remain in the School are evidently greatly benefited by it, and unite with their parents in bearing testimony to the great moral improvement they have made ; but the managers find it so difficult to retain in the School the begging children, and those who have already formed vicious habits, that they feel it better to direct their efforts principally to prevention, giving the preference in their admission of children to those whose destitution renders them most liable to fall into crime, rather than those who are already criminals. It is obvious, then, that such institutions, admirable as they are if wisely managed, cannot prove any effective check to the already existing juvenile depravity, or do much towards removing the ignorance of the 20,000 children, who, it is stated in the same report, "are estimated to be still destitute of any means of instruction in Liverpool."

In Bristol a similar institution was commenced during the last year, in connection with the Ragged School Society, and with similar results.: of the 90 who were admitted during the year, and selected from the Evening Ragged Schools, 25 left without assigning a reason, and 27 from various causes, leaving the number of 38 only in attendance.

It is unnecessary here to enter into any details respecting the management of these or other Industrial Schools; much of their efficacy will depend on the wisdom and experience of their conductors, on the conformity of their arrangements to good principles, and on the degree in which the spirit that animates them is calculated to train up religious, moral, independent, industrious, self-acting beings. We need hardly add that though, in speaking of these Schools, allusion has been especially made to boys, the girls who are to become the mothers of the next generation, require not less, but even more, a watchful and careful training; nor will the elevating effect of the School training be less perceptible on them than on the boys, if women of the educated classes will devote to them a portion of their time and care.

Before concluding this chapter, let it be observed

how powerless, under the *existing arrangements*, even the most influential individuals are, when they desire to rescue these young creatures from a vicious life. We have already seen how ineffectual were the efforts of the Chaplain of the Bath Gaol, to place his young prison charge on liberation in an Industrial School; the same difficulty he has experienced again and again, the young culprits who have felt the irksomeness of imprisonment, not choosing to submit to the restraint of School, and absconding; the establishment has in fact proved useless for the original purpose of reclaiming young vagabonds and thieves, *owing to the want of any legal power of detention there*. The following evidence of Mr. Rushton of Liverpool, before the Lords' Committee, in 1847, is a further illustration of this :—

"There is a lad in the Borough Gaol of Liverpool of 10 years old. That lad was brought before me when he was 9. It was a distressing case. I sent for his mother, and I said, 'Now, if this lad were a piece of meat, or a shilling, you would look after him; you do not look after him at all. He is a thief: you will be answerable if this goes on. I give him up to you, take care that he does not come again.' In a month or so he came back again, charged with a deliberate attempt to pick the pocket of a woman in the market. I sent for the woman again. She cried piteously, and I let her take him home. In a week he was brought again, having then got his hands into a lady's pocket, and laid hold of a purse containing £30. This became a serious matter. A magistrate cannot pass over this; the safety of every one is concerned in it; this poor woman's £30. might have been her whole substance. I then sent for the overseer,—we have an Industrial Parochial School three miles from Liverpool,—and I said, 'Now this is a very clever child, let us try if we can manage him.'   I sent for the woman, and said that she should not have the child any more, that I would certainly deal with him ; I remanded him, and sent him for two days to the Bridewell, and when her vigilance was abated I had him taken off secretly to this Industrial School.   No doubt this was exercising a power beyond the law, but I was anxious to make an effort to save the boy. In three days she found him out, and took him out of the Industrial School, and in one week he was brought back to me, having attempted to pick the pocket of a woman in the market-place, and he was sentenced by me, for that attempt, to three months' imprisonment, and he is now in gaol, where proper classification is impossible, and as his mind is already impressed with the practices of his mother, that lad is sure to be a thief unless something is done.   I instituted accurate inquiries, which I ought perhaps to have done before, respecting this woman, and I found that she had been a convicted thief, that she had trained this child to the dexterous picking of pockets, and that he is one of the most dexterous pickpockets alive. If we had an institution to which I could have sent that lad on a summary conviction, where he would have been under reformatory discipline, he would have turned out a clever and useful man ;   now he will turn out a clever thief.   Now this goes on, day by day, under the eyes of every magistrate, though magistrates do not usually see so much of it as we do in large towns ; we see it daily.   A population of 360,000 persons yields a vast amount of this sort of crime ; and the great object which I think we ought to attend to, is to cut up this cause of crime by the roots, by taking these juvenile offenders, and putting them into places like Mettray, or the Asylum which has been tried at Stretton on Dunsmoor, near Warwick.   In that Asylum it has been shown, even in a financial point of view, that the system has very favourable claims to consideration.   The 14 cases in Liverpool cost 100 guineas each, besides the subsequent expense of transportation ; from 1833 to 1841, 77 boys were put into the Warwick Asylum; the cost of the whole, including maintenance, was £1,026 ; of these 77 boys, 41 have been effectually reformed.   So that if you divide the cost by the number reformed, it will be found that while on our system at Liverpool it has cost 100 guineas in each case, and that 10 out of 14 have been transported, it has only cost 25 guineas in the Asylum, where 41 out of 77 have been reformed."

The experience of four years longer passed in the performance of his painful duties, has only increased Mr. Rushton's sense of the importance of subjecting these young delinquents to other influences than those of a gaol, and the most distressing consciousness that while a different mode of treatment might make them useful members of society, the present condition of the law *absolutely prevented him* from doing what he would have used every effort to do for their benefit.* The anecdote quoted, p. 218, strongly betrays this feeling. On a more recent occasion, 5 intelligent-looking boys, from the ages of 10 to 16 years, were brought before him, with a man and woman, charged with being receivers of stolen goods. (Vid. *Liverpool Mercury*, March 28, 1851). " Will any one tell me," said he to a gentleman near him, " I *cannot* make honest men of these 5 lads ?" " Sir," was the reply, " I would repeat the question, but apply it in a different way ; I would say, will any one tell me, that in order to make an attempt to do so, it is necessary they should pass through a certain career of vice and crime, and be

* Since this passage was written, the news has arrived of the lamented death of this excellent man. May his voice be heard with power from the grave ; and may other labourers rise and supply his place as the earnest friend of the neglected young criminal!

put through the exercises of a gaol, *before attempt is made to convert them into honest men ?*"   To such ordeal is the magistrate now compelled to submit numbers of intelligent youths, whom he feels sure he could convert, by different means, into "honest men."

Though instances might be multiplied without number, in which the benevolent are made to feel that the youthful culprits who are proceeding from one stage of crime to another, from their being left utterly without control, except when in the prison, might, with every prospect of ultimate success, be arrested in their career, if any power could be exercised by the magistrate of sending them to the Industrial School, and keeping them there for a sufficient length of time, instead of committing them to prison ; yet a more forcible one can hardly be brought forward than one given by Sergeant Adams in his evidence before the Lords in 1847, and commented on in his charge to the Grand Jury of the Middlesex Quarter Sessions, in 1849.

"It is the case of a child who was born in May, 1826.— When he was $11\frac{1}{2}$ years old, he was sentenced to 12 calendar months' imprisonment, for passing base coin. He was the son of a coiner, and a boy of quick and lively parts, high courage and good temper. It appeared that this boy had been employed till he was 10 years of age by his father to watch the process of coining, and to give notice when suspected persons appeared.   He was then employed by his father as a passer of base coin.   His father used to give him a base shilling. He used to buy a pennyworth of onions, apples, &c., and bring the change back. And, in answer to a question from me, what his father gave him, he said, 'A penny a-day, and plenty of victuals, if he did well, and *a good hiding if he did not*. While he was in prison, his father was transported for coining, and his mother died. At the end of the year I got the boy into the Children's Friend Society, *where he was doing exceedingly well*, but a clamour arose against the society, and the boy left its protection ; 12 months ago, I transported that boy as a pickpocket. *I entertain no doubt that with proper education and training that boy would have been as good a boy as any child that any one of us may possess*."—p. 31-2.

Now before this little boy of $11\frac{1}{2}$ was sentenced to a twelvemonth's imprisonment, he had been taken to different police offices *fourteen* times, but always discharged from want of evidence, except by one magistrate, who, as he said, sent him to prison for a month, "for being found in a house with intent to commit felony."

Here was a child absolutely trained by his father to vice, and so apt a scholar that he could elude conviction with the skill of an experienced thief. But while this little boy was so well known to the police, and so familiar a visitant to the police stations, was any attempt made to train him up in the way he should go, though so roughly taught the path he should shun ? Not until the latter months of his imprisonment do we hear that he was cared for as a young child to be led into the road of virtue ;—then, says Sergeant Adams, "I conversed with him frequently, pointing out his forlorn situation, and at his own request obtained an admission for him, on his discharge, into the Children's Friend Society." He absconded, it was supposed at the instigation of a relative ; he was apprehended on a charge of vagrancy, again received into the asylum, *but there was no power to detain there this young lad, who was now without parents, and who must necessarily fall into crime if he left it ;*—he again absconded, and was again convicted with a sentence of 10 years' transportation. Most truly remarks the excellent Sergeant, " The sins of the fathers are, and must be visited upon the children, *but the law need not be called in aid of this necessary consequence of evil doing, and will be more profitably employed in check-ing than in promoting it. It has already rendered very effectual aid to the abandoned parent in his education of this wretched boy, and when it ejects him from prison houseless and friendless, it will have accomplished his aim ;—the boy is a thief for life.*"

We have now completed a review of the Schools which are in operation to elevate the perishing and dangerous classes of children, pointing out the dangers and difficulties which may present them-selves in the working of them ; the good which they can effect ; that which *in their present condition is beyond their reach ; and the legislative aid they must receive to enable them to have the effect they contem-plate.* In this review the object has been to *develope principles,* rather than to present any historic view of the various institutions alluded to, still less to give details respecting them, which, interesting as they would be to many engaged in the prosecution of such labours, do not necessarily come within the province of this work.

The *Evening Ragged Schools* have been first considered, as originating the efforts which are now being more efficiently made to give education to this class. The importance of this movement has been shown, as breaking down the wall of partition which had before more completely separated the higher and more educated classes from these children of misery, than if a sea had rolled between them;—it has made the rich and poor meet together with common interests, and inspired a degree of mutual sympathy and confidence which could hardly have been excited in any other way, and which was necessary, to lead to better things. But it has also been shown that as a barrier to the overwhelming flood of ·juvenile depravity, the Evening Ragged School is utterly ineffective; and that it is open to many evils unless conducted with considerable caution, though capable of doing much good if well managed, especially if aided by the personal and home influence of the teacher.

Free Day Schools, for those whose circumstances *prevent* them from receiving the benefit of the British and National Schools, have been shown to be capable of producing a sensible and important effect on a class, who, if not already absolutely among the perishing and dangerous children, will inevitably become so if left untaught, untrained. But that such Schools should produce their effects, they must be conducted, in many respects, very differently from the ordinary existing ones; and that such effect should beneficially influence the population of our large towns, they must be adequate in number to the need of them existing;—this cannot be done without *some special provision for their maintenance in a healthy and effective condition*, as the benevolent public are already sufficiently taxed by demands on their voluntary contributions, and such Schools are more than double the expense of the pay Schools.

Industrial Feeding Schools have been last considered, as adapted to a class below that which the Free Day School can reach, and rescuing from a life of vagrancy and crime those who inevitably must otherwise have been condemned to it by the circumstances in which they were placed. But that these should have their full operation on these classes, it has been shown by experience that attendance on them should be *enforced by magisterial authority* on all children who subject themselves to police interference; and that *legislative sanction must be obtained to make such enforcement*. And that due support should be secured to such Schools, as well as that the burden of *maintaining* the children should fall where it ought, legal sanction should be obtained for requiring from the parochial funds the allowance to which each child in the School has a claim, or from the parents, who have the means of maintaining it, a similar sum;—in all such cases security being afforded that the Schools are properly conducted.

Should such Schools, under such regulations, be generally established, there can hardly be room for doubt that a very material change will be made in the nature and amount of juvenile crime in this country. The views which have been here developed are not mere theory, nor derived from casual observations. They are the result of long and careful consideration, tested by experience. Would that they could have been unfolded by an abler pen, guided by a more powerful spirit! In the remaining chapters we have to consider the condition of those who have already received the prison brand, and who, whether as yet young in crime, or fully experienced in it, are, *as the law now stands*, almost certain to end their career only by receiving its highest penalty.

CHAPTER V.

THE GAOL.

THE only School provided in Great Britain by the State for her children, is—THE GAOL!

When the hitherto neglected child enters this, he is very carefully nurtured;—attention is paid that he is neither too hot, nor too cold;—he has that precise quantity of food provided for him which is found by scientific investigation to be most conducive to the preservation and strengthening of his physical powers; a surgeon watches over his health of body, a chaplain over his spiritual condition, while a schoolmaster devotes his time to the training of his intellectual nature. It would seem that the walls of this school-house are rather unnecessarily thick and massive to confine the tender limbs of a little child;—that the keys used to lock him in are somewhat ponderous;—that the stern military governor and the strong rough-looking turnkeys are rather strange attendants on a creature almost a nursling. But let that go;—the little boy has qualified himself to be taken care of by his country; the young girl has shown that she too is of some importance to society, for she can do harm to it, and so must be cared for;—the child that was a noxious weed is now to be reared as a hot-house plant, and trained into beautiful form,—*for a short time;*—then it is to be thrown again on the cold hard world, to become more rank in its growth, more hurtful, more unsightly, even from the very circumstance of its hot-house abode.

Who is to answer for its increase of sinfulness? The child?

This chapter will be devoted to the consideration of the present system of prison discipline as regards juvenile delinquency. We shall first inquire what have been its positive effects in various individual cases, which may, from being types of classes, fairly lead to some general results as to its efficacy as a preventive of crime in the young, or as a curative measure. The *justice* of such a course as that now pursued in reference to children, will then be considered, and its *wisdom* as regards the well-being of society.

It is no longer a subject for doubt that the old and unreformed prisons, where classification was impossible, where the young child charged with his first offence was exposed to the contaminating influence of old experienced felons, were Schools of vice to the juvenile offenders, which it was nearly impossible that any could enter without being ruined for life. Though numbers of new prisons have been

built on an improved plan, and others altered so as
to secure some degree of separation among the prisoners, yet the Select Committee of the House of
Commons on Prison Discipline, in July 1850, " deem
it their duty to state that several prisons are still in
a *very unsatisfactory condition* ; and that proper
punishment, separation, or *reformation in them is
nearly impossible.*" In Newgate, for instance, the
actual construction of the prison renders separation
impracticable ; there were, the Governor reports to
the Lords' Committee in 1847, and to the Commons
in 1850 ; " 400 boys under 16 out of 3000 annually in
the gaol ; there is an attempt to separate the tried
and untried juvenile prisoners who are kept distinct
from the adults in a school yard. There is no means
of preventing contamination and communication
between the prisoners at night, when from 6 to 15
are in each ward ; in the winter the wards are locked
without light at 5, and unlocked at 7, consequently
14 hours out of the 24 the prisoners are in darkness,
without supervision ; during the day, until recently,
they have not had any employment. Many of the
juvenile prisoners have been frequently in prison,
and are very hardened ; some *from* 9 *to* 11 *have been
in prison repeatedly, and have very little fear of it.*"
It cannot be imagined that many of the 400 can
spend even a few weeks in such a prison, with such
associates, and with so little superintendence, without
being added, almost irrecoverably, to the criminal
population of the country. Such gaols are probably

few in number; and as it will be readily acknowledged, even by the advocates of the present system, that they must be most injurious to children, we need not further consider them.

The Liverpool Borough Gaol may be regarded as a favourable specimen of one not under the separate system; for it can hardly be doubted that all is here done *which can be done under the circumstances,* for the reformation of the juvenile offenders, so earnest has been the interest expressed in them by the late excellent magistrate, Mr. Rushton, and by the chaplain, who have given public testimony of their desire to adopt reformatory plans with them. The following short account of a visit to this gaol, will show how little such a place is adapted to be a reformatory School; even when, as in this case, the schoolmaster and mistress, as well as the officials, manifest a kind interest in the poor children.

"*August* 8, 1850.—Having obtained an order to visit the Borough Gaol, especially with a view of gaining information respecting the juvenile offenders, my friend and I were admitted without difficulty; the officials everywhere behaved with courtesy, answering our questions politely, and appearing kindly disposed towards the prisoners. We saw every part,—the industrial departments, kitchens, chapel, &c.; all seemed neat and orderly, and everything needful was provided. But unhappily there is not room for the present numbers, and from 20 to 30 prisoners sleep in the dormitories, 2 or 3 in the cells;—there are now between 500 and 600 males in the prison, and between 300 and 400 females, the common proportion; there are usually about 80 children; on that day there were 153. A number of the adults are in prison for vagrancy, and detained only about 7 days, the period of im-

prisonment ranging from that to 2 years ; the ordinary number admitted daily is 40, on Mondays 80. The officials all
united in the opinion that when a boy once comes, *he is almost
certain to come again and again, until he is transported.* Only
one or two of all the boys and girls I happened to speak to
were there for the first time ; most of them had been there 5
or 6 times, one 16 times. We first visited the females. The
matron appeared kind and cheerful ; the girls were sitting at
work; she said she was familiar with many of them as old
offenders, though young. It was a melancholy and touching
sight to look upon all these poor girls with the stamp of
crime upon them ; most seemed hardened, but many capable
of better things ; all looked mournful. I spoke to four who
were sitting together, saying to each a word of affectionate
encouragement, and each thanked me as I said it ; I found
that all of these had been in prison six times or more ; one of
them was a sweet looking little girl of only 12 years of age,
who had the habit of picking pockets; they all seemed
penitent, and expressed the determination that this should be
the last time ;—all had homes, yet had received scarcely any
schooling but what they have in prison. This, the matron
said, is the case with many, indeed to some the prison seems
the only true home ; she believes that a great reason of their
so soon falling again into sin after their discharge, is the
want of any helping hand and Christian aid when again in the
world ; tempters often lie in wait for them as they leave the
prison, they know that their character is lost, they yield, and
are shortly again committed. During one part of the day the
schoolmistress teaches such women as wish to learn to read ;
seldom more than 6 avail themselves of the privilege. We
then visited a room for women, one for female vagrants, and
another for males, all at work ; their countenances were *most
painfully degraded*, and I did not like to look at them. Mr.
—— said he saw a hardened smile on the faces of many of
the men ; I observed nothing but shame. We next passed
through many long corridors of cells, which were opened as
we went, and an unhappy youth or man stood at the entrance,
dressed in red if sentenced to transportation, or with badges
denoting the number of their convictions. We spoke to two

or three as we walked on, but the spectacle was so painfully degrading, that not feeling that I could help them, I generally walked on without looking at them. These have only such easy monotonous work as picking oakum, and it seemed to me that they must be brooding over bad thoughts, hopeless of the future. It was a heart-sickening sight, to see so many in a sort of living death to all that makes life desirable. Fortunate, in comparison, were those who had a trade, as they were engaged in some active and useful occupation, which might give a healthy tone to their minds. The school-room was a more happy spectacle, though here also was a deadening coldness, very different from the joyous animation of a good Free School. Half the boys attend in the morning, half in the afternoon, the rest of the time being employed in industrial works :—the master said that only about one-third can read at all when they come, not one-tenth can derive any pleasure from reading ; hence there is very little anxiety to learn evinced by them, and they appear to come rather to escape from work than to improve. Many make, however, considerable progress, but the master agreed with me in believing that learning does not of itself produce any reformation on them. The adult males are more anxious to learn than the females, and improve more rapidly ; there are often as many as 40 at School. I saw the two poor little fellows referred to by Mr. Rushton in his letter to the Town Council, 8 and 9 years of age ; they looked stunted in body and mind ; the officers seemed interested about them, and expected that on their discharge the father would seize them, and again force them to evil practices. There was another poor little child, only 7 years of age, *committed for trial for stealing* $2\frac{1}{2}d.$; this was doubtless in the hope of placing him in the contemplated Penal Reformatory School. We afterwards saw two crying bitterly in dark cells ; one, the officer said, was very unruly and hardened, though this was his first imprisonment ; his mother had been to see him, and had wept over him, but he was quite untouched ; the other was being punished for beating poor little T. H. as they went up stairs ! Solitary confinement, and a bread and water diet, are generally found sufficient punishment ; flogging is resorted to very rarely for insubordination, perhaps only once in six months ; then the men are all drawn out to witness it, and it seems to produce a good effect. Handcuffs and irons of any kind have not been used for many years, except on going to trial. The only pleasing part of the establishment is the chapel, where the prisoners are assembled daily for prayers ; they appear to esteem it a privilege to attend, and are always orderly ; there is a small organ, and many join in the singing. Altogether this was a most instructive though painful visit ; I especially mourned for the poor children who cannot be yet hopelessly hardened, but whose young hearts the prison gloom and necessary restraint cannot do more than curb, for the time, without reforming or quickening to a better life. May a renewed spirit of faith and love be shed on such institutions, where as yet, ' Hope which comes to all, comes not to them.' "

That the foregoing description of the evils of this crowded gaol, which must necessarily produce so much contamination, in the juvenile prisoners especially, is not overstated, is proved by the following memoranda of the chaplain.

" *March* 24*th*, 1851.—In the girls' class there are this morning 54 children, we have occasionally 60 ; for these we have only 12 cells ; one cell is occupied by 2 children suffering from a cutaneous disease, and through the other 11, the remaining 52 children are distributed at night, nearly an average of 5 in each cell. 30 women slept one night in beds on the floor in the square of the reception ward ; and 5 in each of the 6 cells opening into it. It is occasionally more crowded even than this, and it is questionable whether anything worse is to be found in the worst Union Workhouses in Ireland. It must not be inferred that I impute blame in any quarter ; the evil is incidental to the deficiency of room in the gaol. The corporation is erecting a new one, which will be the largest in the kingdom at present ; it will be on the separate system, and is expected to be ready for use in 12 or 18 months."

Would it not be cheaper, (for gold seems almost the only consideration of weight in these matters,) would it not prove in a few years a *great economy,* to build and support a good Reformatory School, such as will be described in the next chapter, instead of a gigantic prison, which sends forth the young children only to return again and again, until sufficiently hardened and criminal for transportation? That end is reached by some sooner than might have been anticipated, notwithstanding their precocity. This can hardly be more forcibly shown, than by the following case related by Mr. Rushton in his letter to the Town Council of Liverpool (1850). Such circumstances, he says, *" are of daily occurrence, and they are increasing."*

"At the October Sessions, 1849, a man aged 40 years was sent by me to trial. He was found guilty, and sentenced to 3 months' imprisonment. This man has 3 sons. Patrick, the eldest, is now 14 years old. He was first brought before me on the 9th of June, 1845, charged with stealing ropes. He was then about 9 years old. I did not wish to send so young a child to gaol, so, as I usually do, I delivered him to his parents with an admonition to them. On the 29th of September following he was again brought before me, and after a remand and a second admonition he was discharged. On the 25th of October, within a month, he was again brought before me, and was sentenced under the summary powers of the local act to an imprisonment of one month. On the 15th of November, after being thirteen days out of prison, he was again accused and sentenced to 2 months' imprisonment. On the 16th of March, 1846, he was in custody on a charge not proved, and discharged. On the 25th of April he was imprisoned for stealing a small quantity of iron, and sent to gaol for a fortnight. On the 4th of June he was again imprisoned for a month. On his next appearance I thought it best, not-withstanding his tender years, to send the boy to trial ; and at the Borough Sessions, in September, he was tried and con-victed for stealing a bag of currants from the dock quays, and sentenced to be imprisoned for 4 months and to be twice whipped. In October, 1847, he was charged with steal-ing, and the case not being proved he was discharged. He was again in custody on the 30th of October, and imprisoned : also in November, 1847 ; in May, 1848 ; in October, 1848 ; in March, 1849 ; in August, 1849 ; and on the 7th of January, 1850, he was again sent to gaol for 3 months, where he now remains. Thus, at the age of 14, he has been 24 times in custody ; he has been 5 times discharged, twice imprisoned for 14 days, once for 1 month, once for 2 months, 6 times for 3 months, and tried and convicted, and sentenced to 4 months imprisonment and to be twice whipped.

" The second son of the same man was brought before me on the 2nd of March, 1849, and since that time, up to the 2nd of February last, has been 8 times charged with theft. He is now 9 years old ; and on Saturday last he was again brought before me for robbing a till, in company with 3 other lads about his own age, and he remains in custody. The third son, Thomas, was brought before me on the 8th of February, 1849, accused of theft ; again in June, again in September, again in January, again on the 4th of February, and again on the 15th of February, and he also remains in custody : he is now 8 years old. Both these last-mentioned prisoners are small of their age: when standing in the dock the lower parts of their faces are not visible. These lads have been trained by a vicious father to the work of plunder ; he has taught them how to steal with dexterity, and he uses them as a means of supply-ing himself with a luxurious existence. Time after time I have remanded these children, and after certain periods of delay, I have sent them by night to places where they might have a chance of escape from the father who is destroying them ; but the father has always discovered them, and, in the absence of power to detain the children, his demands have been obeyed, and here is the sad result. I shall now have to send both these wretched children to gaol. I can no longer permit them to be employed by their father as the instruments of fraud; yet I know that the children are not moral agents; that they know no distinction between right and wrong; that all that is good in them has never been developed, or has been systematically destroyed :—and no effectual means exist without your aid of rescuing these children from worse than death."

These are the little boys alluded to in the visit to the gaol; they have been there again,—one tried and then acquitted, *but since convicted and transported for* 15 *years;* the youngest is under a second conviction of felony. The " sweet little girl " spoken of in the visit, has been since twice in gaol. " She will be discharged to-morrow," says the chaplain, " after 3 months' imprisonment; we are making an effort, (I fear but a hopeless one,) to save her from her evil associations at home by sending her to Manchester."

Judging from the foregoing examples, it must be evident, that even if the imprisonment has not earlier matured the child in crime, it has at least utterly failed to check it. Let us turn to another gaol, conducted on the strictest separate system, and considered very excellent in its arrangements. We find the Recorder of Bristol lamenting, in his charge to the Grand Jury at the recent Quarter Sessions, that of the number to be tried, 61, (of whom 12 were 17 or under)—

" It would seem that there were not more than 37 cases of prisoners who had been for the first time detected in crime; and it appeared, on reference to the depositions, that in 24 cases there had been prior convictions. He was sorry to find *from the great number of cases of the latter description*, in which prisoners had been brought before him for the second, and sometimes for the third time, that *the punishments had not had the effect of reforming them*. Of the 24 cases of prior conviction, he found that 7 or 8 had already been convicted more than once. That was an evil which was, undoubtedly, greatly to be lamented, because it was hoped that punishment would have the effect of reclaiming criminals, and he was *very sorry to find so many instances in which it had failed to do so*."—(Vid. *Bristol Mercury*, April 12, 1851).

An opinion is here, then, publicly expressed by the highest authority in Bristol, one founded on facts forced on his notice in the discharge of his office,—that the system of punishment adopted has failed in its object, that of reformation. Yet it cannot be supposed that this failure is to be imputed to any neglect on the part of the magistrates, of the governor, or of the chaplain of the gaol, in their due administration of the punishment, or to any want of desire on their part to make it beneficial. In the case of the juvenile prisoners, a whipping has been frequently a part of their sentence, one so severe as to draw screams of agony from the young sufferer, earnest entreaties on the bended knees from their companions who witnessed it, that such extreme penalty might be abated, and heartfelt pity even from the turnkey;—they have been subjected to the most rigorous seclusion, the arrangements of the gaol not permitting them the small consolation of even seeing the face of a fellow-prisoner during divine service, nor was the master and friend of some of these poor boys who had obtained an order from the magistrates to visit them, allowed admission to them ;*—yet with this severity, careful attention has been paid to their physical condition, and so much good instruction has been given them, that many who have entered the gaol nearly ignorant of the scriptures, have come out well acquainted with its contents. Surely these boys ought to be both de-terred and reformed !—if indeed severity and solitude can reform them, or crush the strong and buoyant spirit of youth. Let us examine the records of the Free Day and Evening Ragged School described in Chapter III., and learn the effects of such imprison-ment on the 24 boys from that School who suffered it during the last year. The following statement re-specting them is founded on the careful observation of the master, who visits his scholars, and strives in every way *in his power* to lead them to a right course. It must be recollected that no one of these 24 boys was regularly at School when he was de-

---

* It may be doubted whether such severe exclusion of the offenders from visits from those who might influence him for good are accordant with the teachings of Him who charged us to *visit the prisoner*, or even with the spirit of the English law. Mr. Baron Alderson gives as his opinion to the Lords' Committee, "Under separate imprisonment, *I would en-courage as much as possible the society of the good with such criminals. The visits of kind persons should be allowed*, subject, of course, to proper regulations." It was the privilege of Mrs. Fry to visit the most degraded in their prisons ; those who would follow in her footsteps are sternly repulsed from the Bristol Gaol.

tected in crime, and that very few had ever been more than occasional attendants.

" Of the 24 boys who were in prison during 1850, 12 have become *decidedly more hardened and reckless* since their imprisonment; before, they were more or less under School influence, now they are quite untouched by it ; few ever come within the School-room, and then their behaviour is so bad that their dismissal is commonly necessary. Most of these boys have shown at times a desire to do right, and susceptibility of improvement, which might have made them good and useful members of society, if placed under proper restraint for a sufficient length of time. C. and J. are well educated, clever boys ; they are at large, corrupting those around them, and engaged in felonious acts ; C. was lately an accomplice with Z., in stealing lead ;—he escaped, but is now in prison for stabbing his mother ;—Z., was condemned to 9 months' imprisonment, with a threat of transportation for the next offence. B. and A. have been several times in prison, *and each time have come out more bold;* they have no home, and one was provided for them by a friend on their discharge in January last, but they soon deserted it, refused work, and are evidently living on plunder. F. is a passionate, high-spirited boy, whom a few years ago a word or touch of kindness could soften or bend ;—now he is brazen and reckless, one of the well-known juvenile gang who may constantly be seen in Lewin's Mead, unchecked, plotting mischief in open day. The rest are wild boys, ready for every sort of evil. Of the others, 5 were, before their imprisonment, notorious thieves, and were in about the same condition after as before. A. S. *had long been known* as the worst boy in the neighbourhood, but this was his *first conviction;* he has fine talents and a powerful spirit, which can find no scope but in mischief, as he is at present circumstanced ; he shows at times, when he comes to the School, a desire to do right, and seriousness of thought, which makes one mourn for him; his little brother, 10 years of age, was twice in prison last year, and equally wild after each discharge ;—he is now under better influences, and attends

School. The same was the case with G. H., 12 years of age, after his imprisonment last year, and he soon incurred another ; on his discharge last January, he was removed from his family by a friend who had seen much good in him ; he is apprenticed, continues under School influence, and gives hopes of reformation.   Only 3 have been for a time more amenable to instruction since their punishment ; 1 was a little boy who was driven to theft by actual want, (the only case of the kind,) he was placed in the Union Workhouse, remained there a year, and is now in regular work ; another is attending School ; the third, Z., was stated by the governor of the gaol to be the very worst boy there ; yet he was *the only one of the* 24 who got into regular work at once on his discharge, and seemed for a time repentant and striving to do right : but bad home influences, and a vicious neighbourhood, presented too strong temptations to him ; he again fell into evil.   4 besides these are still in prison ; 1 was a notorious thief before he came to School, nearly 5 years ago, yet he has escaped till now ; his mother is a hardened woman, well known to stimulate him to petty theft ; there is no hope for him unless he is removed from all his past associations ; nor is there for 2 of the others ; the fourth, · V., was, 2 years ago, in a respectable bookseller's shop for some months, but, losing his place, he fell into idleness and vice ;—he is not badly disposed, and should he get a place of work on his discharge, might do well ;—but who will take him ?"

Such is the actual effect of imprisonment on these young criminals, who cannot be considered the worst that have inhabited the Bristol Gaol and Bridewell during the last year ; for they had all previously shown some desire for improvement, by coming to School. Can we contemplate it without a conviction that an utterly *useless method* has been pursued, that while some other and better means might have reclaimed them, and made them useful members of society,—as the law with respect to these juvenile offenders now stands, they are almost certain to go on undeterred, unreclaimed, from one degree of crime to another, leading on with them those who, like them, are left unrestrained to the indulgence of their vicious inclinations. And when they happen to be detected in passing the bounds of law, what will be done to check them by our magistrates, our recorders, our judges? The remedies which are found *not* to have the effect intended will be doubled, or tripled; —then more severity will be proposed, as our gaols are overflowing;—then little boys of *six* years old or upwards must be *transported* with or without a remark from the judge (p. 14.); and little girls of *nine* or upwards (p. 16.); and secretaries of state must send them back as unfit subjects for the law's penalty;—the young children must then still puzzle the judges; but the full-grown, daring boys of 14 or 15, who have gone on until now unchecked, uneducated to anything but evil, must, when they are audacious and wicked enough, become " the children of the State," must now be carefully trained at Parkhurst, at great expense to the country, and then sent abroad, where it is hoped they do well! Is such a state of things to continue without remonstrance from the people,—without effort to ameliorate the law on the part of those in power, who daily see the evil,—of the enlightened who think they perceive a more excellent way?

Some who lament the condition of these poor children, leaving the prison with a brand indelibly on them, and returning to the evil influences which had led them into sin, have proposed the establishment of societies expressly to aid and encourage discharged prisoners, and Schools of Refuge for the young delinquents. In the case of Bristol, we are not aware that any institutions of the kind exist, and there is strict exclusion of the visits of benevolent persons who might carry out the good effect of the solitude and severe discipline after the discharge ;—what may not the prison system do for the young delinquent, if followed up by a friendly personal interest in him within the walls, and watchful care beyond them ? The Bath Gaol may furnish us with a good example of this. In this city, for the last 9 years a society has been at work " for the relief and reformation of discharged destitute prisoners ;" a " Ragged Industrial School " has been established expressly for the reception of vagrant and criminal children ; while none who know the earnest and affectionate anxiety of the chaplain for those poor young creatures, can doubt that everything is done for them that a wise kindness can dictate, *under he existing systems.* " If any gaol might have been expected to have succeeded with prisoners of an early age," says Mr. Osborn, " it was the New Bath Prison, where every facility has been supplied, and no labour was spared in the endeavour to inculcate better principles and habits, especially in children ; nor were they on their discharge from confinement entirely disregarded." Let us hear, then, from the chaplain himself, a few instances of the effect of this system under its most favourable aspect; they are cases recorded in his memoranda.

"*December* 28, 1850.—This morning a lad, by name Robert Welch, was dismissed from the gaol. Observe his history.— R. W. was imprisoned (January 15, 1850,) in the Bath Gaol at the age of 7 years, for begging, and committed for 7 days. He was quite unable to read, even a letter, and as ignorant of religious knowledge as if born in a heathen land. Again he appeared in the prison for a like offence and like punishment, 3 *days after his discharge.* A third time, for the same offence, in the following year, now being 8 years old, and punished in a similar way. A fourth time—no longer for an act of vagrancy—he comes for attempting, in company with 2 or 3 others, to steal time-pieces from a gentleman's house in broad daylight. The infant prisoner, now only 10 years old, acknowledges that he has a little sister who goes about singing, while he goes begging, and 'was it not for sister we couldn't live.' His education in reading and scriptural knowledge is now begun in prison. He learns the Ten Commandments, but, being in prison only for a month, he departs with very little more useful knowledge than he had when he came in. His father is blind, and carries about cotton and tapes ; his mother does a little washing ; his eldest brother goes into the country picking up bones and rags, and lives, as the child said, without shame, 'and lives with a gal !' His second brother 'leads father out ;' another brother goes about the streets begging ; there are 2 or 3 more brothers and sisters in this wretched family, making a family of 8 children, some of whom are too young to enter upon the vagrant life. In the winter of the same year, 1847, he is sent to prison for 2 months for a garden robbery. This gave us an opportunity of adding a little more to his religious knowledge, which had to be re-commenced, since he had forgotten all he knew in the lapse of a few months. The sixth time the child is committed for 14 days, for stealing a cocoa-nut ; and on his discharge was induced to go into the Ragged Industrial School, established about this time, where by much perseverance on the part of the master, and much self-denial under control on the part of the child, he was led to remain for some time ; *but the School authorities having no legal right to keep the lad against his will,* being either tempted by others, or impatient of control, or the vagrant life having taken too deep a hold of his mind ; and it is not surprising that he appeared again in prison for the seventh time, as a vagrant, for 4 days. Now surely he has nearly run his course, for his next committal was, the eighth time, as a rogue and vagabond ; sentenced for 3 months. During the time between this and the former, he was in the Ragged Industrial School 6 months ; but, as on the former occasion, he ran away, *and we had no power to compel him to stay or return.* His next, and ninth committal, is for felony—stealing a clock the value of 18s., and he stands at the bar before the Recorder at the Quarter Sessions to take his trial. *His prison life has made him bold and insolent.* He bounds into the dock, casts his eyes round the Court, and with a nod places his head erect, and says ' Not Guilty !' With a knowing look he asks with insolent pride of the witnesses one or two questions. The child of 13 years is found guilty of the offence by a jury of his country, and sentenced to 5 months' imprisonment with hard labour. The expiration of this sentence brings us to the present time ; and now, let me ask, what has the law achieved ? It is only a few days ago that this little urchin was reported for talking in class, for which he was denied for a while the privilege of attending School. I visited him frequently, and perceived a strange vivacity in his countenance, *an unnatural quickness in his manner, and extraordinary versatility in his language. More than enough to be accounted rudeness in another child was endured from him.* Opinions and feelings as to our treatment of this child would have led me to endure anything from him. But a few days after he became insolent to one of the officers, refused to do the prescribed work given him, argues the matter with all the assurance of a man of 30, yea, indeed, with his hand points to the coat given him to mend, he shows more determination than is seen in one of 800 adult prisoners, and then, after venting his passion in words, he burst into tears. This prison offence merit[s] punishment, and it must be brought before a visiting justice. The complaint is legally made, and the chaplain and the governor accompany the magistrate to the cell of the little stubborn sinner. On entering, he pleaded his own case, and laid the blame on the officer. With difficulty would he be persuaded to let the magistrate speak to him, and when a hearing for authority was obtained, many an interruption ensued ; for when addressed, he in a fit of passion broke out, and incapable of giving it sufficient expression, he threw himself on the ground, and beat his head against the iron grating of the wall. The magistrate, guided by mercy, *and the circumstances of the case*, was content with giving kind advice and reproof, and did not order any punishment beyond the keeping the prisoner on bread and water for 3 days."

What is to be the final corrective for this poor little boy, for whom the chaplain laboured so earnestly, but it would appear to many uselessly, may easily be anticipated. This young child has been actually *trained* by the existing laws to utter regardlessness of their penalties, and to a complete contempt of authority. The magistrate was powerless in the cell of the criminal, disarmed by the real innocence of a poor child who has been brought into an unnatural state by circumstances over which he had no control, and from which he had a maddening feeling of being unable to free himself ;—while the chaplain, who is so deeply touched with a sense of the evils of which the little boy is the victim, that he is ready "to endure anything from him," is completely unable to carry out his earnest desires for the child's reformation, for no sooner is the prison door opened, than he can obtain no power to do him good, until he shall again commit a crime. The older brother, who had been his blind father's vagrant companion, has already attained the rank of a transported felon. This is his history :—

"Michael Welch commenced his career of crime as his brother had done. On his fourth committal the magistrates gave him the longest period the law permitted, viz., 6 months and hard labour. During this long incarceration, the child, (being then 14 years old,) appeared very troublesome, but in a peculiar way. It did not appear to arise from a wish on his part to give trouble, so much as *from the nervous and restless state into which he was brought by imprisonment.* He had been discharged only 2 months prior to this commitment, when he had been 4 months in prison, 2 before, and 2 after trial. *During this last incarceration he manifested a rapid and incessant volubility in his cell to me. His health and manner attracted considerable attention from the surgeon as well as myself. A liveliness and vivacity unnatural. His eyes large and prominent.* His resolutions for the future appeared to be sincere ; his entreaties to be taken into the Industrial School were very earnest ; his sorrow for his past conduct appeared to be very earnest also, and he looked anxiously forward to his discharge from prison. He became very much delighted with his ability to mend and make shoes, and never failed to call my attention to his improvement in this respect, making me compare his work with that of others. On discharge from prison, in proof that the child was really in earnest as to going to the School, *he went there direct from the prison without even calling on his father and mother, brothers or sisters, and then I saw him a few hours after his arrival full of thankfulness, fair promises, and good resolutions.* There was no thought about his relations on the first day or so, though I believe he was reminded of them, and would have been allowed to go and see them. There he remained for a short time, but his outbursts of temper being so violent, and *there being no authority to punish or retain the lad contrary to his inclination,* he was let out; within about 10 days of his discharge, he was re-committed for a burglary, viz., breaking into a dwelling-house, and stealing boots, &c., therefrom. For this offence he was committed to the Assizes, and after lying in gaol nearly 4 months, he was found guilty and sentenced to 7 years' transportation. *This is the goal to which his circumstances in life and his crimes have brought him. Now, then, will every pains be taken to fit the lad, (now 15 years old,) for a useful life in the colonies.*"

The Bristol and Bath Gaols probably present as favourable a sample of the effect of the strict separate system, in itself considered, as can be found. The Preston Gaol may at first sight appear to form an exception; for Mr. Clay states that while under the old system of a short imprisonment and a whipping, the boys came back undeterred at the rate of 56 per cent., the number of juvenile offenders decreased from 178 in 1842 under the old system, to 60 in 1846 under the separate system; in 1849 there were only 4 re-committals, and in 1850 there were only 26 juvenile offenders in the gaol, for the whole of North Lancashire, and not one for trial! But with the " austere" discipline here enforced, there is combined that spirit of Christian kindness and *modification of the strict separate system which probably render this gaol unique.* All labour felt to be profitless and inflicted merely as a punishment, is avoided. " *I have been taught repeatedly,*" says the chaplain, " that I must not look on *any case as hopeless.* * * I am gradually brought to this in my own practice with regard to the prisoners, that the proper course is *to bring to bear upon them every humanizing influence that can be made available.* There is a system of watchfulness on the part of the governor and myself, *seeing where an opening into the boy's heart or mind or understanding exists, and availing ourselves of it.* * * The prisoners see each other in chapel, it is a point on which I should be somewhat earnest ;— *earnest in favour of treating the prisoner as if he had something good in him;* as if relying on him thus far, that when he is brought to worship God he will behave himself, *and acting upon that I have never been disappointed."* This treatment creates a degree of mutual confidence which leads to an avoidance of the mischief and insubordination so common among boys in prison, and of subsequent reformation, of which touching instances might be given did space permit. The governor and the chaplain continued their watchfulness over the culprit when he leaves the gaol, obtain work for him, and have often the satisfaction of restoring him to be a useful member of society. But even such treatment is not adapted to a child. Mr. Clay's memoranda respecting the little Dominick alluded to (p. 14), afford a striking illustration of the uselessness of our present system.

"The father is of the lowest grade of hawkers ; his three oldest sons were by a first wife—one is transported, the second is in Kirkdale Gaol under a similar sentence, the third, Thomas, was sent to prison with Dominick for *horse stealing* and robbing a till. 'If you let me and the little boy go,' writes Thomas on a slate in his cell, 'we will not starve, we are too wide-awake boys,—us both. Thomas Rafferty, his history would be worth hearing. In the first place, he is a great thief. He has robbed many a good old house and shop drawer ; and now I repent it. Sometimes he has got 40 shillings at one lift, and never got found out. If you heard my history, though, you would never want to hear another, it is so bad. Tom is always the master, sending the little boy out alone, you may be sure ! *He is up to his business, since Tom has learned him ;* he is just the right size to do that business. Then Tom gets a few pounds some nights, when Dominick comes home. Then Tom gives him sixpence for himself to spend. *The little boy does the robbery while Tom is watching to see if anybody is coming.* Tom receives the money, and then buys a watch and is proud like a gent, walking up and down the streets, looking at my watch for pride, living on the best of meat, but now is poorly off.' *Sentence of transportation was passed on the child in October*, 1846, *the elder brother being at the same time liberated !* I need scarcely say that our treatment of this child, when sent back from Milbank,—though he was in prison, *was divested of almost everything penal.* He was placed under the care of a well-disposed prisoner who had children of his own, and *all which had hitherto been wanting in his training we endeavoured to supply.* He was docile, susceptible of attachment, and very intelligent naturally. He was a particularly handsome child, too ; with a pair of those large dark eyes which indicate southern blood." Mr. Clay, having ascertained that the mother was a superior woman, and would take the child to Ireland away from his associates, took measures for obtaining a pardon for him ;" " our excellent governor himself," he adds, " conveyed him to his mother in Liverpool."

What could or would *the law* have done for this child ? What is it doing for his brother ?

We have now so traced the effect of the prison under various systems, as to leave no doubt on the mind that while in those under the unreformed regulations nothing but utter contamination can be expected from it, under the strictest separate system its discipline fails of effect in the case of children.

Let us now consider the *justice* of the system at present adopted with regard to juvenile offenders.

A single example may be adduced to show the *unthinking cruelty*, as well as *injustice*, of the course pursued by society towards them; it is recorded in the *Ragged School Magazine*, April 1851, as extracted from *Dr. Malcolm's Report on the General Prison for Scotland*, 1850.

" G. M., aged 11 years.   This poor boy died of the effects of starvation and neglect, ' which he had suffered almost all his lifetime.'   I scarcely believe he had *ever* had a regular meal excepting in prisons, and when out at large he usually slept in stairs or pig-styes, as he had no settled home to go to.   Everything was done *here* to invigorate the system, but he was too far gone, and *could* not rally.   He was *never* in a state to be removed from the prison, and it would have been cruel to have sent him out, as *he had no home.*"   The governor states, " Means were used to ascertain the residence of his friends, that they might remove the body for interment if they wished to do so, but without success.   The poor boy had been finally convicted of breaking into a house, and taking therefrom *a small quantity of oatmeal, aggravated by 2 similar convictions of similar thefts*.   This *child* was tried by a jury of 15 *men*, and sentenced to 15 months' imprisonment in the government prison for Scotland."

Has not the Saviour warned us that he will not admit the plea of ignorance in those who *had not seen his image* in the wretched destitute outcast ? And are we Christians ?   Is society just to award the high penalty prepared for the wilfully erring, to a little untaught, uncared-for child, who *cannot* know that it is doing wrong in satisfying the cravings of nature? Is society wise to provide no less ponderous and costly a place than a prison, to be the home and infirmary of a little outcast? Yet we regard with less pain this poor boy removed from so cruel a world to the Heavenly Father's rest, than one, and many such there are, actually, at the present moment, driven by existing institutions to a life of crime.

" A. is homeless, friendless ; he has been so for many years, and of course has been several times in prison ;—thus the master of the School alluded to, Chapter III., found him about 18 months ago, and after some difficulty, admission was obtained for him to the Union Workhouse ; but his vagrant habits were too confirmed ; in a few months he ran away, and was again seen wild in the streets ; the master entreated the Union authorities to apprehend him for absconding with their clothes, and to restrain him, for his condition was such as to excite commiseration in all. *They laughed at the idea of troubling themselves about him, and expressed satisfaction at being relieved of him with or without the clothes.* He was of course soon again in gaol, and for a longer time ; he came out somewhat penitent, and sought admission to the Union Workhouse ; *it was firmly denied to the homeless boy ;* a trifling relief was given him, and he was told to get work. Through the efforts of the master admission to a cotton factory was obtained for him ; a lodging and the necessary clothes were provided for him ; *but his long confinement in a separate cell had not taught him how to live in the world ;* he was soon in the streets a vagabond ! He was again induced to come to the School, and showed a disposition to be amenable to good direction ; he again entreated assistance from the Workhouse, and his utter destitution was pointed out to the authorities ; *he was peremptorily refused any kind of relief.* He is now wild in the streets ; friends are powerless to render him effectual help ;—he must live on plunder, for no one can employ him in his present condition, until he has harmed society enough to be worthy of being prepared at great expense to colonize a foreign country. This boy has good talents, has not shown himself unsusceptible of good impressions ; with proper training and *the curb a young lad ought to have*, he might now be maintaining himself, instead of leading a life of crime."

These two examples exhibit the "perishing" child left to die—the "dangerous" child driven to crime, by their country's laws, or by the administrators of them ;—let us analyze, point by point, the present treatment of criminal children.

The law of England does not recognize the right of a young person under age to contract matrimony, or enter into solemn engagements without the consent of his parents, nor may he even bind himself to learn some useful trade without the signature of his father to the indentures. If he has property at his own disposal, he cannot will it away until the age of 21. The child is very rightly regarded in the eye of the law as incapable of acting wisely for himself, and therefore under the control of his parents ; he acts as the French law well expresses it, " sans discernement." And yet, no sooner does the child *prove to society* his utter incapability to govern himself wisely and well, by falling into crime, than he is deemed worthy, even if of the age of 6 or 7, to be placed on the footing of a man. The father, who might be prosecuted for neglecting to supply the bodily necessities of the child, is now apparently released from obligation to him.

"I think," says Mr. Pearson, the City Solicitor, in his evidence before the Lords' in 1847, " that the law of England is not fairly dealt by in its administration as regards children. By the common law of England, a child under years of discretion is not taken to be *capax doli*. By the theory of our law it is necessary that you should prove against a child charged with crime, a precocious capacity for evil, or, as Lord Hale describes it, a mischievous discretion ; whereas every person above the years of discretion is by law presumed to be cognizant of the law, and unless the contrary be proved, he is held answerable for his acts. A child under years of discretion has applied to him by the law the converse of that proposition ; he is not held to be capable of crime, unless from intrinsic or extrinsic evidence his capacity is proved. I press, with great submission, upon your lordships as legislators, the propriety of applying this principle of the common law in this respect to poor neglected and destitute children. They are dealt with and treated as criminals, by a multitude of acts creating summary convictions, and they are lost for life in reputation and in self-respect, by being committed to prison, and treated as criminals, frequently mere infants, before that period at which the law presumes their capacity to commit crime. I respectfully, but earnestly and ardently, press upon your lordships, that *a child should not be subjected to criminal punishment for petty offences, when, from its ignorance and destitution, arising from parental neglect, it is out of its power to know, or even knowing, to obey the laws.*"

The child is then dealt unjustly by in being exposed to the same severity of punishment, the same brand of criminality as the adult, while he is debarred, and rightly so, from occupying the same independent position in society in matters concerning his own welfare. He is, too, subjected to a number of petty restrictions and punishments for trifling offences, which would never be committed by adults. Flying kites and playing at marbles in forbidden places, taking a toy from a basket temptingly exposed, or a penny tart from an open window, would not be likely offences to bring a man before the magistrate, but for such the young child is to be familiarised with the paraphernalia of "justice!"

"Coeval with this extraordinary increase of commitments and convictions for crime," says Mr. Pearson, in a paper delivered into the Lords'; "has been the multiplication of petty offences punishable by fine, and (failing its payment) by short imprisonment in gaol. All these offences, (many of them mere *mala prohibita,*) it is within the range of mischievous youth to commit, and having no money for the penalty, they of course pay in person, as they cannot pay in purse. Upon summary conviction, short imprisonments are awarded for the smallest offence, and it is no uncommon thing to read in the newspapers, of young urchins found in a state of destitution, or in the commission of some petty delinquency, commiserated by the magistrate, who expresses his pity for their unfortunate condition, and laments that he has no other place than a criminal's gaol to which he may consign them. The mind of the child thus becomes familiarised with a gaol—a prison is at once disarmed of its terrors and its shame."

"I have, sometimes, cases tried before me," says Sergeant Adams, "for stealing penny tarts, oranges, 2 or 3 apples, and articles of that kind. In 1 case, about 2 months ago, (March, 1847) a child 9 years of age, *who was wholly unknown to the police*, was tried before me for taking a little toy hammer, value 1d., from a basketful which was placed at a shop door."

Such severity does not, indeed, affect the children of the higher and more favoured classes of the community. Robbing orchards or hen-roosts is regarded only as a clever feat in the gentleman's son at a public school; and while the boy who steals lead from the top of a house is threatened with transportation on the next conviction, stealing knockers from the door by a young student is considered a spirited feat, to be punished, if at all, only by a fine and a reprimand. Most truly says the excellent Recorder of Birmingham :—

"In my opinion, it is *inexpedient and most cruel* to treat children under a certain age as subject to the criminal law. Discipline, and not judicial punishment, appears to me proper to be applied in such cases. No one thinks of sending school-boys, for their not unfrequent petty larcenies, to the bar of criminal justice : and I think it imperative that the existing criminal law should cease to be applied to such young offenders for larceny. I am deeply impressed with the conviction that some amendment in the law, and change in its execution, is essential, but I do not feel competent to suggest what those alterations should be."

There is, besides, an extra degree of severity exercised in the case of juvenile offenders. We do not hear of whippings being awarded to older culprits for committing larcenies, in their case more culpable ; but the police reports of large towns give the frequent intelligence of whippings for boys, in addition to their other punishment. Of the certain effect of this punishment we have already spoken in Chapter I. Mr. Pearson, who, when under-sheriff, had peculiar opportunity of observing it in Newgate, says, in his evidence before the Lords :—

" We administered personal chastisement in Newgate. Boys convicted there were ordered perhaps to a week's imprisonment, and to be flogged. *We sometimes had those boys back again, after being flogged, in the next session.* It occurred once at the Old Bailey, that in the very same session the same boy came back again, having committed another offence within a week of the time when he had been flogged."

An experienced governor of a gaol says, that while boys who are as yet novices in crime dread flogging so much that they would sooner have a year's imprisonment than endure it, the hardened young thieves will incur it again and again, without appearing at all deterred by it. This punishment is inflicted with a cat-o'-nine-tails, the marks of which are indelible on the person.

"This punishment," says Sergeant Adams, "ought to be abolished, not only as being too cruel, but as being one which *boys do not care about.* We have substituted at Middlesex whipping with a birch rod ; and it is a singular but undoubted fact, that boys who laugh at being put into a dungeon, and *doubly laugh at flogging with a cat,* are upon their knees blubbering and praying not to be flogged with a birch rod—it deters them more than anything. I often sentence a child to a month's imprisonment, and to be well whipped at the end of the first fortnight, so as to keep the terror over his mind for a fortnight ; but I find that those children continually come again."

Is it not cruel injustice to inflict upon boys *a torture which is not awarded to men for a similar offence,* and especially when it is found to be inefficient as a preventative of crime ? And can we do otherwise than admire the courageous spirit of a lad who will dare excruciating torture, but shrink from disgrace, while we mourn that it is not enlisted for good rather than for evil ?

Again,—there is a manifest injustice in awarding
to young boys or girls the highest secondary punishment of the law for a first or second petty larceny,
and so branding them for life, or at any rate severing
them necessarily from all the ties of nature. The
returned convict, A. B., who gave evidence before
the Lords in 1847, had been employed as a clerk
in a mercantile house in Manchester, when, at 18,
being convicted of a petty larceny, his *first* offence,
he was sentenced to 7 years' transportation ; he was
11 weeks in Lancaster Castle, *associated with his
fellow-convicts,* and then 6 months in the hulks,
before leaving the country. It was 31 years before
he could leave the colonies, all of which were passed
in punishment, except 5 or 6, during which he had
not the means of leaving ; a subscription was at last
raised for him by a number of emancipists who knew
him, and who thus enabled him to return. The
moral condition of the convicts in the penal settle-
ments, as described by various witnesses of high
official position to the Lords' Committee in 1847, is
such as to make any benevolent mind revolt at the
idea of subjecting the young to its contaminating
horrors.

" The population of Norfolk Island," says one witness, " is
composed of all classes of persons ; some who had been sent
there from Van Diemen's Land, doubly convicted. There were
persons sent there from England, *many of them of tender age ;
some of them could hardly have shaved before they landed in
the island ; and their appearance, young and fresh, was very
striking under the circumstances, when you went round the*

island and saw the marked contrast of the people around them."
" In the large prison of Norfolk Island," says Dr. Willson,
" there were 800 men, 500 old prisoners, and 300 fresh men
from England, mingled. These slept in a large building containing from 16 to 80 men, who were there shut up in darkness, without supervision, from 8 o'clock at night to 5 the
next morning. I never saw men in such a state as they
were when I first landed, so much so, that I could not call any
portion of my flock together to address them ; and I thought
it prudent not to force the thing, but I spent 3 or 4 days in
visiting them at their work, or when they were at their meals,
and they came round me in knots of 10 or 20, or 30 or
40, and they stated the grievances under which they were
labouring." Dr. W. adds, in answer to questions :—" From
what I have seen of the system of transportation, as it now
works, *I certainly do not consider it, looking at it morally, a
mode of punishment lawful for a Christian nation knowingly
to inflict, nor do I think that any amount of necessity of
deterring crime will justify the continuance of such a punishment as that at present administered.*"

The returned convict, A. B., gives this fearful picture :—

" The men were in an island by themselves, under sentence,
with nothing before them but misery, and they cared nothing
about their lives. I have seen so many murders that I do
not know which you refer to. I have seen men cut up in the
barracks just as you would cut up meat. I have seen 21 men
executed in a fortnight, in New South Wales : they were
hanged for little or nothing. Those horrible murders were
committed in Moreton Bay. The men were pressed with
hard labour, and heavily ironed, and very badly clothed and
treated. The system was rather too severe, and they killed
individuals alongside of them when they were in this state.
They were in a state of frenzy."

Could any previous training protect youths introduced to such a state of society ?

"*I remember the case of a boy of* 16," says Mr. Stonar, "who had been accused by his overseer. He watched his time, and came behind the overseer with a hatchet in his hand, and struck him down with it. He cut the man's leg so severely that it was amputated. The boy was tried, and he was executed. I remember another case which occurred at Point Puer in 1843.—In that case there were 3 boys on their trial. The head of one of them hardly rose above the bar of the Court. In that case the overseer was destroyed with a stone hammer, a small hammer with which stones were broken. The boys who were concerned in it were striking at him for a long time, and a great many other boys were looking on and not interfering. Their defence was conducted by one of the barristers of the Supreme Court, frequently employed by the prisoners. He was very severe in cross-examining the witnesses. He asked each of them what was the reason which prevented his coming forward and interfering. One of them stated that his only reason for not coming forward was, that if he had, he would have been called a dog, and his life would have been rendered miserable in the gang. Another stated that it was no concern of his ; and the other answers given by the boys were equally brutal and unfeeling. The boys were acquitted of the murder, but found guilty of manslaughter."

That numbers of unhappy children have been so circumstanced is clear from the evidence of Captain Groves, Governor of Milbank Prison, where prisoners sentenced to transportation are first sent.

"In 1844," he says, "I received 31 transports under 12 years of age ; from 12 to 14 years of age, 75 ; and from 14 to 17, 233 ; making a total of 339 under 17, out of 3,669 who passed through my hands. I do not recollect that any young person has been ever transported under 15 years of age ; but many have had this sentence passed on them by the judge, expressly with a view of their being sent to Parkhurst. In 1845, there were 34 under 12 years of age, 82 from 12 to 14, 796 from 14 to 17 ;—in 1846 there were 16 under 12, 29 from

12 to 14, and 226 from 14 to 17 : and then in the middle of
last year the system of sentencing young lads to transportation
with a view of being sent to Parkhurst, was stopped, and it
is only now and then when it appears the judges are not aware
of the order, they do it. The convicts were so unmanageable,
and so unfit for the discipline of Milbank, and there were so
many of them, that it was obliged to be put a stop to. In
those 3 years the proportion of the juveniles to the whole
number was about 1–8th ; 1,271 was the total in 3 years."

A feeling evidently existing among judges of the
injustice and undesirableness of sentencing lads to
transportation under such circumstances as have
been here described, has led to a degree of diversity
in the system pursued in sentencing young persons,
which must give rise to an uncertainty of punishment, utterly subversive of its deterring influence.
Lord Chief Baron Pollock, and Mr. Justice Coleridge
state, in answer to questions proposed by the Lords'
Committee—" I do not remember ever to have
transported a mere lad or young girl for a first
offence, except as to the former, *where the circumstances have made me desirous of placing him at
Parkhurst.*" Mr. Baron Alderson says, that the boys
brought before him are " supposed to be of confirmed
habits, rather than offenders for the first time. *The
punishment I impose is most generally that of transportation.*" The same diversity of system may be
observed in the answers of all the judges. Even in
the same city and in the same court, boys who are
acquainted with each other's crimes and characters
see conviction receive such very different punishment for similar offences, as must destroy in

their minds all idea of just and certain retribution. For examples of this we may refer to the School described in Chapter III. J. is spoken of in the public papers as the head of a juvenile gang, and glories in it ; he is the only one who is known to have committed an absolute theft in the School, and has been many times in prison. His removal from the neighbourhood would prove the greatest benefit to it, as well as to himself and to his family ;—but he escapes transportation. L. (p. 89.) has been since in prison, and each time comes out with greater audacity ;—he escapes,—though already one of the dangerous class. Z. on the other hand, who was the only one who came out of prison ready to work and to submit to School influence, on being recently again convicted of a petty larceny, had 9 months imprisonment awarded him, with a threat of transportation for the next offence. At the same Sessions, a man of 36, whose criminal neglect had left his little son to give the city the expense of imprisonment, and who was now convicted himself of robbing his employers, was awarded only 4 months. P. was, after 3 or 4 imprisonments, transported ; while his acquaintance D., whose family and friends all expected him to be transported, he had proved so incorrigible by all past discipline, only received a sentence of a year's imprisonment ; J. D. was taken up for picking a lady's pocket ; it was fully proved against him, and he was committed for trial, but *released* on the interference of the lady ; two days after, his schoolfellow J. P., was taken up for stealing half a pound of butter; he was sentenced to a month's imprisonment and two whippings.

A certain and inevitable punishment may, if it ever has that effect, deter from crime; such uncertainty of it, combined with the numerous chances of escape, never can, among the young and thoughtless.

Let us now inquire whether the gaol is injurious to the child physically and mentally.

At Wakefield, when the separate system was carried out to nearly the same extent as at the Model Prison at Pentonville, *it was obliged,* says the Inspector, *to be dropped in reference to the juvenile offenders.* In that prison there were at the time of the report from 70 to 80 boys, some of them from 10 to 11 years of age. The boys were at first put under close separate confinement, but they soon suffered from debility and contraction of the joints; premonitory symptoms of sluggishness and feeble-mindedness appeared, and there was evident danger to their minds;—the authorities then relaxed the plan, sending the boys to work in the garden instead of the sedentary occupation of picking oakum and wool,—and permitting them to play at leap-frog during certain hours; nor have they thought it right to return to the former system.

" I believe," says Rev. Whitworth Russell, " that in the case of very young children, separation is not productive of good effects, unless where it is employed for very short periods. There is an *elasticity about childhood and youth which it is essential to maintain, but which I think can hardly be maintained under a system of separation.* The adult, having his character and habit: formed, and his mind stored, has resources upon which he can fall back ; the child has no such resources. *Now a child ought not*, I think, to be placed *in circumstances which improperly interfered with the due formation of its character, and the due development of its opening faculties. To this essential process separate confinement, I believe, is not adapted.*"—(Second General Report of Prisons, p. 162.)

The cases of the young Welches, related by Mr. Osborn, strikingly illustrate the injurious effect produced on the excitable nervous temperament of a child by the unnatural seclusion in which he is placed in gaol. Those who are well acquainted with the characteristics of childhood will feel assured that these were not solitary instances, but the natural effect of such treatment on temperaments of that kind. A mother who had detected her little son, for the first time, in dishonesty, desired, by timely punishment, to save him from future shame and suffering. She locked him up in *complete solitude,* carrying him herself the necessary food, and so confined him—herself suffering, she said, even more than he did—*until she saw his health begin to fail, which it did in a fortnight ;* she then *very gradually* admitted him to the family, but did not allow him to mix with his schoolfellows, until she had good evidence that he was reformed, which he now appears to be. Such being the results of experience, we cannot wonder that Dr. Baly, the principal medical officer at Milbank, states in his evidence before the Commons in 1850, that while the number of insane among adults was only $\frac{1}{10}$th per 1000, the proportion among juveniles was 4 $\frac{6}{10}$ths per 1000.

" I think so great a difference," he says, *" cannot be altogether accidental, and it seems to me an important fact.* The treatment of the juveniles in Milbank Prison was the same with that of the adults ; during a portion of that time there was a juvenile class, and they were in association, *but the cases of insanity, with one exception, did not occur among that juvenile class.* It occurred to me that it was wrong to submit juveniles to separate confinement. At the ages of 13, 15, and 16, at which those cases of insanity occurred, *youths are in an excitable state of body and mind ; they have not the power of reflection, but they feel intensely ; and it seems to me dangerous to subject them at such a time to such a punishment."*

The child is then placed in a condition perfectly discordant with his nature. The exercise of his buoyant animal spirits is severely visited as a prison offence : he must not even raise his voice in those loud and joyous sounds which seem a necessity of his nature ; all exercise of his social feelings is cut off, no voice of tenderness is heard, and the spirited boy who will be softened to tears by the gentle reproof of his teacher, vents his energy in ingenious attempts at mischief in the prison cell. If the seed of religion is sown, it is sown in a hot-bed, and dies when exposed to the outer air. He learns only how to be a good prisoner—if he learns that lesson at least—and when he enters the world, he is even more unfit to act in it, or to resist its temptations, after this period of unnatural seclusion. But it is the common experience of official persons, that juvenile prisoners are by far the most audacious, disobedient and intractable. " Experience has taught me," says Mr. Field, the chaplain of Reading Gaol, " that, contrary to the general opinion, the youthful occupants of our prison are among the most difficult of correction, and are insensible to many arguments by which those of mature age may be convinced and persuaded."

The governor of the same gaol, Lieutenant E. Hackett, says in evidence before the Committee of the Commons in 1850,—

" Under the present (the strict separate system), there are as frequent offences against discipline on the part of juvenile offenders, as under the old. *Boys are more inclined to mischief under the new system than they were under the old*, because when they are shut up in a separate cell, they amuse themselves by committing all sorts of petty offences, writing their names, scratching off the paint, boring holes in the doors, injuring the gas pipes, and breaking the thermometers."

Here is a picture of the class, by Mr. Osborn, of Bath :—

" The present system deals with children as with adults. All the ceremonies of the law have to be regarded. ' They alter not.' These juveniles are, when in prison, of all its inmates the most troublesome ; they strut from cell to chapel, and from chapel to cell, with such an air of impudence and self-importance, as is seldom seen in older criminals. Their manner, and their questions in the dock, declare how the present mode of discipline operates on their minds. The expression of their conduct, if not of their lips, is of this kind : ' There's the policeman ; he must mind and not ask me any questions about my offence. There's the turnkey ; he is my servant to bring me my breakfast, dinner and supper, and if he don't give me enough, I'll send for the scales to weigh my bread and meat. There's the schoolmaster ; he must give me instruction, and supply me with books. There's the doctor ; he must come and ask me how I am twice a week, and every day that I want him. There's the chaplain ; he must visit me frequently. And the governor must not neglect me ; and the magistrates, they come twice a week, and ask me if I have any complaint to make. The officers are obliged to mind what they are about.' This swells the frog into an ox."

Nor must the effect of subjecting a child to the hardening effect of public exposure in a court of justice be overlooked. He is here not only branded for life by being seen in the felon's dock, but if the modesty natural to childhood does not render his position overpoweringly distressing to him, the very repression of all childlike feelings makes him audacious and brazen, and the imposing solemnity of a court loses all power to touch him.

" I was inexpressibly shocked," says a teacher, " at seeing H. enter the dock ; he had been for a short time my scholar, and had then been gentle and quiet in his demeanour, and manifesting a desire for improvement, though giving indications of considerable slyness. I had been grieved to hear of his crime, but still more so was I to observe the bold hardened look with which he stared round to recognize his acquaintance, quite unawed by the assemblage of persons collected in due form to try him. He cross-examined the witnesses, even with more acuteness than the barristers had done in the preceding cases, endeavouring to falsify their evidence, and asserting his innocence with a coolness and tact which were shocking to us, who were quite convinced of his guilt. His six weeks of solitary confinement had not done much to inspire him with penitence."

Here is an exhibition at the last Quarter Sessions at Bristol :—

" T. W., aged 13, for stealing meat. The last named prisoner, though of such tender age, *is a very hardened offender*, and, on being sentenced, *began dancing in the dock in a very defiant manner*."—*Bristol Mercury.*

It was the belief of one who knew him, that this was a dance of disappointment and passion at the length of his sentence; but whatever may be the cause of it, are such scenes consistent with the majesty of justice in England? Must judges, councillors, juries (not indeed of *peers*), continue to assemble, to attempt in vain to crush the spirit of a child of 13, now hardened by repeated imprisonments into a criminal.

A perception of these evils led, in 1847, to the passing of the Larceny Act, which gave to magistrates the power of committing to prison, with or without a whipping, for periods not exceeding 3 months, all children charged with theft, whose age did not exceed 14. It was hoped that such an act would diminish crime by saving young criminals from the brand of public prosecution. That act has been followed by very contrary results, and so, we believe, will all such attempts to adapt to children the criminal law for adults. The benevolent and experienced Sergeant Adams has demonstrated its evil results in his charge to the Grand Jury of the Middlesex Quarter Sessions in 1849, and in 1850. He has collected returns of committals from the various London prisons, and finds the increase of the committals after the Act, in the first year, was 107; in the second year 173; and " that since the Act came into operation, the committal of children has been rapidly and steadily increasing." Many persons, he believes, who would have hesitated to brand a child as a felon, have appeared as prosecutors since the Act has been in force, thus familiarizing the young with the interior of the gaol; and he arrives at the conclusion, the soundness of which he has tested in various ways, *that with the increase of power of summary jurisdiction, there is a corresponding increase in the number of commitments.*

Let us now consider the *wisdom* of continuing to pursue the present system with regard to juvenile offenders. We shall quote the opinions of various experienced persons, highly qualified to form a correct judgment respecting it. The following are testimonies on the subject, given before the Select Committee of the Lords in 1847 :—

"Mr. Smith, the Governor of the Edinburgh Gaol, states that he 'considers short commitments of young offenders to have the most mischievous effect possible ; it inures them to imprisonment by slow degrees, till it becomes no punishment at all. * * The fact that a boy has been imprisoned goes far to ruin him for life. * * On comparing the sentences, we see that 62 out of every 100 are sentenced to not more than 20 days, 21 out of every 100 to no more than 10 days, and nearly $2\frac{1}{2}$ out of every 100 to no more than 5 days each. * * One person has been 110 times imprisoned in 15 years, the sentences ranging from 5 to 60 days. * * It is sad to think that 34 out of every 100 new criminals are such by the time they reach the age of 20 years ; 19 out of every 100 at 16 ; and 4 out of every 100 at 12 years of age."

"I think as to children," says Sergeant Adams, (confining the term to children from 7 to 12,)—"prison discipline is incompatible with their reform. * * I have not the slightest doubt, that with children it would be better to apply ourselves to a reformatory than to a deterring process. * * It is doubtless still necessary to hold out imprisonment as a terror to adults ; but as far as a child is concerned, I do believe that prison discipline of any character operates as a retarder rather than as a promoter of reformation. Confinement is needful ; but it should be the confinement of a School, not of a prison. The mind of a child loses its elasticity and is injured by imprisonment."

" The discipline of prisons," says Rev. Whitworth Russell, " gives but little hope of the reformation of children, and I am confident that in the great majority of cases the juvenile delinquent is rendered much worse, and much more dangerous to society by imprisonment. I have visited prisons when children have been brought in for the first time, and I have seen them overwhelmed with fear and distress, clinging with instinctive dread even to the officer that brought them there ; and I have seen those very children, 3 or 4 days afterwards, laughing and playing in the prison-yard with other convicts, and I felt then that the dread of a prison was gone from those children for ever."

Mr. Baron Alderson.—" As long as juvenile offenders are mixed up in our gaols with adults, no effectual improvement can take place. I have known an instance in which a regular plan for a robbery, which took effect and was tried before me, was laid in one of what is called our best regulated gaols, and on the tread-mill. The instrument there was a boy, and the principals were adult thieves. * * I do not think that im- prisonment with hard labour in a prison, as prisons are now managed, is a judicious mode of punishment for juvenile offenders, as I believe that without other efforts it is not found by experience to produce any great or real reform, and that most generally it is followed by a re-committal."

" Mr. Justice Coltman.—" It is to be borne constantly in mind that it is in a great degree from ignorance, and the im- matured state of their reasoning powers, that children offend, —' Nequeunt curvo dignoscere rectum,'—and they are entitled to be treated with great indulgence until they are able in some degree to understand the grounds on which the rules of right and wrong are founded ; and a gaol, however well conducted is, I fear, a bad school for them, and it fixes too dark a stain on their characters."

" So far as I have experienced or have understood," says Lord Cockburn, " Imprisonment has very seldom, if ever, reclaimed juvenile offenders. It is chiefly for thefts that these boys were brought before us ; and the case of a truly reformed thief, whether young or old, who has already defied 2 or 3 convictions, is a phenomenon, I believe, of very rare occurrence indeed. A thoroughly reformed thrice-convicted thief, I should like to know a well authenticated example of. And the reformation of the juvenile is what I despair of most. The various and peculiar attractions of thieving, strong to the adult, seem nearly irresistible to the young, to whose unformed minds, moreover, the habits of even the best conducted gaol are particularly hurtful."

The total number of juvenile offenders over Scotland," says the Lord Justice Clerk, "has greatly increased since 1830, and they are now found in numbers in small quiet provincial towns, where formerly such were wholly unknown. The short imprisonments to which such offenders are subjected on summary convictions in police courts, or before the sheriffs, generally produce no other effect than *to render them utterly indifferent to that punishment*, especially as the separate system in many places cannot be acted upon in regard to them. We have seen cases of lads of 16 or 17, who from the age of 10 or 12 and upwards, have been 6, 8, or 10 times convicted ; sometimes tried before the sheriff and a jury, and sentenced to long imprisonments, in which the separate system was acted upon, but returning *undeterred and unreformed.* But I ascribe the failure, as to boys, very much to the evils of association with bad companions during the short imprisonments to which they are at first subjected, and to the impossibility of making any impression on them, during say 40 or 60 days. * * Certainly at present the *short* imprisonments seem only, in the ordinary case, to *harden* the offenders."

"There are generally in the prison at Tothill Fields," says the governor, Lieutenant Tracy, "600 convicts, a third of them being of the age of 16 and under. In March, 1847, there were 10 under 8 years of age, 36 at the ages of 8, 9, and 10 ; one-third of the whole throughout the year being females, but not so young as the males ; one poor little child had been

committed there *under* the age of 6, an object of wretchedness and misery."

The bulk of these poor children are regarded as
hardened offenders, sent there for the first offence,
and lamentably ignorant.

" I think," says Mr. Tracy, " that we produce but little
improvement upon them in prison, according to the new
system (separate confinement,) with our best attention ; their
short sentences are, in my judgment, most objectionable.
Nor do I believe that giving the magistrates the summary
power of punishment and discharge, without subjecting these
young offenders to the contamination of a prison, would be
effectual. Their association out of prison in the early stages
of crime, and the localities and densely populated districts in
which they are, have a very demoralising effect upon them ;
for the most part they are both neglected, and, in truth,
outcasts. * * I have traced London thieves, step by step,
from very tender years to manhood, who have over and
over again been inmates of our prisons. It appears most
distinctly that most of the juvenile offenders are set on by
receivers of stolen goods, or by other thieves."

The following is from the *Second Report of the
Surveyor-General of Prisons* : —

" There is great difficulty in maintaining a really effective
system of discipline suitable for juveniles in almost all
prisons, in consequence of the small number of prisoners not
justifying the expense of an adequate staff for their special
instruction and management. Hitherto, criminal youths
committed to prison have, in too many instances, been
thoroughly corrupted by the contaminating influences around
them, and others who have escaped committal through the
anxiety of magistrates that they should not be exposed to
such evils have been encouraged by impunity. Indeed, the
whole system hitherto pursued with this class appears to be

open to the most' serious objections, both as regards the practice of sentencing mere children to transportation, or committing them to the penal discipline of a prison."

"A prison," says Mr. Carter, the Chaplain of the Liverpool Gaol, in his Report to the Mayor and Magistrates in 1847, "may have a deterring influence to a certain extent, so long as a boy is unacquainted with its interior ; but on the present system, when a boy is committed for 3 or 5 days, it loses all its terror ; * * he leaves the prison more callous than when he entered it."

"My decided opinion," says Mr. Chalmers, the Governor of Aberdeen Prison, before the Lords' Committee, "(formed on an experience of 22 years,) is, that if a first imprisonment, however short, be not effectual in deterring persons from committing new offences, it is *in vain to expect that repeated short imprisonments will lead to different results.*"

In his Report for 1850, of the prisons in the county of Aberdeen, after stating the large number of persons committed during the year, 943, of which 451 were old offenders, he adds :—

"The present system has not only proved inefficacious in deterring from crime, but also in reforming the criminal. This may be illustrated by the following incident :—' 14 male convicts were lately removed from the Aberdeen Prison to the Government Prison at Milbank. Whilst they were proceeding in a van from the wharf at London to the prison, one of them, a boy of 16, who had been repeatedly in confinement, and who was very expert at pocket-picking, after gazing in astonishment at the crowds in the streets, exclaimed,—' If I were but placed down there, (meaning Fleet-street,) I would soon fill my pockets with something of value, —I would, in a short time, make a complete fortune !' "

Did space permit, we might quote the opinions of numerous other persons of great experience, who have given their evidence on various occasions as to the utter uselessness of the present system as regards the treatment of juvenile offenders; the Select Committee of the House of Commons on Prison Discipline, elicited from various witnesses, testimonies strongly corroborative of what has been already stated. Abundance of additional proof might be adduced, were it needed, to show that this system quite fails of its effect, either in deterring or in reforming young children; but we trust that it is not needed.

Let us now consider a little the expense of these short imprisonments, attended, as we have seen they are, with only a hardening effect to the child.* In the town of Ipswich, there were, in 1849, 26 juveniles in prison, the average detention of each in prison averaging 4 weeks; the daily expense of each was 2s. 1¼d., making a total cost for their maintenance £74. 12s. 10d. The expenses attending their examination before the magistrates and committal, averaged 8s. each, making £10. 8s.; 7 were prosecuted, with an expense of £33. 5s.; the rent of a cell for the 104 weeks may be reckoned at £12.; making each child an average expense of £5. to the public for a punishment which is almost certain to throw him for life into the criminal class. We have seen that he might have had a year's schooling with food provided, for £4., in an Industrial School. Is such a plan an economical one to the public?

* *Moral, Social, and Religious Condition of Ipswich,* by John Glyde: Simpkin and Marshall.

The careful calculations of the Chaplain of the Bath Gaol for a series of years, afford us yet more striking results. In the following table, derived from his yearly records, we have the numbers of juvenile offenders who began their course of crime respectively in each year. The table for each year is prepared as that for 1844, in p.   ; we give here only the results.

Commitments during the year ending July.	Number of juvenile prisoners committed first time.	Length of imprisonment at different times.	Number of summary convictions.	Number of committals for trial.	Number of these transported.	Whole expense.	Time calculated.
1844	55	32½ yrs.	183	64	15	£3063	in 6 yrs.
1845	46	17⅙ yrs.	105	33	7	3575	in 5 yrs.
1846	31	11¼ yrs.	51	25	4	2127	in 4 yrs.
1847	46	14½ yrs.	77	27	2	1931	in 3 yrs.
1848	50	10⅓ yrs	59	14	1	1263	in 2 yrs.
1849	42	14 yrs.	37	18	1	1191	in 1 yr.
Total . .	270	100 yrs.	512	181	30	16150	in 21 yrs.

This enormous sum of £16,150. can of course be only an approximation to the truth;—it may fall far short of the real expense to the country of these 270 young offenders; for though the *known* imprisonments in other gaols, and trials elsewhere, are included in the calculation, it was of course impossible to ascertain the whole extent of them elsewhere; an imaginary estimate has of course also been made of the expense to the public which these young vagrants who have been living in Unions or supporting themselves by begging or stealing when out of prison. The sums levied on the public by pickpockets and thieves, have been stated, p. 35. In the *Ragged*

School Magazine, May, 1851, is the confession of a reclaimed thief, as related by the Rev. J. Burns, at a recent meeting of the Dundee Industrial Schools. In one expedition, he and a companion cleared above £289. at different places, in sums of from £1. to £50.; they had only once the interruption of a month's solitude in Durham Gaol. In the *Ragged School Report,* for 1849, it is mentioned that,—

" The industrial class in Brook-street School, New-road, is composed of 14 lads and young men, formerly reputed thieves. 8 of these have been in prison, on an average 4 times,—in custody, 15 times,—and the number of robberies committed by each, about 200. For the property stolen, they received only about 1–5th of its value, and yet the amount they often realized *amounted to £3. each per week.*"

" Mr. Burnall stated at a public meeting, at Hanover-square Rooms, April 17, 1849, that the 18,000 prisoners in the prisons of Middlesex alone, cost, on an average, first and last, £120. to £150. each. Also, that 550 persons, under 17 years, convicted in one year, at Clerkenwell Sessions, for stealing, cost, in prosecutions, £1,200. ; while the whole amount of the property they stole only amounted to £160."

It is stated in the *Edinburgh Review,* July, 1849, Art. I., that,—

" The number of convictions for felony in the metropolitan district, in 1848, was 3137, and the value of the property lost was £44,666., in addition to all those robberies which do not come under the notice of the police. The number of known thieves in the metropolis alone is 6,000. In England and Wales the number of persons living wholly, exclusively of those living partially by depredations, is estimated at 40,000. From the testimony of a thief, it appears that at one of the lodging-houses for trampers, not one spent less than 3s. a-day ; as they obtain from receivers of stolen goods only from 1–8th to 1–3rd of the value of the property stolen, we cannot place the loss to the community at less than from 10s. to 12s. a-day. In other words, a thief costs the community about £130 a-year, while at liberty ; in prison this may be reduced to from £20. to £30. But, if reformation be not effected, one or other of these charges must continue during the remainder of his life."

" In my own experience," says Mr. M'Neel Caird, " I could point to a single family who have cost in prosecutions and punishments not less than £1,000., and £20. timely spent on their education and training might probably have saved it all."

Shall we go on to pursue a system fraught with such evil to the child, and to the public. That such a system is most injurious is acknowledged by the Committee of the Lords appointed in 1847, to consider this subject. "The evidence," they state in their Report, " throws some light on the treatment of young offenders. *That the contamination of gaols, as gaols are usually managed, may often prove fatal, and must always be hurtful to boys committed for a first offence, and that thus for a very trifling act they may become trained to the worst of crimes, is clear enough.* But the evidence gives a frightful picture of the evils which are there produced."

We shall, in the concluding chapter, consider the remedy which may prove effective to check this growing evil.

CHAPTER VI.

In the early part of this work a series of Schools
were described, which, as far as existing social regulations permitted, have been proved to be eminently
effective in checking the process of juvenile delinquency; and it was shown what legislative aid is
needed to enable such a system to be so extensively
carried out as to produce the desired effect. The
gaol has been next considered, as a deterring and
reformatory agent for the correction of criminal
children; we have seen that under the most favourable circumstances its influence on the young is
rather for evil than for good. Notwithstanding all
our severity, Mr. Neison informs us, in a table he
laid before the Committee of the Commons last year,
that after deducting re-committments from the
annual register of prisoners tried at assizes and
summarily convicted, the yearly average in 9 years,
ending with 1847, of male prisoners 12 years of age,
was 683; 12 and under 14, 1,181; 14 and under 17,
4,352; so that above 7,000 youths are annually

added to our criminal population, without including the children under 12, who, as we have seen, have often already become, under the present system, hardened offenders,—nor the females, who at this age are about 1-5th of the number of the males.*

Better to prepare a small portion of these for the colonial life assigned them when sufficiently vicious, the Parkhurst Prison, in the Isle of Wight, was established by Government a few years ago, for the reception of boys sentenced to transportation. It is in name and in fact a prison. Great expectations of the benefit to result from it were entertained by the benevolent, and we have already seen that kind-hearted judges frequently endeavoured to escape from the perplexity and incongruity of their position,

* It is to be hoped that this enormous annual increase is subject to some of those errors which no science or care can effectually guard against in such returns ; Mr. Neison himself says that the proportion of re-committals must be very much greater than is stated in the reports. The Governor of the Bristol Gaol has kindly prepared returns of the number of persons under 17 years of age committed and re-committed during the last 3 years.

	Committed in				Re-committed.						
	1848	1849	1850	Total	Twice.	Thrice.	Four times.	Five times.	Six times.	Seven times.	Total.
Males .	142	91	98	331	31	14	4	2	1	1	53
Females	10	8	19	37	4	—	—	—	—	—	4

The fluctuations in this table are remarkable, as well as the varying proportions between the sexes. These numbers, from a large seaport town, would lead one to hope that there may be an over-statement in Mr. Neison's table.

when little children accused of the grave crimes of felony and housebreaking were brought before them, by sentencing them nominally to transportation, in the hope of their being sent instead to a good Reformatory School,—until such use of the establishment was checked by the government.

The following account of Parkhurst Prison is derived from the evidence of Captain Hall, the Governor, before the Committee of the House of Lords in 1847, and of Lieutenant-Colonel Jebb, the Visitor :—

" This is a penal establishment for boys who have been sentenced to transportation, usually between the ages of 10 and 18, but even at 8 or 9 many have been thus sentenced with a view of getting them here, and not long ago there were as many as 60 or 70 at this tender age. On the boy's first arrival at the prison he is placed in a probationary ward, where he is kept in separate confinement for 4 months or more. During this time he is not allowed to hold any intercourse with the other boys, but for at least 5 hours he is at different times in the presence of others, either for exercise, instruction or religious service, and during the time he is in his cell he is supplied with occupation and books, and is visited by the officers of the establishment. This is not, therefore, a stringent separate system. The boys appear in good spirits, cheerful and happy, nor does their health in any way suffer ; indeed boys have frequently asked to go back to the probationary ward after having left it, from feeling there a degree of security from temptation to commit prison offences, and consequently to incur punishment. After this the boys are placed together where they learn trades, and converse or play with each other, under the eye of warders—the meals being taken together, 360 in a large hall. The boys remain at Parkhurst from 2 to 3 years, sometimes longer, during this time a highly favourable change is generally perceptible in the whole disposition of the boy ; there is a great difference between the first and second year, and a still greater difference between the third and the former year. The state of health has been remarkably good, only 14 deaths having occurred during 8 years, among nearly 1200 boys. On leaving Parkhurst they are generally sent to the colonies, and much depends on the circumstances in which they are there placed. In Western Australia, there is an officer of the government, styled the Guardian of Juvenile Emigrants, who is appointed to apprentice the boys and to see that the conditions of the indentures are fulfilled, visiting them once in 6 months. It is feared that in other colonies such provision has not yet been made, and that the boys are consequently exposed, on arriving, to much danger of falling back into dishonest means of gaining a livelihood. Excellent reports have been received recently of the conduct of boys sent out to Western Australia ; —of 62 boys, 50 were first-rate lads, but 12, about 1–5th, were very troublesome, and great difficulty was felt in disposing of them.* This has also been experienced in making satisfactory arrangements for those sent very young to Parkhurst, who, after passing through the appointed time, and having received the requisite instruction, were not old enough to be sent abroad, and having a prison brand affixed to them, could not be otherwise placed out. For such cases, Colonel Jebb feels it would be most desirable to provide District Penal Schools similar to Parkhurst, where they could be properly arranged for, leaving only the boys above the age of 15 to come into the hands of government for transportation."

Thus far the establishment would seem a good one, were it restricted to such boys of 15 or 16 and upwards, as have so thoroughly resisted every attempt to reform them, that their absolute removal

* A gentleman who has been many years resident in Australia, declares that the worst class of convicts landed there are the Pentonville and Parkhurst prisoners.

from society is the only safeguard from their evil
influence on it. But what is to become of the young
boys,—of the female convicts altogether? These
have been quite uncared for in the provision made
for the older boys.

Above 2000 of the annual fresh supply of male
juvenile delinquents are under the age for Parkhurst. Mr. Neison's statistic tables show that,
during the 9 years for which the tables are drawn,
females constituted one-fifth of the total tried at
assizes; about one-fourth of the summarily convicted, and of the whole number re-committed, one-
third were females. But of those 14 years of age
and under, only between one-seventh and one-eighth
were girls. A yet more striking fact is derivable
from a paper delivered into the Lords' Committee
in 1847, by Mr. Chalmers, Governor of Aberdeen
Prison. The per centage of female prisoners in
all the prisons of Scotland is nearly one-half; of
juvenile female prisoners under 17, between one-fifth
and one-sixth; but the per centage of *re-commitments
of juvenile female prisoners is greater by one-half* than
that of males. This statistic fact would indicate
that young girls are generally much less prone to
crime than boys of the same age, but that their tendency to it rapidly increases with their age, and that
when they have once embarked in a criminal career,
they become more thoroughly hardened than the
other sex. The correctness of these painful results
is proved by the testimony of the Bishop of Tas-

mania before the Lords. After speaking of the
fearful condition of the female convicts in the
colonies, which surpasses in degradation and vice
even that of the men, he adds :—

"Female felons are so bad, because, before a woman can
become a felon at all, she must have fallen much lower, have
unlearnt much more, have become much more lost and depraved than a man. Her difficulty of regaining her self-
respect is proportionally greater. There is nothing to fall
back upon—no one to look to. I believe that the experience
of almost every parish priest in England would lead him to
the conclusion that there are many cases in which our village
girls are kept straight, not so much by their own good principle, as by the check imposed upon them through the dread
of shame, the fear of fathers, mothers, friends and relations.
Let that check be once removed, and their future progress is
rapidly downward. When they go out as convicts every thing
is gone, every restraint is removed, they can fall no lower."

An experienced temperance advocate has stated
that, while the cases of drunken men who have become reformed and steady teetotalers have come
very frequently before him, *he has never known an
instance of a woman, given to intoxication, being
really converted;* this will probably be common experience. The records of the teacher's journal are
quite in accordance with these painful facts.

"One little girl only, at all connected with our school, has
been taken before the magistrates, while such occurrences
among the boys are frequent. We have not, then, in the school,
the criminal class of girls, and only in a few cases the sisters
of the boys who have been convicted of theft ; that many
girls who are already known thieves exist in Bristol, the
weekly police reports sufficiently show ; *but these will not come
to school.* Nor will the low and degraded girls that infest the

neighbourhood ; in the early period of the school several of these came for a time, but have since discontinued. The girls who attend are rather the very poor and low than the vicious. Their general appearance usually strikes strangers as superior to what would be expected in such a school ; this arises from the circumstance that girls are more easily able to improve their dress by their industrial habits, and also that girls are more quickly susceptible of improvement than boys. Any effort, therefore, soon tells on them ; but this very flexibility of nature renders them more liable to fall when under bad influence. On the other hand, it is far more difficult to call out their intellectual powers than those of the boys, and thus to interest them in their lessons ; this arises not only from the difference in their natures, but from the circumstance that while the boys have been sharpening their powers by roving the streets, the girls have been confined to their wretched home. The dulness and stupidity they manifest, united with great vulgarity, is a serious hindrance to their improvement, but persevering effort has done much for them."

When we reflect that the early moulding of the young child's mind depends almost entirely on the mother, and that these neglected children, who are in great danger of joining the criminal class, if they have not done so, are to become the parents of the next generation, surely express provision should be made for their training and reformation. As yet they have been unprovided for by the government, and Parkhurst only exists for the boys.

Let us now endeavour to ascertain from public documents how far the juvenile prison at Parkhurst is fulfilling its mission. As confinement here is the only authorized mode of disposing of young transports rather than subjecting them to the system adopted for adults, Sergeant Adams frequently sent juvenile offenders to it before the rules of admission were defined as at p. 27, yet this is the opinion he expressed of the Institution before the Lords in 1847 :

" I was about three weeks ago at Parkhurst, in the Isle of Wight. They there act upon the principle of cooping up, and it seems to me a mistaken one. They have 40 solitary cells, and every child who is sent to Parkhurst is locked up in one of those cells for 4 months after he goes. I call it solitary ; perhaps the word ' separate' is the term used, but it is solitary in this respect, that he is there for the whole 24 hours, with the exception of when he is in chapel, and 2 hours when he is at school, where he is in such a pen that he can see nobody but the minister. His sole employment is knitting, and reading good books. No good conduct can make him there less than 4 months, and if his conduct is not good, he is there until his conduct is good. At this time there are several boys who have been in those cells from 6 to 12 months. It seems to me that it can only make them sullen. * * When the prison was first established, the boys were allowed occasionally a game of play ; that was entirely put an end to. Within the last 3 months they have been allowed occasionally to play at leap-frog, but no other game. Of course, if boys are allowed to play at leap-frog and no other game, leap-frog will be the only game at which they will not care to play. I asked what were the rewards held out for good conduct, and they told me the only rewards were permission to attend the evening school, and the privilege of going to the governor to get information of their friends. Why, one half of them have no friends to ask after, and as to the other half, the less they know of them the better. The privilege also of attending evening school, though a great and proper one, might be rendered more valuable if accompanied by the privilege of half a holiday, and a game of cricket. That they can behave ill in their solitary cell is quite clear, because otherwise a boy could not be there for 12 months ; but what that ill behaviour is, or what the good behaviour is, I did not ask, for I thought I ought not pry into those questions."

Such is the opinion of the prison expressed by a benevolent and experienced man. Let us turn for further particulars to the printed reports presented to both Houses of Parliament.

" The number of prisoners, 79, sent back to Milbank for transportation in 1846, was, from peculiar circumstances, unusually great. A number of ill-disposed and discontented boys having been discovered, who manifested no desire to avail themselves of the course of instruction and training pursued at Parkhurst, but mischievously employed themselves in unsettling and perverting others, it was deemed expedient to remove the greater portion of them in the month of April, and the salutary effect of that step has been very apparent since that time in the improved conduct of the remaining prisoners. The other individuals returned for transportation were boys, who having repeatedly incurred minor punishments for misconduct, had been placed in the penal class, and, while there, did not evince any real desire to amend."

It seems, then, that after some years of experience, sufficient moral power was not obtained to control as many as 79, who were therefore sent back to people another country. At Mettrai, the number of morally incurable was, even from the earliest times, only occasionally one or two. We see also that even this strict penal discipline cannot preserve the less vicious from moral contamination, from " ill disposed and discontented boys." The last report will show whether any great progress in moral influence has been made in five years. The Governor reports :—

" The number of attempts to escape has been very large this last year (1849), 34 prisoners in all have run away, 30 of these while out at farm labour. All of them, however, were speedily re-captured. None of the boys who made these attempts had, so far as I can ascertain, any hope or expectation that they would really be able to secure their liberty ; but having found that 2 boys who had run from the land, and had committed a robbery previous to their re-capture, were removed to Winchester Gaol, they determined to try to get relief by such a course of proceeding, from the restraint and discipline of Parkhurst, which they found to be intolerably irksome. Having no power of forethought or rational consideration, they yielded to the impulse of an unfounded notion, that *any* change from Parkhurst would be for the better."

When a youth who had twice attempted to escape from his former confinement, was asked why he did not make a similar effort at Mettrai, he replied, *" because there are no walls ;"* from that penal asylum there have been for many years no escapes ; here there are " enclosures long believed to be impassable," sentinels with loaded guns, and a certainty that there is no possible escape from the island ; yet the inhabitants of the surrounding district are in constant fear of finding runaways in their houses, nor is the apprehension diminished by the fact of two conflagrations having been kindled by the prisoners during the last year.   Why does this state of feeling exist at Parkhurst ? The Visitors give in their report a sufficient clue to it.

" Among youths such as are confined at Parkhurst, who are precocious without experience, very restless and adventurous without being guided by reason, very excitable, credulous when one of themselves asserts a fact, or advances a proposal, yet suspicious of all that may be stated or urged by their officers, even to an extent that could hardly be believed by those who did not continually watch the workings of their minds, it is most difficult to make them understand what is for their immediate, as well as their prospective benefit."

What wonder is it, that with such a state of feeling, with nothing to exercise and give free vent to their " restless and adventurous" spirit, with no " direct and sufficiently powerful stimulus in the way of remuneration for work efficiently done," their pent up energies should break out into frequent acts of disrespect to the officers, violence, wanton damage of property, and even theft, as well as disorder and prohibited talking, for which an average of 445 boys incurred, in 1844, 4105 separate punishments (among them 165 whippings), making an average of above 10 per diem! If the governor is able to state in the last report, that the behaviour of the majority " was generally, quiet, orderly, and obedient;" he feels obliged to add :—

" That while there has been a general observance of outward regularity and attention to the prison rules among the greater portion of the boys, and serious breaches of order have been of comparatively rare occurrence, there has not been that evidence of a general and growing desire to improve in moral conduct and industrial energy which I anxiously looked for, and the apparent absence of which causes me much disappointment. Prisoners are generally indolent, boys especially."

Those who have accorded in the principles of reformatory action which were laid down in the first chapter, and have been our guide in the consideration of all the schools that have passed before us, will feel no surprise that the governor's hopes are unfulfilled, not, it may be, through any fault of his own, but through the radical error of the whole system. It attempts to fashion children into machines instead of self-acting beings, to make them obedient prisoners within certain iron limits, not men who have been taught how *to use their liberty without abusing it ;* without this knowledge, and the power of employing it, we have seen that the best instruction, the Word of God itself, but little avails its possessor. Such a system must fail; for the boy whose heart has never been purified and softened by any good home influences, who has always done " what is right in his own eyes," will never give a *willing* obedience where his powers can have no free exercise, where there is no softening power of love to subdue him, where he can never hear from woman what should have been the entreating tones of a mother, where he regards with profound suspicion the appointed agents of his reformation. It is utterly vain to look for any real reformation where the heart is not touched, and where the inner springs of action are not called into healthful exercise ; this cannot possibly be done for children under the mechanical and military discipline of Parkhurst.

We have thus endeavoured to scrutinize the system adopted in this establishment, and to point out its radical defects, because it is the only reformatory prison for boys existing under government direction, and is regarded by many as a model one. Of the details of its management it is unnecessary to speak ; they appear, from the reports to be well planned, and carried out with due attention to the health of the boys, and their instruction in mental and industrial pursuits, while the expense is probably as moderate as is possible under the circumstances. There is only one other point to which we would draw attention. Parkhurst is especially intended for the training of boys, who at the end of two, or at most three years, will be prepared to go out as colonists, and the regulations now laid down make 14 and upwards the age of admission. The governor has, in his report, stated his opinion—

"That the admission of youths of 18 and upwards, or of lads who have pursued a course of crime for several years, till they have become habituated to and hardened in it, is very much to be lamented, as it seriously impedes all efforts made for the reformation of our inmates. Such characters as those above described, having been many times imprisoned, have lost all sense of degradation, have no desire to become respectable characters, and have no intention to earn their subsistence by honest means whenever they may regain their liberty. Abject slaves themselves to sensual appetites and propensities, the only voluntary activity they manifest is a continual effort, by persuasion, by threats, by false promises, or by ridicule, to make other prisoners pursue their vicious example in opposing all means which may be tried for their moral improvement."

But at the end of the preceding year there were 393 out of 622, 18 years of age and upwards, some of them " convicted of atrocious crimes," which, he justly feared, would " afford subject for eager investigation and debasing discourse among a certain class of the prisoners." When young men have arrived at that degree of audacious depravity, can it be doubted that, unless sufficient moral force is in action to neutralize their influence, they must be most unsafe companions for boys ? And if youths have been allowed thus to go on in a career of crime until they have been " so many times imprisoned, that they have lost all sense of degradation," surely a school for boys is a most unfit place for them.

Let us now consider an institution in a neighbouring country, which, from its great success in the reformation of young offenders, deserves our minute and careful examination.

La Colonie Agricole, at Mettrai, in France, has for its object *to restore to society, as honest and useful members of it,* those young persons who have subjected themselves to punishment, and to do this by substituting the discipline of a school and a family for that of a prison. This is a higher aim than that of Parkhurst, which prepares its inmates only for expatriation. The Mettrai school owed its origin to the devoted efforts of M. Demetz, aided by a few gentlemen, who, animated by his spirit, formed a " Societé Paternelle," to assist in the execution of his plan. The public at first doubted and held back, " but *we* did not doubt," says their report, " because we knew the men who devoted themselves to this generous mission ; we believed as they did ; we were convinced that if the great experiment could succeed, it would be *by their hands, by their intelligence, their ardent faith.*" M. Demetz matured his plans, trained some teachers, and received the first inmates of his school selected from different prisons, in January, 1840. In 18 months the president could say in his address, "Its success is no longer contested.

Government, which ought to lend itself to no hazardous project, nor endanger existing order by Utopian schemes, *but whose province it is to aid realized attempts,* can no longer withhold from us its co-operation."

The following account of the establishment, is derived from a report on its system and management, by the Rev. Sydney Turner, Chaplain of the Philanthropic, and J. Paynter, Esq., Police Magistrate, in the Appendix to the Second Report of the Surveyor-General of Prisons. It is corroborated by Mr. M. D. Hill's account of Mettrai, after a recent visit there (1848), in a charge to the Grand Jury, and by extracts from the Reports of the Societé Paternelle in the *Christian Teacher* (1842).

" The establishment is intended for young criminals, whose vicious habits are to be corrected, and who are to be prepared to be useful members of society. The principles which guide all the arrangements are enlightened by a high religious aim, and tend to infuse into the unfortunate young beings confided to it high motives of action, to awaken in them pure desires, by letting them feel the happiness of virtuous social intercourse, and to give them such habits of life as will be likely to be permanent, when the necessary restraints of the institution are removed from them. Hence, for the spirit of fear, which is usually the controlling one in such Schools, is substituted to a great extent that of love, guided by wisdom and the experience of a sound mind. To carry out this principle an internal organization is adopted very different from that of other such Schools. Instead of making the boy, now separated from his natural ties, at once a member of a large community, where, among several hundreds of his own age, he cannot imagine that his own individuality is of more importance than as one of a number, or that his own actions are more regarded than to check him in the commission of faults, or to provide for his bodily wants; he is placed in a family where each member is personally interested in the moral well-being of the others, and where his good or bad conduct must materially influence the prosperity of the whole. The Mettrai School, containing about 400 boys, is so arranged as to be a collection of families. The boys are divided, with a careful regard to the varieties of their character and disposition, into a number of separate portions, each containing about 40. Each of these portions, or 'families,' has a master, and two assistant masters specially connected with it. Each family resides in a distinct house, having no connection with the other inmates of the establishment, except during the hours of work, recreation, or divine service, or on occasion of any special assembling of the whole number. The master, or père, as he is called, and the two assistants who act under him, live and *constantly associate with the boys, sharing in their amusements, and having in the main the same accommodations. The responsibility of the master is thus made far more personal and individual.* These 40 boys are *his* especial charge. He is answerable, not for the whole in general, but for them in particular. Hence the masters are led to exert themselves more definitely; an emulation is created among them as to who shall show the best moral and intellectual results from his labour. *The boys and the master are much more closely connected, and a more real influence, as well as a more kindly one, is produced.* By this daily association confidence is generated, a higher moral feeling roused and nourished, and the esprit du corps, usually so strong in Schools, is silently thwarted and destroyed. The boy feels that his master is not a mere officer to watch him and enforce discipline, or a mere instructor to teach him, but is a relation, —a friend—to sympathize with him and assist him. More officers being thus employed than would be necessary in ordinary Schools, *there is a greatly increased amount of moral agency on the boys,* which much assists in their discipline, and facilitates in their progress and improvement. *The boys are themselves interested and employed in maintaining the discipline and order of the establishment.* Two boys called 'Frerè ainés' are elected monthly in each family by the boys, to assist in its regulation ; their being chosen by the boys themselves under the sanction of the master, prevents jealousy of them being felt by the other boys, who readily obey them. The scholars are also permitted to select those who are to receive rewards for good conduct, and their concurrence is appealed to when any are to be punished. With regard to the discipline of the establishment, and the rewards and punishments in use, the principle is, that no part of the boy's conduct, however inconsiderable, be unnoticed or overlooked. 'The least fault is punished,' is the expression of the directors. The punishments are,—making the boy stand apart from his companions —privation of meals and of recreations—admonition in the 'parlour' of the director—imprisonment in a light or dark cell, with or without a dry bread and water diet—and finally, expulsion, which is synonymous with the boy's being sent back to the prison from which he was received. Corporal punishment is utterly prohibited. But strict as the discipline is, the number of masters and officers, and their continual association with the boys, prevent the occurrence of many faults and infractions of the rules which would else arise, save it from being vexatious, and insure its being really, and justly, and kindly enforced. The principle of the School instruction is, that the boy shall only be taught as much as the average of agricultural and other labourers acquire, viz., to read, to write, and to cypher. The more advanced boys are taught the elements of drawing and geography. The instruction is in all points made as individual and personal as possible. All the boys are taught music. Industrial training occupies a large proportion of their day. It is a principle that the boys shall be continually occupied, and thoroughly fatigued. There are about four hours allowed for meals, recreations, morning and evening prayers, dressing, &c. The rest of the day, with the exception of one hour appropriated to instruction in the School, is devoted to labour. The accommodation, dress, food, &c. of all the inmates, officers as well as boys, are of the plainest description. M. Demetz lays it down as a principle that self-denial in yourself is the essential condition of usefulness to others, and he teaches this in his own example, living himself in all respects as he requires the officers and boys to do. With all these regulations there is the inculcation of a religious motive on the boys, and the cultivation of religious principle among them. Nothing is merely routine, merely mechanical ; all is pervaded and animated with the real earnest character of the resident director.

" The moral results have fulfilled the most sanguine expectations of its directors. Since the first establishment of the institution in 1839, there have been received 521. The number of present inmates is 348, leaving a remainder of 173. Of these, 17 have died ; 12 have been sent back to their prisons for misconduct, 144 have been placed out in various situations in the world. Of the 144 thus placed out, 7 have relapsed into crime, 9 are of doubtful character, and 128 are conducting themselves to the full satisfaction of the directors.

" A great portion of the singular success which has attended the efforts of the directors is attributable to the attention paid to the education and training of the masters, and the youngest assistants. M. Demetz commenced his operations by establishing a Normal School, and by devoting himself for some months to the education and preparation of young men, to undertake the superintendence of the families which he proposed to form. There is still a Normal School attached to the colony, in which there are always from 12 to 18 pupils, preparing to replace the masters, as any of these leave for similar institutions which are being formed in various parts of France.

" The direct influence of the School does not cease with the expiration of the time appointed for residence there. After remaining at Mettrai for about 3 years, situations are readily obtained for them with farmers and tradesmen, there being more applications than can be satisfied. Whenever a boy is thus placed out, a ' patron' is obtained for him, i. e. some gentleman of the neighbourhood who will interest himself in his conduct and welfare. Reports from these patrons are obtained every 6 months, from which a list is made out and suspended in the large school-room. If the lad behave well, he is presented, on arriving at his 20th year, with a ring, engraved with an appropriate device. If he turns out ill, while under 20 years of age, he is either received back for a further trial, or is sent to the house of correction from whence he originally came, and remains there till the expiration of his sentence."

Now it is evident that, to carry on such a work as this, there are needed first of all fitting and efficient instruments, who address themselves to it, to use M. Demetz's words, " with the Gospel in their hands," —who unite intelligence, self-control, and the knowledge of human nature, with devoted christian earnestness ;—and next, these men must be invested with such power as to give them a sufficiently strong hold on the objects of their care to enable them to carry out their plans. The French law gives this legal hold upon the boys to the directors of Mettrai, thus enabling them to dispense with walls, exercising only moral restraint, while they exert an effectual control over the scholars by their liability to be sent back to prison for the rest of their term if they grossly misconduct themselves. In Mettrai these two conditions *have* been fulfilled ; the *personal influence* of the directors has been directly or indirectly felt by every individual boy, while a power has been given to that influence by the fear of being sent back to the house of correction. Through this combined influence walls and sentries are dispensed with; the boy is allowed that liberty of action which is so important to a true reformation of the character, and since the first year there has been no attempt to escape from the establishment.

It would be useless to point out the difference, which must be most striking to all, between the two penal establishments of Parkhurst and Mettrai:— the one under the guidance of strict discipline and military rule,—the other under that of Christian love. The example of Mettrai has been extensively followed in France; the immense importance of such Schools becoming evident, many other such have been established, and the excellent M. Demetz, whose spirit is still the presiding one in his own original School, sends forth teachers into all parts of France, who have been trained under his influence.

A yet greater monument of the power of faith to overcome mountains of vice and ignorance exists in the Prussian dominions. Near Dusseldorf, on the right bank of the Rhine, rises Dusselthal Abbey. This is rather a refuge for wretched outcast children than a Penal Reformatory School, but it must not be passed over in our consideration of such, because it affords a most striking instance of the power of such principles as were developed in the first chapter, to overcome the greatest moral obstacles. The following short account of it is extracted from a small work entitled "*Illustrations of Faith,*" Nisbet and Co., 1844:—

"In 1816 Count Von der Recke, a member of a noble Prussian family, renounced the pursuits and pleasures belonging to his station in life, to devote his time, his fortune, and his talents, to the care and education of poor fatherless and destitute children, and of such grown-up people as have sought his protection. His country had been recently devastated by war ; numbers of unhappy children, deprived of their natural protectors, had become absolutely savage, living, when unable to gain any subsistence by begging or stealing, on wild herbs and roots. His father and he first received a few of these wretched little beings into their own home ; then the father gave up a house for their use, and finally, by the sacrifice of his own fortune, and with the help of friends, he purchased an estate, which forms their present abode. Many were so confirmed in their wild habits, that any degree of restraint was intolerably irksome to them ; they would run away and live in the woods, until compelled by hunger to return. Yet they were often successful in cases which would lead one to despair." The history of several is given in the narrative. " One of these, Clement, was supposed to be about 13 years of age ; more depraved characters have been received into the asylum, but none so nearly resembling the lower animals in appetite and manners. It was not known where he came from, and he could give no account of his earlier life ; his language was scarcely intelligible, and partook of the sounds of the four-footed companions of his infancy ; among his most pleasurable recollections seemed to be his familiarity with the Westphalian swine, and his most frequent stories related to these favourite animals. While yet a child, he had acted as swineherd to a peasant, and was sent to the fields to eat and sleep with the swine ; but his unfeeling master, less attentive to the miserable infant than to his bristly charge, scarcely allowed him food sufficient to sustain nature : when hungry and faint, the poor little wretch actually sucked the milch sow ! and to satisfy his craving appetite browsed upon the herbage ! At his first reception into the institution, he would steal secretly on all fours into the garden, and commit great devastation upon the salad beds ; nor was he induced, till after repeated chastisements, to give up his unwonted luxury. The sequel of the story is encouraging :—After unspeakable pains, the more amiable qualities of Clement began to develope ; he discovered an uncommonly kind and obliging disposition, which gained him the affection of his companions, and by his humble and submissive deportment he became not only a favorite with his teachers, but an example to others who had previously enjoyed much greater advantages. He requited his benefactors by cheerfully employing his strength in the lowest services, and continued a faithful Gibeonite, a hewer of wood, and a drawer of water for the institution."

Such is a specimen of their scholars, and yet in an early report the Count and his friends could say,—" Come, ye dear friends of humanity, come and see what the compassion of God has already done for this little flock, once wild, corrupted, debased beyond conception,—sunk almost beneath the level of the brutes. Oh! come and admire the wonderful transforming power of the gospel, which of these fierce lions' cubs hath made tame meek lambs. Come, *and rejoice over the modesty and obedience they evince ;* their love and attachment, not only to their teachers and benefactors, but even to strangers ;—*see their industry, activity, and desire to be useful ;*—come, listen to the harmonious songs with which they praise their Creator and Redeemer, and hear from their tender lips their gratulations over their deliverance! Especially come, oh! come, and unite with us in prayer and thanksgiving to our Lord and Saviour, who has never left himself without a witness among his creatures."

This will seem to many the language of enthusiasm; it is so if we apply that term to deep and ardent faith pervading our daily life, and inspiring with a quickening spirit even the daily drudgery of the work he had undertaken. *Ora et labora,* was his watchword. He had constant and harassing difficulties in raising the necessary funds. In many instances, his own ardour kindled that of others, and unexpected supplies arrived at a moment of need, which he received as a gift and encouragement from his Heavenly Father; but he had frequently trying disappointments,—still greater trials arose from the condition of the children :—

"Great wisdom and prudence," continues the narrative, "as well as incessant labour and attention, were required in managing such children as have been described, even so far as to prevail on them to remain under any partial restraint, and to receive any instruction.   Their ideas of right and wrong had to be corrected, and their sense of enjoyment rectified, even in the lower capacities of animal enjoyment. They had no distinct conceptions with regard to property, nor could they perceive any injustice in applying to their own use whatever suited their convenience, and might be easily obtained.   Bodily privation, cold and hunger, were the sources of their several suffering ; and their highest enjoyments the luxurious indolence of basking in the sunshine, or before a comfortable fire, or a nauseous gluttony indulged in to repletion. * * The vitiated appetites of the children, till corrected, derived more gratification from gluttony at one time, and almost starvation at another, than from the equable and moderate supply received at stated hours, which the rules of a well ordered household provided.   Nor was the properly prepared diet itself agreeable to their taste ; they relished sour and wild fruits, raw vegetables, half-raw flesh, and a superabundance of bread, more than the same articles properly cooked, and fully but frugally administered.   The discipline required was uniform, steady and strict, yet kind. To gain their affections, without indulging their early vicious propensities, was no easy task, but until this was accomplished, nothing could be done effectually for reclaiming such wayward vagabonds.   The training is threefold ; and while the object of each division is distinct, they are all three carried on together in harmony with one another.   In the industrial department, mechanical aptitude and such practical habits as may tend to secure a livelihood are aimed at ;—in the mental department, an endeavour is made to develope the powers of the understanding, and impress it with religious truth ;—the moral department is conducted so as to awaken the conscience, to inspire the love of God, and to open the heart for the reception of the Holy Spirit."

"The Count considers the 220 persons collected together within the walls of Dusselthal, whether as scholars, servants, or teachers, as one family ; he lives among them as a father, taking the most lively interest in everything that concerns their welfare, bodily or spiritual ;—he shares their joys and sorrows, pointing both to the same great end."

Did space permit, it would be interesting to watch him in his family at the Christmas fête,—at the funeral of his little daughter, which consecrated their cemetery—" Das Himmels-garten." But we must conclude this brief account of Dusselthal, and cannot do so better than in the words of its founder, which so vividly exhibit the spirit in which it is conducted :—

" Everything in Dusselthal tends, either directly or indirectly, to the promoting the kingdom of God ; it is this that makes all my labours so pleasant. Every walk, every step, every employment, all are connected with the kingdom of God ; and, oh ! it is blessed to labour for that kingdom. I desire life only for this end !"

It is a mournful sequel to this touching record of devotion and love, that the Count's health and strength have been exhausted by his exertions, which have not been supported by others as they ought. The energy and talents which should have been left unimpaired for the sustaining of the spiritual life of the establishment, have been wasted by pecuniary difficulties, and now the inhabitants of the neighbouring town feel obliged to do what they should ungrudgingly have done before, form a regular fund for the support of the establishment. It is individual love and zeal which alone can rightly guide such institutions, but this *must* be

sustained and encouraged by the aid of the many.
This was done at Mettrai; Dusselthal and its
founder languished because it was withheld.

The Rauhe Haus of Hamburgh is already well
known to the public, from the account given of it
by Horace Mann in his *Educational Tour*.* But
the powers of the spirit of love and of domestic influences is so strikingly shown by Elihu Burritt, in
an account of a recent visit, that we must transcribe
a few passages.†

" On the 1st of November, 1833, J. H. Wichern, an earnest
man, whose heart is a living gospel of Christian love to his
kind, took possession, with his family, of a small one story
straw-roofed house, fronting on a narrow lane, leading out of
the village of Horn, about three miles from Hamburgh. ✶ ✶
About an acre of land covered with sprawling bushes, ditches,
hillocks, &c., formed, with the smutty cottage, the foundation
of the new institution which was to solve another great prob-
lem in the mysteries of humanity. ✶ ✶ After the lapse of
a week spent in purifying this little cottage, and preparing it
for a home for the unfortunate little beings who were to be
gathered to its hearth, three were brought in from their
lairs on the frosty pavement or door-stones of the city. In
the course of a few weeks, 14 of these young vagabonds
were introduced within the fold of that family circle, varying from 5 to 18 years of age, yet all old in the experience
of wretchedness and vice. Each had become a hardened
veteran in some iniquitous practice or malicious disposition ;
and, as such, had been pronounced or regarded as incorrigible.
Nearly all of them had been left and trained to beggary, lying,
stealing, and to every vicious habit. Some had the organ or

---

* This has been printed separately : Oberlin Tracts, No.
xii., Horsell, Paternoster-row.
† Bond of Brotherhood, April, 1851.

disposition of destructiveness, developed to such a frenzy, that the first thought of their life seemed to be the mutilation of everything they could reach ; others had acquired a ferocious force and obduracy of self-will. One of these adepts in crime had been convicted by the police of 93 thefts, and yet he was only in his 12th year. They had been treated or regarded as a species of human vermin, *baffling the power of the authorities to suppress.* They had slept under carts, in doorways, herding with swine and cattle by night, when the begging or thieving hours were past. Such were the boys that found themselves looking at each other in wonder and surprise the first evening they gathered round the hearthstone of that cottage home. There was no illusion about this sudden transformation in their experience. There was that bland benevolent man in their midst, with his kind eyes and voice, looking and speaking to them as a father to his children. And there was his mother, with the law of kindness on her lips, in her looks, in every act and word ; and he called her mother, and they called her mother ; and the first evening of their common life she became the mother of their love and veneration; and they—ragged, forsaken, hopeless castaways, conceived in sin, and shapen in iniquity—became the children of her affection. As far as the east from the west, was their past life to be separated from their future—to be cut off and forgotten. And this cottage, away from the city and its haunts, with its bright fire by night, and the little beds under the roof, with its great bible and little psalm-books, was to be *their home.* And the great chesnut-tree that thrust out its arms over it, and all the little trees, and the ditches, hillocks and bushes, of that acre *were their own.* Some hymns and sweet spirited ballads were sung after the frugal supper ; and then the mother of the circle told them some nice stories, with her kind voice ; and the father, with his kind eyes, asked their advice about some little plans he had in his mind for improving their farm. The feeling of home came warming into their hearts, like the emotions of a new existence, as he spoke to them with his kind voice and eyes, of *our* house, of *our* trees, of *our* cabbages, turnips, potatoes, pigs, and geese and ducks, which *we* will grow for *our* comfort."

Could Parkhurst, with its impassable walls—its bolts and keys—its sentinels with loaded guns—and officers regarded by the boys with profound suspicion —its military discipline and solitary cells—have so subdued these boys who had baffled the power of the authorities ?

" The boys at once set to work. At the end of the first week they had made a year's progress in this new life, and its hopes and expectations. The earth mound gradually disappeared ; and *the faith that they could do something, be something, and own something grew daily within them ;* and they sung cheery songs at their work ; for almost every evening they practised on some ballad, under the instruction of the mother of the circle. So eager did ' they become to accomplish the undertaking,' says the first report of the Institution, ' that they frequently worked by lantern-light in the evening, rooting up bushes and trees, in spite of snow and rain.' " As their number increased, they themselves built, with unwearied exertion, a new cottage, to which a colony was sent, under the care of an " earnest young disciple of the law of love, who had come from a distance to discipline his heart and life to the régime of kindness, and who had lived in their midst as an elder brother. ' On a bright Sabbath morning,' says the Report, ' it was dedicated, in the presence of several hundred friends, to the Good Shepherd, through whose love and help already twenty-seven boys had taken up their residence therein.' " Mr. Burritt found quite " a cottage village of boy-families, with workshops and dwelling houses, a little chapel, a wash and drying-house, a printing-office, bake-house, &c. There are now about 70 boys and 25 girls in this establishment, who constitute 4 boy-families, and 2 girl-families ; both sexes vary in age from 8 to 16 years. There are from 36 to 40 'brothers,' and 8 ' candidates,' or theological students, preparing for the ministry, by taking lessons in the law of love, as here put in force. Thus, not only are these young creatures rescued from ruin, and transformed to a new life

but scores of earnest young men are trained for superintend-
ents and founders of similar institutions in other countries."

We cannot speak of the cost of this establishment;
in gold, it can be but small, though there is so large
a proportion of teachers, for there is no useless outlay, no magnificence wasted on buildings, as in some
of our palace gaols and splendid Ragged Schools,
which look as though they would dignify vice, and
make a mockery of rags to display the founder's
munificence; but there is a priceless amount of
Christian love and effort lavished upon it; and this
has been repaid with large usury.

The three establishments we have been considering, are directed to the reformation of boys who are
already in the eye of the law convicted felons, by
substituting, *under the sanction and with the aid of the
government,* a home and an Industrial School for a
prison; and of those who have become outcasts from
society, being first deserted by it, and perishing—then
necessarily becoming its enemies, and dangerous.
The same kind of treatment has been adopted, and
with the greatest success, towards both classes, for
both have been morally neglected, their affections
blighted, their powers perverted. In our own
country, it would appear to the superficial eye, that
the Government has well provided for its " state
children" at Parkhurst, for the outcasts in its union
workhouses; we have seen with how little success—
how ineffectually! Private philanthropy has endeavoured to supply this want, and two institutions

especially, the Philanthropic, and Stretton-on-Duns-more, have been for many years doing all that their crippled finances and the existing state of the law permitted the earnest and devoted labourers in them to accomplish. A short examination of each of these will show what such institutions can do, and what legislative enactments are needed to render them effective agents in the reformation of juvenile offenders.

The following account of the Philanthropic Insti-tution is derived from the two last reports, and from information given by the Rev. J. Turner, whose evi-dence before the Committee of the Commons, 1850, contains most valuable statements :—

" The society from which this institution emanated, was established more than 60 years ago, for the improvement of depraved and destitute children infesting the metropolis. Many changes were made in its constitution, until the school was removed to a farm at Red Hill, Surrey, early in 1849. It is now designed solely for those boys who have entered on a criminal career ; they come either as volunteers after com-pleting their imprisonment, or at the desire of their parents, or having received a conditional pardon. Over these last alone is there any legal hold ; but many of them have proved the most difficult to manage ; they have been selected from gaols, as among the best, to finish their sentences, and become effectually reformed ; ' but as a general rule,' says Mr. Turner, ' the best prisoner makes the worst free boy, the most difficult and trouble-some boy to deal with, because he has been so accustomed to de-pend upon the mere mechanical arrangements about him, that he finds self-action almost impossible ; such are the most reluctant to work, and the most untrustworthy ; directly they are free, certain dispositions develope themselves, which under the restraint of the prison were mastered and hidden.'* The boys are provided with coarse wholesome food and clothing, and taught to be indifferent to weather, and to work just as the labourers who teach them, a short portion of each day being allotted to direct instruction; strict moral discipline is enforced, with a constant stimulus to self-control. 50 entered on the Farm School, mostly between 14 and 18 years of age, the majority fresh admissions, and unused to labour, ' yet,' says the report ' thanks to the power of religious influence, to the attractive and subduing force of kindness, to the self-respect, thoughtfulness, and sense of personal responsibility created (especially in the older lads), by their *free position and the confidence reposed in them*, and last, not least, to the interest attaching to the varied and active occupations of agricultural life—the steadiness and industrial exertion of the boys have been greater, the faults and offences committed have been much fewer and of lighter caste, than during any corresponding period of the society's operations, on its former system of sedentary employment, and restriction within walls and gates.' The idle, lounging city lad, though at first he grumbles at fare so inferior to his prison diet and exposure, for which his warm cell has but little prepared him, soon lays aside his indolent habits (the Governor of Parkhurst has truly remarked that *prisoners* are always idle), soon becomes imbued with the industrial spirit of the place, and learns to dig and thresh as well as the rest. Frequently those who would generally be considered the most hopeless, who have been in prison six or seven times, work with most earnest purpose at

---

* The following entry in the *Teacher's Journal*, is a commentary on this :—" May 9th, 1851. O. and V. came out of prison last Saturday ; the character given of them was, that they were ' ill-behaved and refractory during their confinement.' They were described by the schoolmaster as ' idle, slow to learn, and inattentive.' They came to School the next morning much softened, and appearing resolved to alter their course ; so they have continued since : they are among the very few who have shown a sincere desire on their discharge, to remain under School influence and to get work."

their own reformation. ' I have been greatly struck,' says the chaplain, 'with the amount of obedience and regular attention to our school rules and discipline the boys have yielded, especially as to not leaving the boundaries of our school farm ; that above 100 lads, mostly fresh inmates, or gathered from the class who by habits and early instruction are most full of independent action and licence, should be here without a wall or barrier, except the regulation, 'No boy must leave the farm without a pass ; and that very few of them should have been guilty of breaking the regulation, is a remarkable circumstance.' The few boys who run away, are those who in an early period of their stay are unable to endure the restraint ; on the whole, experience leads to the belief *that four-fifths of the boys yield to the influence of the school.* A number of them are assisted to be free emigrants, and from these, very interesting letters are received, showing their deep sense of the value of the instruction they have had, and grateful affection to those who have given it."

The institution at Stretton-on-Dunsmore, for the reformation of criminal boys, has now borne the test of above 30 years' experience, and has proved by its operations that it is cheaper to the country to reform boys than to punish them, and that their reformation is possible. We may gather the following particulars respecting it from recent reports : —

The Asylum is adapted to receive from 12 to 20 boys, who are hired as labourers from the Warwick and from the Birmingham gaols, the magistrates occasionally shortening the sentence of the boy when it is known to them that he will go from the gaol to the asylum. The means employed in their reformation are : Placing them under a certain degree of restraint. Making them feel the advantages and comfort of a well-ordered family. Inspiring them with the hopes and fears of religion, and a principle of obedience to the will of God. Endeavouring to keep up a preponderating moral influence in the Institution in favour of virtue and religion. From the earliest period, the cases of decided reformation have been steadily increasing from between 45 and 50, to between 60 and 70 per cent ; of the cases which are regarded as failures, it cannot be said that the efforts employed have been entirely wasted, about half only being known to have fallen into crime. This establishment, then, has been fully answering the object proposed, and its supporters have continually hoped that the important benefits it was conferring on society, would lead to the supply of adequate funds. In this they have been disappointed. Application for aid was made, in 1848, to the Council of Education ; it was not granted. The annual subscriptions are year by year rapidly declining ; and the increasing actual deficiency in the receipts of each year, compel to that inroad on the funded property, which must shortly lead to the dissolution of the establishment, unless it can be placed on a different footing.

In both of these Reformatory Penal Schools, two great difficulties are felt;—first, that of obtaining funds adequate to the necessities of the establishment, or its powers of usefulness ;—the other, that arising from no legal power of detention residing with the master. It has been already shown that justice would demand that the public being the party benefited by such establishments, should, in some way or other, be made to bear the expense. Likewise it is essential to the completeness of the system of Penal Reformatory Schools, that such degree of forcible detention and authority should exist in the conductors of the establishment, as to prevent the absconding of boys before the system has had a fair chance of influencing them. It has been found, both at the Philanthropic and at

Stretton-on-Dunsmore, that there is very little in-clination to run away after the first 6 months, when once the boys have been brought under School influence. The same difficulties were felt in a School of a similar character, established in Bath by Mr. Osborn, and were set forth in a memorial of the Committee of Management of the Ragged Schools of that city, addressed to the Secretary of State :—

"* * * * The total number received since the open-ing of the School has been 125, of whom 73 are known to have been in prison.

"Your memorialists have not been without encourage-ment in the result of their endeavours, inasmuch as several boys have, by these means, been reclaimed from pilfering and vagrant habits, and are leading industrious and respectable lives. Sanguine hopes are also entertained respecting others who are now in the School. Great difficulties are, neverthe-less, found to exist in the way of fully carrying out your memorialists' design, to some of which they desire to draw attention :—

"1. The want of clear authority to detain the boys who have voluntarily entered the institution, and compel them to submit to reasonable and needful discipline. In consequence of this great defect, very many boys, who might have been reformed by a lengthened residence in the institution, have left, after a few days or weeks ; and others, by irregular at-tendance, or by finally withdrawing themselves after repeated re-admissions, have entirely failed to receive the benefits which your memorialists are anxious to confer upon them.

"2. The entire dependence of the establishment on volun-tary support. It is feared that the present outlay cannot be permanently continued, still less could it be enlarged to the extent which would immediately become needful if a power of detention were conferred on the Committee,—or the Institution, in any other way, made available for all who really need its assistance."

In the last chapter we saw that the chaplain's unwearied efforts with the poor young Welches were frustrated from want of the necessary power; *these two difficulties have since caused the dissolution of the School.*

The Schools considered in this chapter have furnished abundant proof of the influence on the young of withdrawal from the evil influences which had led them into crime, and placing them under good ones. An experiment has been tried in Birmingham, by the Recorder, which is even more encouraging, because the circumstances are not so favourable. The peculiar nature of the business of this town presents great facility for petty theft, and Mr. Hill has ascertained from the criminal returns that the juvenile offenders under 16 constitute one-fourth of the whole. Feeling anxious that the young offender should not be subject to the injurious influence of the gaol, Mr. Hill has attempted a new system with them. He states in his evidence before the Lords, that many of the children having friends or relatives, or masters who are kindly disposed, he sends for them, and allows them to take back the child, under the following guarantee. The master enters into an obligation to take care of the child; his name is inscribed in a register, and at certain frequent but undetermined periods, he is visited by an officer of the police without notice, for the purpose of ascertaining what has

been the conduct of the boy, and how he has been
treated, and of this a very accurate register is kept.
Now such a mode of treatment must be attended
with many disadvantages and difficulties, and it
would obviously be better to remove the child from
his temptations and bad associates, and place him for
a time in a reformatory institution.   Not only must
much depend on the child's natural disposition, and
whether he committed the theft from a sudden
temptation or from a dishonest spirit, but even still
more on the master, and whether he undertakes the
trust from a sincere desire to benefit the object of
his care.   Mr. Hill has found, however, that the
masters are, as a body, kindly disposed, and he considers the results to be, under the circumstances,
decidedly favourable.   At Michaelmas, 1846, there
had been 113 so tried since the experiment began
in 1841 ;—only 40 had relapsed; of 29 from different causes there was ignorance; but 44 had maintained their position without a relapse.   Such a
course must, to be beneficial, be adopted with great
wisdom and caution, as well as benevolence ; some
of the judges who sent in their opinion to the Lords'
Committee, state that they have occasionally pursued
a similar one; others say that they were not aware
that they had the power of doing so.   It is evident
that it is only under peculiar circumstances that it
can be attempted ; but the experience of Mr. Hill,
when contrasted with that of Mr. Osborn, only 5 of

whose 55 young prisoners were in any degree reformed, is most striking.

With respect to the expenses of such Reformatory
Schools, as compared with those of Gaols, it is not
perhaps easy to make a perfectly exact estimate of
them, because they necessarily vary with the system
adopted in them;—yet the annual expenditure of
each prisoner must, under the most favourable circumstances, be much greater than that of scholars
in Mettrai, the Philanthropic, Stretton-on-Dunsmore,
or even Parkhurst. The prison diet per head in the
Bristol Gaol is, indeed, only £7. 4s. 3d. per annum,
but little more than that at Parkhurst, which is £6.
7s. 11d.; but this constitutes a very small item in the
expenditure;—besides a share in the establishment
expenses, in some prisons the annual expenditure
of the staff of officers is £15., and even £20. per
head; * at Parkhurst it is about £8. 10s. per head,
while at Mettrai, where the instructors and attendants average 1 to every 5 scholars, it is only £4.
10s., nor is the item of salaries larger at the Philanthropic. The cost of the building is often overlooked, but ought to be included in the prisoners'
expenses as his house-rent. Lieutenant-Colonel
Jebb states, in his evidence before the Commons,
that each cell in York Castle cost the enormous sum

* Vid.—Article on the Management and Cost of Prisons in
the *Law Review*, Nov. 1850.

of £1200., those in other prisons varying from £120. to £500. The Model Prison at Pentonville cost up to the period of its occupation, £84,168., making £161. per cell. Surely accommodation for 500 or 600 children, on the Mettrai system, need cost but a very small portion of this sum.

"The Borough of Birmingham," said Mr. Hill, in his charge to the Grand Jury in 1848, "was paying £20. per annum for every one of its prisoners at Warwick, and notwithstanding the union of skill and kind feeling of which the Warwick Gaol had the benefit in its management, it did so happen, from causes beyond present control, that its inmates were far more likely to advance further into crime than to be reformed. And even if it should be said that even £12. per annum is much to pay for the benefit of those who are in hostility to the laws of God and man, the answer, as far as pounds, shillings, and pence are concerned, is, that offenders must be maintained either in prison or at large ; and that, even if the expense of reformatory training were greater than that of training to deeper corruption, it would be true economy to prefer the former to the latter."

The gross annual cost of the establishment at Mettrai is £20. per head ; but the produce of the labour of the scholars averages £8. each ; if, then, every scholar remains 3 years, and the average loss from failures be reckoned at 6, be added, the reformation of each youth will cost only £42.

We arrive then at the following results from the evidence and facts which have been brought forward in this and the preceding chapter :—

First,—That, as a general rule, all children, however apparently vicious and degraded, are capable of being made useful members of society, and beings acting on a religious principle, if placed under right influences, and subjected to judicious control and training. The comparatively few exceptions that would occur do not invalidate the principle.

Secondly,—That the present system adopted towards offending children renders them almost certainly members for life of the criminal class, for it neither deters nor reforms them; while, by checking the development of their powers, and branding them with ignominy, it prevents them from gaining an honest livelihood.

Thirdly,—That good Penal Reformatory Schools conducted on Christian principles, where there is a wise union of kindness and restraint, have produced the desired effect of enabling the most degraded and corrupt to become useful members of society;—but that such institutions cannot be efficiently carried on, or maintained, without a steady income, which cannot be certainly or justly raised by individual effort alone, and without such legal authority as will impose sufficient restraint over the scholars to keep them under the School influence.

Fourthly,—That the parents being in reality the guilty parties rather than the children, since juvenile delinquency usually originates in parental neglect, every parent should be chargeable for the maintenance of a child thrown by crime on the care of the state, as much as if the child were at large, and should be held responsible for the maintenance of a child in a Reformatory School, or made in some way to suffer for the non-discharge of this duty.

If these four results are true ones, *legislative enactments will be needed to carry the spirit of them into operation.*

A sufficient number of Reformatory Penal Schools must be established under the guidance of enlightened Christian benevolence, sanctioned and mainly supported by government inspection and aid.

Magistrates and judges must be empowered to send all convicted children to such Schools, instead of committing them to prison ; power of detention being vested in the masters, for such length of time as may seem needful for the reformation of the child.

The parents, or, if none, the parish of the child, must be held responsible for such weekly payment as may cover the cost of his maintenance during his detention.

The need of such provisions has been already brought before the notice of the legislature ;* the importance of such institutions was forcibly stated to the Committee of the Lords in 1847, and of the Commons in 1850. Perhaps the opinion of no one of the many witnesses is entitled to more respect than that of the late Rev. Whitworth Russell.

" I think," he says, " that there should be what may be called Penal Schools formed in different districts of the country. There should be a power of detaining the children in those Penal Schools till the age of 18, but at the

---

* Introductory Chapter, pp. 44—47.

same time that those who have the government of such establishments should be at liberty to receive such bail as would be satisfactory to them for allowing the discharge of a juvenile offender, previous to that period of 18 years. I consider that those institutions should be really and pro- perly training Schools, rather than prisons. There should be a certain amount of penal restraint in those institu- tions, inasmuch as the reckless and disorderly habits which the juvenile delinquents have almost universally acquired, will demand a long, steady, and, to a great extent, penal re- straint, in order to the extirpation of those habits. I think that, attached to these penal Schools, there should be land for agricultural training, gardening, &c., workshops for in- dustrial training, and good School arrangements for intel- lectual training, so that the physical, the moral, and the intellectual powers, would be trained and developed at the same time ; while those who conducted themselves well should have their names placed upon a record, for recommendation for employment, apprenticeship, enlistments in the army or navy, [?] or emigration, as opportunities might offer. *I be- lieve that such institutions, properly formed and conducted, would lead to a great diminution of the number of juvenile offenders.*"

The Committee of the Lords, one of whose direct objects it was " to inquire into the execution of the criminal law, especially respecting juvenile offenders," thus state their views in their report :—

"The question of punishment of juvenile offenders is a further and distinct one beside that of the juris- diction and power of conviction in their case. Very important evidence has been given in favour of deal- ing with such offenders, at least on first convictions, by means of Reformatory Asylums on the principle of Parkhurst Prison, rather than by ordinary imprison- ment ; the punishment in such asylums being hardly more than what is implied in confinement and restraint, and reformation and industrial training being the main features of the process. Without going beyond the principle which should be followed on this question, the Committee are disposed to recommend the adoption, by way of trial, of the Reformatory Asylums as above described, combined with a moderate use of corporal punishment. The Committee also recommend the trial of a suggestion made by witnesses who have given much attention to this subject, that, wherever it is possible, part of the cost attending the conviction and punishment of juvenile offenders should be legally chargeable upon their parents.

" Upon one subject the whole of the evidence and all the opinions are quite unanimous,—the good that may be hoped from education,—meaning thereby, a sound moral and religious training, commencing in Infant Schools, and followed up in Schools for older pupils ; to these, where it is practicable, *industrial training should be added.* There seems in the general opinion to be no other means that affords even a chance of lessening the number of offenders, and diminishing the atrocity of their crimes.

" The Committee, therefore, deem that they should not be discharging their duty if they did not earnestly press these momentous subjects upon the attention of the legislature. Without raising any speculative questions on the right to punish those whom the State has left in ignorance, *it may safely*

be affirmed that the duty of all rulers is both to pre-
vent, as far as may be possible, the necessity of pun-
ishing, and when they do inflict punishment, to
attempt reformation. The Committee, therefore,
strongly recommend the adoption of effectual measures for diffusing generally, and by permanent provisions, the inestimable benefits of good training,
and of sound moral and religious instruction; while
they also urge the duty of improving extensively the
discipline of the gaols, and other places of confinement."

Such are the views of that Committee, but they
have not yet been so carried into action as to make
any change in the juvenile criminal population of
our country. These young beings continue to herd
in their dens of iniquity, to swarm in our streets, to
levy a costly maintenance on the honest and industrious, to rise up to be the parents of a degraded
progeny of pauper children, or to people our gaols
until they are audaciously wicked enough for transportation—in either case to be a drain on our resources, a festering plague-spot to society. There
are many earnest and Christian workers in this
cause, who see these evils, and know what only can
be a cure for them;—let them not be weary in their
exertions; let them not be daunted by discouragement, apathy, repeated disappointment;—but let
them with one heart and voice unite in striving
that the perishing and dangerous children of our
land shall no longer remain in this outer darkness.

Surely the people will listen when earnest words of truth and soberness are addressed to them;—the legislature will move when they hear the united voice of the nation.

This work is now brought to a close;—to many it will seem far too long, and full of uninteresting details;—it is far too short, when compared with the vastness of the subject, and the abundance of the material from which, with difficulty, a selection has been made. All those whose aid has been solicited in furnishing information, have, by their ready and most kind acquiescence, shown how deeply they have at heart the cause in which they are labouring;—to all, the thanks, not only of the writer, but of the reader, are due, for they " have spoken that they do know, and have testified that they have seen."

May many labourers arise in this deserted vineyard, and may the blessing of the Lord of the Harvest descend on this, and every humble endeavour to serve Him. Amen !

BRISTOL, MAY 7TH, 1851.

INDEX

355